Myron Cohen's
BIG
JOKE BOOK

Myron Cohen's
BIG JOKE BOOK

Illustrated by Sheila Greenwald

Citadel Press   Secaucus, N.J.

First paperbound printing
Copyright © 1958, 1960 by Myron Cohen
All rights reserved
Published by Citadel Press
A division of Lyle Stuart Inc.
120 Enterprise Ave., Secaucus, N.J. 07094
In Canada: Musson Book Company
A division of General Publishing Co. Limited
Don Mills, Ontario
Manufactured in the United States of America
ISBN 0-8065-0853-1

Volume One

Laughing Out Loud

**Volume One
Laughing Out Loud**

**by
Myron Cohen**

with drawings by Sheila Greenwald

Dedication

TO THE TIRED BUSINESSMAN . . . WHO'S ALWAYS CHASING HIS SECRETARY AROUND THE OFFICE . . . NOW YOU KNOW WHY HE'S TIRED!

PREFACE

Material has always played an important role in my life. A comedian needs good material if he's going to get laughs, just as a silk salesman needs good material if he's going to sell his product. And that's what I was before I became a comic—a silk salesman.

Without boasting, I'd like to say that I was probably the most popular silk salesman in the Garment Center—and the poorest one, too.

Every time I'd approach a prospective customer and try to sell him silk, he'd ask if I knew any new jokes. Of course, I did. Then I'd tell him one, he'd tell me one, I'd tell him another . . . and thus it went all day. Finally, he'd say, "Myron, you're great. You ought to be on the stage."

But when I'd ask him about buying some silk, he'd shrug his shoulders and say, "Sorry, Myron, but busines is bad and I. . . ." Then, instead of feeling blue, I'd say something like, "Speaking about business, did you hear the one about the salesman who was stranded in a small backwoods town due to a critical power shortage who wired his boss: I DON'T KNOW WHEN I'LL BE ABLE TO GET OUT OF HERE. IT MIGHT TAKE WEEKS. Upon receiving the wire, the head man immediately replied, AS OF TODAY YOU START YOUR TWO WEEKS VACATION."

Meanwhile, whenever there was a smoker, a banquet, or any other affair, I was always invited to perform . . . for nothing, of course!

Finally, after much coaxing by my associates, I decided to try my luck professionally.

When all the great comedians heard that I was starting out, they came to my aid. First Danny Thomas sent me some jokes. Jimmy Durante sent me some jokes. George Jessel sent me some jokes. And Jack Benny . . . he sold me some jokes.

And that, dear reader, is how a silk salesman became a spinner of yarns.

CONTENTS

Garment Gaities	13
Comedy at the Copa	44
Miami Mirth	56
The Best From Tex	67
Gay at the Chez	79
Amusement in Atlantic City	91
Las Vegas Laughs	101
Catskill Capers	113
It's a Pleasure to Meet the Press	127
There's No People Like Show People	149
Gags for Gourmets	165
Cohen at Home	176

Laughing Out Loud

GARMENT GAIETIES

Whenever I hear anyone use the term, "The Garment Jungle," I always feel that the speaker has missed the boat and the point —it's always said sardonically out of the side of the mouth. This just isn't *my* Garment Center—a world gilded for me by wonderful memories and continuing pleasant associations. The Garment Center has been good to me. After all, I got my start telling stories at Garment Center socials—like many another comedian who apprenticed in the Catskills or small night clubs.

Yes, I grew up in the Garment Center, developed my style in the Garment Center, got my experience in the Garment Center, and although I don't get too many opportunities to frequent my old haunts, I'm proud to have once been associated with all the wonderful people in the clothing business.

As I said in my preface (if you're one of those people who don't skip over prefaces), I was trying to be a silk salesman when the show business bug bit me and caused the worm to turn. One day I just decided to give up pushing silk and become a *full-time* comedian.

I was working for A. E. Wullschleger at the time. Let me hasten to explain that Wullschleger had been a wonderful boss. After all, he laughed at my jokes even if he didn't pay me, so my decision had nothing to do with him.

But he *was* my boss, so it wasn't the easiest thing to do to go in and tell him I was quitting. I squared my padded shoulders, stuck out my chin and strode into his office. Henry Roth, his junior partner, was there.

I must have looked funny because Henry asked, "Anything wrong, Myron?"

"Well, yes and no," I faltered. "It's just that I'm—I'm leaving."

"Leaving?" Wullschleger looked up, surprised. "You got a better job?"

"You might call it that," I told him. "I'm becoming a full-time comedian."

Wullschleger didn't look impressed. "And how much are they paying you?"

That look and tone got me. "Oh, about $1250 a week," I said nonchalantly.

He was incredulous. "For that guff you tell? . . . that—that *trash* you say?"

"Better than the stuff you sell and the cash you pay," said I sweetly.

For all that, A.E. is a great guy. Once when I was appearing at the Copa, I invited him to be my guest and catch my act. I glanced at him now and then while I was performing and it always seemed like he was laughing his head off. So when the act was over I went over to his table and asked eagerly, "Well, A.E., how did you like it?"

He looked at me gravely and said, "Remember, Myron, there's always a place for a good silk salesman in my organization."

Of course, good old A.E. had to have the last word. I mean, it was obvious he was getting back at me for that last act in his office. . . . He just didn't want me to get the best of him, that's all . . . Yessir, good old A.E. had to have his little joke. Didn't bother me a bit. Not a bit. . . .

I also worked for Jack Geizler and Sidney Frankel of Duval Fabrics. Jack and Sid are two swell guys who are never too busy to tell, or listen to, a good story.

The last time I saw Jack he told me about a Garment Center manufacturer named Saul Gold who had an eye for pretty girls. One afternoon his male secretary—Mrs. Gold insisted on a man for the job—tip-toed into his boss' office. "There's a woman outside who wants to see you," he said.

"Is she pretty?" asked Gold eagerly.

"Very," assured his secretary.

"Show her in. Show her in," said the boss, rubbing his hands.

After the woman had gone down in the elevator, Gold confronted his secretary. "Look, here, man," he said, "what made you feed me a line like that?"

"I'm sorry, sir," said the secretary. "It was just that she didn't

give me her name. For all I knew she might have been your wife."

"Dammit all, she was!" answered the boss mournfully.

Sid's favorite is also about a Garment Center character—a Silk manufacturer who had really prospered. He had started off as a cutter, taken courses in business administration at night school, jumped to the rank of executive, and eventually reached the top as a full partner in the firm. When his partner died, he was head man.

One morning, near the end of one of his most profitable years, his secretary brought in some checks for him to sign.

"This one," she explained, "is for the house you're buying in Long Island. It's for $200,000."

"That's wonderful," said the manufacturer.

"And this one for $825,000 is for that new office we're opening in Paris."

"Good."

"This one covers your son's wedding present. It's for $125,000."

"He deserves it. He's a good boy."

"And now," said the secretary. I'd like to ask you for a raise.

I've been with you for more than two years now. Would $15 be all right?"

"Fifteen dollars!" shouted the manufacturer. "What do you think I am, a millionaire?"

☻

Then there is the one about the mother who was telling her friend about her three sons.

"Sammy is a doctor," she said.

"Is that right?"

"Ben is a lawyer."

"I'll bet you're proud of him, too."

"And Joe is a silk manufacturer."

"A silk manufacturer?"

"Yeah, and you know what? He supports Sammy and Ben."

☻

Bosses in the garment industry are always worrying about business. Of course, this is a common disease in every line of endeavor, but Garment Center businessmen seem to have the most acute cases.

Recently, Randy and Mel Rosenthal, of Rona Dress, told me about the two partners, Irving and Bob, who owned a small business in the Garment Center.

One afternoon, the pair, who oddly enough were good friends, went rowing in Central Park. It was a beautiful day and they floated to the middle of the lake. Suddenly, right in the middle of the water, the boat developed a leak and overturned. When the spray cleared, Irving was sitting on the upended boat and Bob was struggling in the water.

"Irving, help me!" Bob yelled, "I can't swim!"

His partner looked around. "Wait a minute, I'll get help," he said. "Can you float alone?"

Struggling valiantly to stay above water, Bob sputtered, "A time like this and you want to talk business?!"

☻

Irving and Max met walking down Seventh Avenue.

"How's business?" asked Max.

"Well, you know how it is," replied Irving, "business is like sex. When it's good, it's wonderful. When it's bad, it's still pretty good."

☻

Ginsberg and Levy met each other on the train to Philadelphia. They had been schoolboy companions and hadn't seen each other for nearly twenty years.

"How are you, Ginsberg?" asked Levy. "Where are you going?"

"Me, I'm going to Philadelphia."

"So am I."

"Is that so? And what business are you in?"

"I'm a silk salesman. And you?"

"What do you know about that! I'm a silk salesman, too."

"Ginsberg, do you remember the great times we used to have at those parties at Rose Lieberman's house in Brooklyn and how we used to fight over Rose? Remember those parties, old man?"

"I'll never forget them."

They continued reminiscing, but half of Ginsberg's mind was busy elsewhere. Somehow everything didn't seem kosher to him. He began to think:

"This Levy is a smart guy. He says he's going to Philadelphia, but why should he tell me the truth? He's in the same business. I'll bet he's going to Pittsburgh. Why should he go to Pittsburgh? He must be going to see Abe Cohen. Abe is probably going to place a big order for silk and he's trying to get the whole thing.

"No, that can't be. He must know that Abe Cohen always divides his order among three of his favorite salesmen. Maybe he's going to see Max Gold. No, Max placed his order weeks ago. Say, wait a minute, Lieberman and Sons moved from Brooklyn to Pittsburgh, and old Lieberman is Rose's father. What did he bring up Rose for? I bet he still has a case on her. That's it. He's going to Pittsburgh to get himself engaged to Rose Lieberman."

He turned to his friend. "Congratulations you old faker, you!" Ginsberg chuckled.

"How did you know?" gasped Levy.

Ginsberg shrugged, "It stands to reason!"

Sam Frontman, of Paramount Dresses in Philadelphia, knew a Garment Center cutter who approached his boss and asked, "Could I have Thursday off? It's my silver wedding anniversary."

The boss snarled, "Do I have to put up with this every twenty-five years?"

George and Wally, my haberdashers, had a friend who opened a men's clothing store in the Garment Center. About a week after he opened, the fellow was shocked when a hysterical woman raced into his store.

"This shirt I bought for my husband has a hole in it."

"Well, what do you expect me to do?"

"I'd like to get my money back."

"There are no refunds here, lady."

"No refunds! What about this notice right on the sales slip: MONEY CHEERFULLY REFUNDED IF NOT SATISFACTORY?"

"Sure," said the fellow, "but there was nothing wrong with your money."

A big business tycoon died and went to his eternal resting place.

When he arrived in the other world, he was greeted by a salesman who used to visit him on earth.

The salesman greeted him with a big hello. "Max, ole boy, I'm here for the appointment."

"What appointment?" barked the businessman.

"Don't you remember?" asked the salesman. "Every time I used to try to see you at your office, you'd tell me you'd see me here."

A Garment Center manufacturer was interviewing applicants to replace his private secretary who was resigning because of expectant motherhood. His right-hand man sat with him as he looked the applicants over.

The first girl was a beautiful buxom blonde. She turned out to be intelligent and had excellent secretarial skills. The second was a dark-haired beauty who was even more intelligent and proficient than the first. The third one was cross-eyed, had buck teeth, and weighed 190 pounds.

After interviewing all three candidates, the boss informed his associate that he was hiring the third applicant.

"But why!" asked the astonished employee.

"Well," boomed the boss, "in the first place, she looked very intelligent to me. In the second place, it is none of your damned business. And in the third place, she's my wife's sister."

☺

Calvin, of the T.V. Coffee Shop, swears this happened: After discovering that he had had a very poor season, the angry manufacturer walked into his office and shouted, "Why is it that every time I walk into this office, I find that nobody is working!"

"Simple," came a voice from the back, "it's those damned rubber heels you wear."

☺

Two Garment Center partners once hired a new secretary. The girl was extremely pretty but very dumb.

"One day," said the first partner, "I asked her to get me the phone number of Zelda Zinc."

"And you know what?" added the other, "Two hours later I came out and asked her how she was doing with that phone number."

"I'm doing fine," she said, "I'm up to the D's already!"

☺

The boss of a big dress house took his wife to Florida for a vacation. He decided that he would like to go by car and see the various states along the way.

During the first day out, they ran into a brutal storm and had to pull into the nearest motor court. As they did so, a young attendant came out and was about to give them a room when an old woman peeked out of a door.

"Do they have a marriage license, Fred?"

"No, we don't."

"When were you married?" the woman demanded.

"Uh, in September, 1938," the husband replied.

"Idiot!" the wife snapped. "It was October 14, 1939!"

"Let them have the room," said the old lady. "They're married."

☻

As Jack Silverman, of the old Roumanian put it: a shoulder strap is "a little piece of ribbon designed to keep an attraction from becoming a sensation."

☻

And then there's the Harry Hershfield classic about the big manufacturer who walked into a clothing store and told the salesman, "I like that suit in the window. What are you asking for it?"

"This is a high class establishment," the salesman told him, "I'm not going to say $100, $90, $85 ... with me, it's one price—$80."

"Isn't that funny," said the manufacturer, "I'm exactly the same nature. I'm not going to say $75, $70, then $65. By me it's one price also—$50."

"Sold."

☺

Nat Sherman, who supplies the Garment Center with all those cigars and cigarettes, knows a salesman who has 100 suits ... and they're all pending.

☺

After a particularly dismal season, an associate of furrier George Becker was trying to cheer up his partners. "After all, fellows," he said, "we have to be optimistic. The only thing we have to fear is fur itself."

☺

Marcia Parker and Bill Felstein, of the Junior House of Milwaukee, attended a party where they met an old acquaintance.

"Hello Sam," greeted Bill, "how's business? I heard that you lost a lot on that fall shipment of dresses. Is that true?"

"It's true."

"And that you almost went bankrupt?"

"That's true, too."

"But I understand you made a big profit on another shipment and wound up having had a pretty good season."

"That's right. Then you heard about it, Bill."

"Yeah," said Bill, "but this is the first time I'm hearing all the details."

☺

Abe Goodman once employed a cutter who was always having hard luck. The fellow invariably seemed to be in debt, and as time went on his bills grew larger and larger. Finally, he reached a point at which he had to do something drastic. Winter was coming, and he couldn't afford to buy overcoats for his three young children.

In desperation, the fellow broke into another firm's storeroom and stole three coats. While he was making his escape, he was caught.

Brought before a judge, he told his story. "I'm not a criminal, your honor. I only stole to keep my children from freezing to death. Is that a crime?"

Then the manufacturer who owned the dress house which was burglarized was called to the stand.

"Do you wish to press charges against this man?" asked the man on the bench. "Or would you rather settle this matter out of court?"

"I want to press charges," the manufacturer said sternly.

The judge was surprised. "But he's not really a criminal."

"Listen, Judge," began the fellow. "If he would have taken those coats last week, I wouldn't have cared, and if he'd taken them next week, I wouldn't have cared. But this week, I'm taking inventory!"

Boris and Joe Alper of Glass and Company love the one about the rich manufacturer who married his secretary and went to Florida on their honeymoon.

No sooner had they checked into their hotel room than a rough-looking thug climbed through the window and poked a gun in the manufacturer's ribs.

"This is a stickup," the fellow announced.

Then he drew a circle on the rug with his heel and gruffly ordered the groom to stand inside it.

"Move one inch outside," snarled the crook, "and I'll pump lead into you."

Then the fellow stuffed his pockets with their jewelry, money, and other valuables. Next, he embraced the sobbing bride and made violent love to her.

"How could you just stand there," wailed the girl later, "and watch a monster like that make love to me? What are you, a man or a mouse?"

"I'm a man, of course. And I didn't just stand there, either. Every time he had his back turned, I stuck my foot outside the circle."

Morris Degan, president of the Gilatzyaner Association, had a friend who approached his lawyer and told him, "I won't pay you unless you are certain that there are grounds for legal action."

"Well, tell me the case," asked the lawyer.

The fellow explained the whole situation and when he had finished, he asked the mouthpiece what he thought.

"The case is airtight," the lawyer informed him. "The other fellow hasn't a leg to stand on. My advice will cost you $100, and for an additional $150, I'll start suit."

"No," said the fellow, "I guess I'd better not."

"But why?" demanded the lawyer.

"Because I gave you the other fellow's side of the story!"

☻

In the Garment Industry, as in all other industries, the workers feel that they're not appreciated by the boss. Charlie Morris often tells the one about the faithful cutter, who after 25 years of work, approached his boss and asked him for a raise.

"Well," began the head man, "business is bad now, Sam, and I just can't afford to give you a raise."

"But I'm doing three men's work, and I always have," retorted the sad Sam.

"Three men's work!" exploded the boss. "Tell me who the other two men are, and I'll fire them!"

☻

Henry Blank of Lehigh Frocks tells about the Garment Center cutter who stormed into his boss's office and screamed, "I've been killing myself for you! I want a raise!"

His boss looked up calmly, smiled, and said, "Why Ben, there must be some mistake. I gave you a raise three weeks ago."

"You did?" exclaimed the embarrassed Ben. "And my wife never even told me!"

☻

Models, as I stated before, are a very important part of the Garment Center. Thousands of words, both fact and fiction, have been written about these shapely lasses.

Agent Phil Consolo overheard a model being interviewed by

her prospective boss. "What are you around the neck, Miss Green?"

"Twelve," she replied.

"What are you around the hips?"

"Thirty-three," she smiled.

"And how are you around the waist?"

"Just wonderful," she cooed.

☻

Al Rosenstein of Roseweb Frocks had a model who once told him: "The nicest thing about money is that it never clashes with anything you're wearing."

☻

A garment manufacturer, who was quite a wolf, grew extremely fond of one of his new models, a remarkably comely lass.

One day when she was coming out of the fitting room, he approached her, gave her a peck on the neck and whispered, "How about coming up to my beach house for the weekend? We'll have loads of fun."

"All right," she smiled. "And I'll bring my boy-friend."

"Your boy-friend? What for?"

"In case your wife wants to have some fun, too!"

☻

Two prosperous Garment Center manufacturers hired a new model. She was beautiful but she wasn't too bright. The two partners were attracted to the girl, but the interest was not of the paternal nature.

"Look," one told his partner, "being that she's so young and pretty, she might be taken advantage of by some fast-talking fellow. I think we ought to take it upon ourselves to teach her what's right and what's wrong."

"You're right," agreed his partner. "You teach her what's right."

☻

Al Frischer of Frischer Carpet Co. employed a young salesman who took a pretty model to see "A Streetcar Named Desire" at one of those off-Broadway theatres. As soon as they found their seats, the girl excused herself and looked for the powder room. Since the theatre was in an old building, the poor girl wandered through winding corridors for several minutes until she finally found the place. It was empty except for a girl seated on a sofa. The model quickly fixed her make-up, adjusted the seams of her stockings, took a final glance in the mirror and with the remark, "God, I look a mess tonight," departed.

Then she went back into the corridor and found her way back to her seat. As soon as she arrived, she asked her boyfriend, "What happened?"

"Not much," he told her, "one girl was sitting on a sofa, then some girl walked in, fixed her stockings and said, 'God, I look a mess tonight,' and walked off."

☻

Noel Kramer, manager of Rock 'n Roll singers, knew the wife of a prominent garment manufacturer who suspected that her husband was carrying on with one of his pretty young models.

Accordingly, she went to a detective agency with her problem. The agency took the job. They put their best investigator to work, and within a week the talented sleuth discovered that the wife's suspicions were well-founded. Hubby was very sweet on a cute blonde model.

"I'll get him," the wife told the head of the detective agency. "How much would it cost to get concrete evidence—enough to sue?"

The agency chief made a few notes on his pad. "With one investigator, a photographer and a witness, it will come out to $500."

The wife nodded. "Get started right away! I think I can borrow that much from my boy-friend."

☺

A.D. Frank, of Topaze Frocks, knows a manufacturer who recently interviewed a model for a job in his show room. He asked the girl about her experience, background and measurements. When the interview was completed, the fellow thanked her for her interest and said, "Where can I get hold of you?"

"I don't know," she answered, "I'm awfully ticklish."

☺

A wolfish manufacturer, who was sweet on one of his pretty young models, couldn't get to first base with her.

Finally, in desperation, he called her into his private office. "Ruth," he asked her. "Why do you spurn my love? Is it that you find me unfriendly?"

"Oh, no" she admitted. "I like you, Mr. Gold, but I have a boy-friend and I love him very much."

With that, the manufacturer walked over to a huge closet and pulled it open. "Look in this closet," he told her. "Do you see all those expensive hand-painted ties? Does your boy-friend have any of those?"

"No."

"And do you see those imported shoes? They're all hand-stitched. Does your boy-friend have any of those?"

"Well, no," she admitted.

"And those shirts," he said, pointing to a stack of expensive, monogrammed shirts. "Does your boy-friend have any like them?"

"No."

"Well, what the devil does he have?" barked the boss.

"He's got sex appeal," the girl barked back, "and I'd like to see you find that in your closet!"

☻

Johnny Frumkes, who manufactures coats, was talking to his brother Joe when an extremely striking model walked by.

"That's a nice dress you're wearing," complimented Joe.

"I change my clothes three times a day if the occasion demands it," said the model.

"Oh that's nothing," replied Johnny, "my sister changes 10 times a day."

"Ten times a day! How old is she?"

"Six months."

☻

Two catty models met in a show room. The first was of the ultra-thin fashion school, while the second was the full-blown, buxom type.

"To look at you, one would think there was a famine in America," said the buxom one.

"And to look at you," the thin one retorted, "one would think you were the cause of it!"

☻

Oriole Elias, of Royal Frocks, laughed when I told him this one:

An extremely attractive model appeared to be the perfect choice to display the manufacturer's new spring line.

"Yes, you're just what we need," he told her. "You have the right face, the right figure . . . everything my models must possess. By the way how much do you expect a week?"

The girl told him her figure.

"Sorry," said the boss quickly, "you're too tall!"

☻

Boss: Whisper the three little words which will make me walk on air.

Model: Go hang yourself!

☻

Alfred and Eliot Oshins, of Sportlane Deb, were talking over business when one of their models walked in. She was a pretty girl, but on this occasion she looked very unhappy.

"What's wrong, Helen?" asked Eliot.

"You're looking at the dumbest girl who ever lived."

"Why do you say that?" asked Al.

"It's this way," began Helen. "I was on the way home from work yesterday when this Cadillac convertible pulls up alongside me."

"What happened then?" asked Al.

"Well, this tall young fellow in the car whistles at me."

"Yeah."

"I told him, 'I'm a lady, get out of here before I call a cop.'"

"Did that scare him off?"

"No. He tells me he'll take me to the best clubs in town and the finest restaurants. He says he's got a lot of money and he's lonesome. Then he says, if I don't want to do anything tonight, all I have to do is give him my phone number and he'll call me tomorrow."

"And what did you do?" asked the brothers Oshins.

"What could I do? I wrote the number down, and when I gave it to him he pressed something into my hand and drove away."

"Then what are you feeling so low about?"

"Because," wailed Helen, "what he put in my hand was a hundred-dollar bill! And like an idiot, I gave him the wrong number!"

Red Ruster and Jack Kay of Sandra Sage Fashions knew a model who was the vainest one of them all. When one was in the presence of this girl, he could never get a word in edgewise.

All she would talk about was herself. One day, however, she met a salesman, a handsome young fellow, whom she liked very much.

"Remember, dear," a friend told her, "men like to talk about themselves. If you don't let him say anything all night, he'll be bored and you'll lose him."

The model took her friend's advice. That night after she had spent three hours talking about herself, she asked, "And what do *you* think about my dress?"

☻

A salesman has to be many things. He must be a diplomat, a psychologist, a good speaker and even more important, a good listener. He must show a sincere interest in his product. But perhaps the most important thing a salesman must have is a repertoire of stories and the ability to tell them. For a salesman without a good collection of stories has handcuffs on his order book.

☻

Public Relations and advertising man, David Green, tells of the salesman who had just obtained a new position. One day while he was on the elevator with his new employer, the boss asked, "By the way, Morris, why did you leave your last job with Goldstein and Goldberg?"

"Well," explained Morris, "they were always arguing and I just couldn't take any more of it."

"Arguing?"

"Yeah, when Goldstein and I weren't arguing, Goldberg and I were."

☻

The brothers Lackritz—Harry, Joe and Sam--like the one I told them about the traveling salesman who arrived at a small town hotel one evening without any luggage.

"Where are your bags, sir?" asked the girl behind the desk.

"I don't have any," he replied.

"But you're a salesman and salesmen always carry samples with them."

"That's true in most cases, Miss, but not in mine, because I sell brains."

"I can't get over it," she exclaimed. "You know you're the first salesman I ever saw without samples."

My brother Phil, who is sales manager for Forge Mills, and a great comedian in his own right, knew a salesman who had been on the road for more than six months. The fellow was the sentimental type and when he got back to the city, he decided to get a record of his girl's favorite song. Accordingly, he called a record store, or at least he *thought* he had dialed the store.

"Have you got 'Ten Baby Fingers And Ten Baby Toes'?" he asked the voice at the other end of the phone.

"No," came the reply, "but I have 18 kids in Alabama."

"Is that a record?" asked the salesman.

"I don't think so, but it's sure above the average."

Phil's boss, Mal Malvin, told me about a salesman who had car trouble on a back country road. He opened the hood and inspected the engine.

"The trouble is in the battery," came a voice from behind him.

The salesman turned around quickly to see who had spoken, and the only thing in sight was a sway-backed old horse watching him over the pasture fence. Naturally, this completely unnerved the fellow, and he took off down the road. About twenty minutes later, he came to a filling station. After he caught his breath, he told his story to the owner.

"You mean to say that you saw no one near the car but that horse?" asked the garageman.

"That's right."

"Was it by any chance a black horse, sway-backed with bow-legs?"

"Yeah, that's right."

"Oh don't mind him," said the gas pumper. "He doesn't know a thing about engine trouble."

☻

Cye Martin, of Stage Clothes, loves the one about the tie salesman who walked into the busy executive's office.

"How about buying some ties?"

"Don't need any. Scram!"

"They're pure silk."

"I said beat it."

"Look at these beautiful linings."

His patience exhausted, the big wig picked up the salesman and tossed him outside. Sample cases were scattered all over the place. Picking up his wares, the salesman brushed off his clothes, and walked back into the executive's office. "Now that you've got that off your chest, I'm ready to take down your order."

☻

Advertising and P.R. man Charles Schlaifer knew a salesman whose hobby was entomology. His dream was to take a trip to Africa in order to hunt down rare specimens. Finally, he found the time and cash to realize his dream.

Making his way through the jungles of darkest Africa, he was surprised to come upon a small village and astonished when he ran into his old friend Benjamin Gross who'd been missing some months from the Garment Center.

"Benny, old pal," he cried, "what are you doing here?"

"I'm a witch doctor," explained Benny. "But what are *you* doing here?"

"I'm looking for a certain bug to add to my collection."

With this, Benny ran to a tree, cupped a small bug in his hand, and brought it to his friend. "Is this the one?"

"No, that's not it."

Benny went to another tree and went through the same procedure.

"Sorry, Ben, that's not it, either."

Benny picked up a leaf that was crawling wtih insect life.

"No," said the entomologist sadly. "All of those are a dime a dozen. The one I'm looking for is very rare."

"Well, I guess I don't have it," shrugged Benny. "But thanks for letting me show you my line."

☻

Two salesmen, one from St. Louis and the other from Chicago, went deer hunting in Pennsylvania. Arriving at the main hunting lodge in the area, they were dismayed to learn that there were no vacancies. However, since they'd traveled so far, they decided to go hunting anyway.

That evening, coming out of the dense woods, they knocked at the door of an isolated farmhouse and asked the woman if she would be willing to put them up for a week. Although she was a widow and all alone, she agreed.

About six months later the businessman from St. Louis telephoned his friend in Chicago.

"George, I just received a wire from an attorney in Pennsylvania, and frankly I'm puzzled."

"Yes?"

"By any chance did you have an affair with that farm widow?"

"Well, look, Steve, I meant to explain that to you."

"And also, did you happen to give my name to her?"

"Well, er, I meant to explain that, too."

"Well, don't bother. The widow died and willed her farm to me."

A salesman's relatives gathered for the reading of his will after his death.

"Being of sound mind," read his lawyer, "I spent every last cent before I died."

The salesman had had a tiring day. He was glad that it was near closing time and hoped that he wouldn't have to wait on anybody else. But no sooner had the hope been formulated than a woman customer appeared at his counter.

"Do you sell men's bathrobes?" she inquired.

He told her that he did and took a couple of boxes off the shelf. Neither was appropriate. He took down two more. They weren't right either.

And so it went until the counter was strewn with boxes, tissue paper, and bathrobes of every color and description. Just as the harried salesman was about to reach for the last box, the woman remarked airily, "Oh, well, I wasn't planning on buying anything anyway. I'm just looking for a friend."

The salesman, whose back was turned, stopped dead. He turned around slowly and faced her for a long moment. Finally he said sweetly, "Madam, I'll take the last box down on one condition."

"Yes," she asked, wide-eyed.

"If you can give me any reason to believe," he exploded, "that your friend is in it!"

A girl was telling her friend that she'd just become engaged to a traveling salesman.

"What's he like?" asked her friend eagerly. "Is he good-looking?"

"I wouldn't say he's handsome, just passable."

"Does he have a good personality?"

"He'd never stand out in a crowd."

"Does he have money?"

"If he does, he won't spend it."

"Does he have any bad habits?"

"Well, he drinks an awful lot."

"Lord, girl, if you can't say anything *for* him, why ever are you marrying the guy?"

"He's on the road all the time. *I'll* never see him!"

Joe Marsh, of the Spindletop Restaurant, loves this one:

The salesman stood sadly at the front door of the farmhouse.

"I hate to tell you this, ma'am," he said, "but I just ran over your cat. I'm terribly sorry and I would like to replace him."

"Well, don't just stand there!" she snapped. "There's a mouse in the kitchen!"

☻

My brother Milton, of Kay-Windsor, loves this one:

It was a brutal night. The rain was coming down in sheets. The wind was blowing fiercely and visibility was almost nil. The salesman was having trouble driving.

"This is a rough one," he told his pet dog, Fido, who accompanied him on all his trips. "Looks like we're in for it!"

But no sooner had he stopped speaking than he spotted a small motel by the side of the road. He couldn't have been happier. He drove up and parked in front of the office, picked up his pup and walked in.

"I'd like a room for tonight," he told the proprietor.

"Sorry, mister," said the man at the desk. "We're all filled up."

"I could sleep on the sofa," suggested the salesman.

"That's where I sleep."

"But you can't turn me out on a night like this," protested the salesman.

The man at the desk simply shrugged, and the salesman realized it was useless to plead. He turned to go, but the proprietor stopped him before he got to the door.

"Just a minute, mister," he said. "Leave the pup here. I wouldn't turn a dog out on a night like this!"

Since Bill Fine was a traveling salesman, he was forced to spend a large portion of time away from home. This might have made him the envy of some married men, but Bill was married to a remarkably beautiful girl—a statuesque blonde, flawless of face and figure.

No one could blame Bill for worrying about his wife when he had to leave her alone so much. What's more, he had reason to be jealous. There was evidence that she was not alone when she was alone. Suspecting, and not knowing, was driving him crazy and during one of his stopovers at home he hired a private detective to follow her while he was away on his next trip.

When he returned, he immediately called the private eye. "Tell me the truth," he begged. "Were my suspicions well-founded? I've got to know! It's the element of doubt that's driving me out of my mind."

"Well," began the detective, "it looks bad. As soon as you left the house, a tall, handsome guy went to the door. In a few minutes your wife came out and the two of them got into a car. I followed them in mine. They went to a night club and I went in behind them. I watched them dance cheek to cheek and hold hands at the table.

"After about three hours, they drove back to your house. Again I followed them and watched through the window. I saw them walk into the bedroom and embrace, but then they turned out the lights and I couldn't see any more."

"What did I tell you!" cried the salesman. "That element of doubt again!"

☻

Meyer Robinson, of Manischewitz Wine, knew two salesman who went wild game hunting in darkest Africa. While they were walking, they came to a clearing in the jungle.

Suddenly Jack whispered to Milton, who was directly in front of him. "Don't t-t-turn around t-t-too quickly, but is that a lion behind me?"

"You're asking me?" retorted Milton. "Am I a fur salesman?"

☻

Al the cutter was eating lunch with a salesman friend. Al ordered chicken noodle soup and his friend ordered borscht. When the waiter returned, he brought Al his bowl of chicken

noodle, but instead of borscht, he brought Al's friend a bowl of potato soup.

"I don't got borscht," the waiter told the fellow. "I brought you a bowl of potato soup instead. Taste it—it's very good."

He did and immediately his face lit up. "It's great. The best I ever had!"

Then he let Al taste it.

"It is good," Al agreed. "Waiter, why didn't you bring *me* some potato soup since it's so good?"

The waiter shrugged, "Did you order borscht?"

☻

Max Asnas, of the Stage Delicatessen, says, "Clothes don't make the man . . . but a good suit made many a lawyer."

☻

A salesman took a girl driving along a lonely country road. They came to a quiet spot and the car stopped.

"I guess we're out of gas," the salesman leered.

With this announcement, the girl carefully opened her purse and pulled out a bottle.

"Wow!" exclaimed the salesman. "You've got a whole fifth! What kind is it?"

"Esso regular," replied the girl.

☻

Irving Stempel, of McKettrick Williams, recently went to a baseball game with two of his friends. One was a sales manager and the other was the star salesman of the same firm.

At the game the salesman bet his boss that the Yankees would win. His boss picked Cleveland. The final score was New York, 5—Cleveland, 3.

"Thanks, boss," the salesman smiled as he was handed the $25 they had bet. "You know what I'm going to do with this money? I'm going to frame it so I can always show people I'm smarter than my boss."

"In that case," said the sales manager, "give me back the $25 and I'll give you a check."

Irving Nelson and Carl Rosen, of Puritan Dresses, prefer the story about the salesman who had tried unsuccessfully for five years to sell a tough prospect. After each visit, the salesman grunted, "I wish I had a hundred like you."

When the customer became curious and asked him why he kept repeating that phrase, the salesman replied, "I have a thousand like you, but I wish I only had a hundred!"

AND BEFORE WE LEAVE THE GARMENT CENTER
REMEMBER WHAT CONFUCIUS COHEN SAYS:
FAVORITE SLOGAN OF
PEOPLE IN THIS INDUSTRY IS
"PIECE GOODS ON EARTH
GOOD WOOL TOWARDS MEN"

COMEDY AT THE COPA

Almost every comedian begins his act with, "A funny thing happened to me on the way to the theatre . . ." Well, nothing at all ever happened to me till I met Jules Podell, the famed impresario of the Copa.

In the many years I've known Jolly Jules, we've always been great friends on and off the job. Like his club, his home is fabulous and decorated in the best of taste. He must have spent a fortune just for the decorator's thought waves. I'll never forget the first time I visited him there.

Right away I noticed that he had pictures of comedians scattered all over the place. See what I mean about good taste? He has a terrific picture of Joe E. Lewis in his living room, a vivid (what else?) profile of Jimmy Durante in his study, and a striking oil painting of Danny Thomas in his bedroom. I can't tell you where my picture is . . . but every time I went to wash my hands, I saw it.

Seriously, though, the Copa is one of my favorite night spots. It better be. It's buttered a lot of my bread. And as a New

Yorker, I get a big kick out of entertaining the home folk, especially the wandering salesmen who are there in droves every opening night to cheer me on. In honor of this fraternity, many of whom make the Copa their home away from home, and office away from office, it seems only fitting that I should kick off with the one about the Knight of the Road who...

☻

... was riding down an old dirt road when his car jerked convulsively to a stop. Looking around, he saw an old house, not fifty feet from where he broke down. He walked over and spotted an old farmer sitting on a rocking chair on the porch.

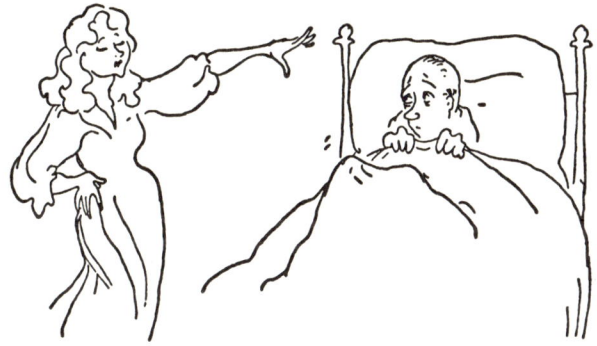

"Could you tell me where the nearest garage is?"

"It's closed for the night," the farmer informed him, "but you can stay here and I'll take you there in the mornin'."

That night while the salesman was fast asleep, he heard a loud knock on the door.

"Who's there?" he asked.

"It's only me," came a sweet voice from the hallway.

Then, before he could say another word, a beautiful blonde dressed in a revealing negligee entered the room.

"I'm the farmer's daughter," she cooed.

"W-w—well, what do you want?" he stammered.

"Don't you know?"

With this, the salesman jumped up, pulled on his pants, whipped on his shirt and bellowed, "I'm getting out of here!"

Amazed, the lovely lass called after him as he tore out of the room, "Brother, are you in the wrong joke!"

☺

Another salesman I knew wasn't so naive. Returning home after a long trip on the road, he immediately went to see his girl-friend.

As luck would have it, her little brother was seated in front of the TV set watching his favorite western program.

Annoyed by the little brat's presence, the guy decided to use some child psychology on him.

"Bobby," he suggested, "look outside the window and for every man you see wearing a red hat, I'll give you fifty cents."

"Sounds great," answered the little terror. Then he ran upstairs to look out the window.

Not ten minutes later, while the salesman and his girl were just getting reacquainted, the youngster suddenly dashed into the room.

"Didn't I tell you to watch for men with red hats!" shouted the irate salesman.

"But I did," the boy explained, "and while you were talking to my sister, a Shriner's Parade passed by. You owe me twelve hundred bucks!"

☺

However, there are many others who can justifiably point to money—or the lack of it—as the root of all their miseries.

I'm thinking specifically of a one-time prosperous manufacturer who had gotten himself into quite a predicament. He had run up large bills with three piece-goods firms, and all three were literally howling for his scalp.

In desperation, the manufacturer consulted his attorney. "Let's notify the newspapers that you've committed suicide," suggested the lawyer. "After that we'll hold a mock funeral, and if we carry it off convincingly enough, it'll solve all your problems."

It was an impressive funeral. Flowers were generously spread throughout the chapel and the house was good. At the proper time, everyone walked solemnly around the bier, and bid a final farewell to the deceased.

Then it was the three creditors' turn.

"Poor Irving," sighed the first. "He never paid his bills on time, but I'll sure miss him."

"S'long, Irving," said the second man, "too bad it had to end this way."

But the third creditor was enraged. "You louse," he snarled, "Pulling a fast one to get out of paying your bills! Even though you're dead, I'm going to get personal satisfaction!"

With that, he pulled out a revolver from his coat pocket and aimed it at the prone figure.

"Look, don't get excited," cried the corpse, sitting up. "You I'll pay!"

☺

During one of my engagements at the Copa, Ed Sullivan phoned and asked me if I'd like to appear on his program. Naturally I was flattered and accepted his invitation.

The next day when I arrived at the studio to begin rehearsals and I saw Ed, I thought he was sick . . . he was smiling. While I was waiting to begin my act, I thought I'd cheer him up, so I told him this story:

After ten hectic years of marriage a battling couple had the worst spat of their marriage. Every piece of china was broken and the house was a shambles. Thoroughly disgusted, the husband grabbed his hat and coat and stormed out of the house.

Not knowing where to go to cool his ire, the steaming spouse took the subway to Grand Central. When he arrived in the center of town, he decided that a visit to some of the local bars would make him forget his troubles. He marched into the nearest one and started downing highballs.

A few minutes later he emerged from the gin mill slightly besotted. He imbibed the fresh night air, and after a short walk, entered another bar.

By 3 A.M., the hapless husband decided that he had gotten up enough courage to take anything his wife could mete out.

He left the bar and started walking up Eighth Avenue looking for the nearest subway station.

Suddenly, he found himself in front of Madison Square Garden. He looked up and there in bright neon lights glared the sign: BIG FIGHT TONIGHT. He paused, re-focussed his eyes, and sighed:

"Home at last!"

☻

Everyone who has ever been associated with the garment industry knows that almost every manufacturer employs beautiful, shapely models to display his latest fashions. Most of the buyers and salesmen they come in contact with are men, and being men, it is only natural that they appreciate how attractive these girls are. Models, of course, have to learn to be diplomatic in dealing with wolves. A show of outraged virtue, after all, could seriously hamper their careers.

Take the case of the two models who were discussing an out-of-town buyer who was dating one of them.

FIRST MODEL: I have a date with Sam.

SECOND MODEL: He's a wolf. He'll tear your dress off.

FIRST MODEL: Thanks for telling me. . . . I'll wear an old dress.

☻

All models must be mindful of their appearance, and a few are especially vain. I'm thinking of one girl in particular—a very self-conscious lass, and I don't mean that she lacked poise.

Dress manufacturer Mike Levine swears he heard this from someone who heard it from someone who heard it from the model herself.

She had just entered her dressing room to change for her next stroll in a fashion show when she spied an elderly window washer working on the other side of the glass.

She had plenty of time so she decided to indulge in a little teasing. First she loosened one strap and let it fall from her shoulder. Then she loosened the other. She watched the window washer out of the corner of her eye.

No reaction.

Surprised and irritated, she wriggled out of the dress and slowly began to remove her slip, all the while keeping her eye on the old man behind the window.

Still no reaction.

"I'll teach you a lesson, you old goat," she muttered to herself. Quickly, she stripped off her remaining garments and walked boldly over to the window. She stood directly in front of the old man and glared at him.

He continued with his work, glancing at her blankly now and then. Finally, he stopped.

"What's the matter, lady?" he asked. "Haven't you ever seen a window washer before?"

☻

Bosses are another big source of conversation in the Garment Center. But, of course, it's nothing like the old days. Now that unions are here, a modern boss who wants to pull the wool over his employees' eyes, needs a much better yarn. Employees are independent and are not afraid to speak up for their rights.

This could be typified by the recent conversation between a cutter and his boss.

"You're nothing but a *capitalist!*" shouted the disgruntled employee.

"A *capitalist!*" screamed his boss. "Listen to me, Hymie. When I have a good season, I make money. When I make money, I pay taxes. When I pay taxes, I'm broke. When I'm broke, I have no money. When I have no money, I'm a bum . . . and a bum, *you* call a *capitalist!*"

Every time I'm at the Copa, I always make sure that I get to see my old friend Leonard Lyons, the *New York Post* columnist. Besides being a terrific writer, Lenny has a wonderful sense of humor. Once while lunching in Lindy's, I told him this one:

An old waiter who had worked at Lindy's since it had opened, suddenly passed away.

Heartbroken, his wife, who had loved him dearly and had been very dependent upon him, didn't know what to do.

Then, as always happens in cases like these, she was swamped with advice from relatives and friends eager to help.

She was urged to see fortune tellers, spiritualists, magicians and cultists. She was told to attend seances where they communicate with the dead. But all these things proved disappointing, and she was getting progressively worse. Finally, her cousin, Irving, came up with a new solution.

"I've heard," he said, "that if you want to speak to a dead person, you have to go to the place where he spent most of his time."

Having tried everything else, the wife decided to go to Lindy's

and try out this theory. When she arrived there, she sat down at a table and started calling her husband. "Seymour," she asked, "can you hear me?"

"Of course I can hear you," came the low but clear reply.
"Seymour, can you speak louder?"
"No."
"Well then," motioned his wife, "come a little closer."
"Can't."
"Well, why not?"
"Because that's not my table!"

Phil Schwartz, of Red Cross Shoes, tells of the Copa chorus girl who, after seeing her name linked romantically with a noted romeo commented: "We have nothing in common. He's interested in girls and I'm interested in boys."

A lush hailed a cab outside the Copa. "Take me to the Copacabana, Driver," he shouted, as he hopped into the taxi.
The disgusted hackie got out and opened the door.
"You're in front of the Copa now, fellow," he snapped.

The inebriated character got out and glanced up at the awning of the nitery.

"Thash okay," he grumbled. "But next time don't drive so fast!"

☺

Whenever I'm at the Copa, I try to size up my audience and then tell the stories which I feel will amuse them most. However, there are many stories which are so universal that they amuse everyone.

For example, husband and wife jokes are always very popular with the customers. Because after all, every husband has a wife and vice versa. But marriage isn't the sacred institution it used to be. In fact, these days it seems that many a girl gets married just to keep herself occupied while she waits for the right man to come along. Just the other day, I heard two actors discussing the merits of a rising young starlet.

"Say what you want about her," said the first, "but before she's through that girl will probably make a good wife for five or six guys!"

Even more unbelievable was the conversation between the young movie queen and her fiancé: "Sweetheart, we'll have to postpone our marriage for a little while."

"But why?" he demanded. "Don't you love me?"

"Of course, darling. But I just married another man."

☺

But it seems that divorce is a luxury only for the rich. A poor man can't get divorced because he can't afford the alimony. You know what alimony is, don't you? It's the same as paying installments on your car—after the wreck.

☺

A Chicago housewife wanted to put her philandering husband in jail for not paying his alimony.

"Look," he pleaded, "I'll make it all up to you. We'll take a trip to New York. We'll take in the sights, see a show, have dinner, and then a few drinks in a nice little spot. Maybe we'll be able to rekindle the old flame."

His wife agreed. They took the train to New York and checked in at the Waldorf Astoria. Then they went out on the town. He took her to the Stork Club where they had some drinks and a steak dinner. Then they went to the Copa. When they left the Copa, the husband was so drunk that his wife had to help him back to the hotel and put him to bed.

When he was all tucked in, she began to worry about her children back in Chicago. Unable to sleep until she'd calmed her fears, she decided to call the maid long distance despite the lateness of the hour.

"Hello, Operator," she said, as she picked up the phone. "Get me Export 3-2333."

As soon as the drunken husband heard the phone number, he roused himself from his stupor, crying, "Hey, honey, don't call that number! It'll connect you with my wife!"

Furrier Sol Shulman told me this one:

He was a silk salesman and she was a buyer for one of the leading manufacturers. They met whenever he came to sell his latest items, and eventually he proposed. She accepted.

For their honeymoon, they went to Niagara Falls. They arrived on Friday night and had a wonderful time. Saturday and Sunday, too, were blissful days that he would never forget.

But when he awoke on Monday morning, she was gone. He quickly dressed, ran downstairs and searched all over for her.

Not finding a trace of her, he packed his bags and took the next train back to New York.

First he went home, but she wasn't there. Then he went to his office and sat down, brooding over his fate.

"What's the matter, Sam?" asked one of his co-workers. "Why are you so blue?"

Heartbroken, Sam told him about the events of the last few hours.

"Don't worry," his friend reassured him, "you know she never sees salesmen on Mondays!"

Secretaries never seem to please anyone. If they're good . . . then their bosses dislike them . . . and if they're bad, their bosses' wives dislike them.

Of course, most secretaries are competent, efficient workers and are above reproach. However, there are good and bad of every kind . . .

Take the case of the cutie who was transferred to the New York office of a large garment concern.

When she was introduced to the boss, he told her, "All right, Miss Stone, do exactly what you did at the Chicago office."

"Okay," she answered. "Kiss me!"

An equally forward secretary went to an Atlantic City convention with her boss. At the hotel desk, he did his best to get separate rooms. However, he was informed that due to the convention, only one was available. As they took the elevator up to their room, the manufacturer sternly warned his secretary that once they got upstairs she was to keep her mind strictly on business. The girl agreed.

But, that night after the lights had been turned out, the secretary impulsively decided that she wouldn't be averse to a little play. "Yooo, hooo, Mr. Gold," she cooed.

"What is it?" growled her boss.

"Can I have more of the covers? I'm awfully chilly."

Angrily, the boss tossed the cover her way. There was quiet for another minute. Then she cooed again. "Mr. Gold, yooo-hooo."

"Now what is it?"

"Would you like to do me a big favor?" she asked seductively.

"What?"

"Would you get me a glass of water? I'm very thirsty."

There was a slight pause. The manufacturer turned toward her, asking softly, "Miss Blatz, how would you like to be Mrs. Gold for just tonight?"

Excitedly, the girl cuddled closer. "Oh, I'd just love that!"

"All right," he bellowed, "then go and get your own glass of water!"

AND AS WE LEAVE THE COPA
REMEMBER WHAT CONFUCIUS COHEN SAYS:
A SMART SECRETARY IS ONE
WHO CHECKS BOSS'S ADVANCES
UNTIL BOSS ADVANCE HER NEXT WEEK'S CHECK.

MIAMI MIRTH

Miami is God's country... He's the only one who can afford it! It's the land of the palms... all open. It's got hotels and motels. Some motels are built so poorly that you can hear the lady next door changing her mind.

When you get to Miami... you'll know it. No matter how hot it is, the women who have them will be wearing their mink coats.

Pepi Einstein, Leonard Lyon's wonderful mother-in-law, tells of one Park Avenue society girl who arrived in Miami on a day in which the temperature had zoomed well over 100. As she

got out of her car, she was overcome by the heat and fainted. A crowd of concerned bystanders gathered around her.

"Get a glass of water!" shouted one.

"Get a doctor!" screamed another.

"Open up her mink!" yelled the third.

The first time I was in Miami, I appeared at the Terrace Cafe, which was owned by Lou Walters. I have also appeared in the Eden Roc, the Fountainbleau, the Sans Souci and the Five O'Clock Club, when it was owned by Martha Raye.

Martha's a great gal, and it was fun working with her. She's got a terrific sense of humor and really broke me up when she told me this one:

Willie Gordon, a cutter from the Garment Center, had had a good season. His boss had given him a lot of overtime, and being the thrifty type, he was able to save enough money to realize a life-long dream—a trip to Miami.

Neither Willie nor his wife had ever been to a really fancy hotel and naturally they were a mite nervous about the whole thing. One thing that bothered them was when and how much to tip. But they consulted with friends who were more experienced and learned what was the appropriate amount or percentage for various services.

Determined to appear poised and worldly, they set off for the southern resort city. When they arrived, they checked in at the swank hotel at which they had reservations, went to their room, and began to unpack. They congratulated one another on the smooth way the tip to the bellboy had been handled.

When they had finished unpacking, they changed into their bathing suits and set off for the beach. Mrs. G. couldn't wait to compare the Florida ocean to the Jones Beach waters. She dashed into the surf immediately and began swimming out. She swam so far and so long, that when it came time for the return trip, she became fearful she'd never make shore.

In a panic she screamed, "Help! I'm drowning!"

The lifeguard, who had been watching her from his perch, dived in and pulled her to safety. He carried her to the blanket where Willie sat frozen with fear and deposited her limp form beside him.

"Better not try that again," he advised her.

She opened her eyes and pulled her husband close.

"Willie," she whispered into his ear, "how much do we tip?"

Sales manager Fred Perlberg was seated in a Miami restaurant with two of his associates when the waiter stepped up to one of his companions and asked, "What'll you have?"

"I'll have a salmon sandwich on rye bread."

"What do you want salmon for?" scoffed the waiter. "Tuna fish is much better. And instead of rye, take whole wheat. It's healthier for you."

"Good," agreed Fred's friend, "make it tuna on whole wheat."

"And you?" the waiter asked as he turned to the second man.

"I'll have bacon and tomato on toast. And give me a cup of coffee."

"Ha," scoffed the waiter, "do you think bacon's so good for you? And coffee, all it does is keep you up at night. Why don't you take a nice roast beef sandwich with a cup of tea."

"All right. Make it roast beef on whole wheat with tea."

Then it was Fred's turn. "And what do you suggest?" he asked, turning to the waiter.

"Suggest!" barked the waiter. "Who has time to make suggestions?"

Jean Suits, manager of the Sans Souci, was host to a salesman who was vacationing in Miami. The man had taken an expensive course at Arthur Murray's dance studio before he left New York and, as a result, he was the picture of grace on the dance floor. At the Charleston, which was experiencing a revival in popularity, he especially excelled.

The first night he was in Miami, he received a wire from the home office that an emergency had arisen which necessitated his return on the morning plane. Instead of sulking, he decided to make the best of his only night in Florida.

When he entered the hotel lobby that night, he spotted a curvaceous cutie seated there. He engaged her in conversation and then took her dancing.

As they danced the Charleston in mad abandon, he romanced her. "Look, Ruth," he gasped, "I really go for you in a big way. But I don't have much time. I have to be back in New York in the morning. Can't we speed things up between us?"

"What do you want from me!" She panted. "I'm dancing as fast as I can!"

Miami *Herald* columnist, Jack Kofoed, tells the one about the tourist who pulled up in front of the Eden Roc, handed his suitcase to the porter and announced: "I've come here to spend the winter."

The porter shook his head and replied, "You come to the wrong place. We don't have any winter here!"

And Herb Rau, of the Miami *Daily News*, counters this with the one about the Miami man who died and went to his final resting place.

When he arrived, he noticed the palm trees and bright sun

beating down on all the inhabitants. "Gee," he remarked, "heaven is just like Miami."

To which one fellow quickly replied, "This ain't heaven!"

☺

Variety's Florida representative, Larry Sollaway, loves this story:

Three elderly men were sitting in the lobby of the Sans Souci. To pass the time they were discussing the effects of old age on them.

The first man, age 73, said, "My hearing is going. People have to shout when they speak to me."

"That's pretty bad," agreed the second man, age 79, "but I think I'm worse off. My eyesight is beginning to fail me. When I walk down the stret, I can't make out the faces of my friends. Even worse, I can't tell a blonde from a redhead."

Then they both turned to the third man who was 93. "And what's your trouble, Max?" one asked.

"Well," he began, "my trouble is much worse than yours. The other day, I was at home with my wife. We had dinner and then some wine. Later I fell asleep on the sofa. When I awoke, I noticed that my wife had gone into the bedroom, and when I entered, she was asleep. Shaking her gently, I said, 'Move over, honey, and we'll have a little fun.'

" 'But,' she protested, 'We had a little fun only twenty minutes ago.' "

The old man tapped his forehead thoughtfully. "My problem, gentlemen," he sighed, "is that my memory is slipping."

☺

Once, while I was flying to Florida, I was accompanied by Paul Yampole, of Miss Jane Inc., on his way to Miami for a well-earned rest.

A wolf who was seated behind us tried to make a play for the pretty hostess.

Moving close to her he said, "How about stepping out, sweetie?"

"Why not?" replied the girl, and opened the door of the airliner for him.

☺

Buyer Sid Kay, of R. and K. Originals, and I were seated in the lobby of the Fountainbleau when we overheard a cynic and his friend having the following conversation:

"When someone builds a better mousetrap the world will beat a path to his door."

"Bunk," scoffed his companion, "when someone builds a better mousetrap . . . some rat will steal it!"

☺

Paul Bruun, of the Florida *Sun*, had a friend who came from a family of writers. His sister wrote books that no one would read. His brother wrote songs that no one would sing. His mother wrote plays that no one would see and his father wrote checks that no one would cash.

☺

Two of Harry Mufson's recent Eden Roc guests were a New York buyer and his wife. He was a Garment Center buyer who had courted and eventually fallen in love with a shapely advertising copywriter. They wanted to have a June wedding and a honeymoon at Miami's Eden Roc Hotel, but the ad agency where the bride worked was in the midst of a hectic promotion campaign and the head of the agency was reluctant to grant her a leave.

Luckily, however, the girl was able to induce a close friend, Susan Rose, an unemployed copywriter, to take over for her

61

during her absence. Since Miss Rose was an exceptionally pretty girl, the male copywriters at the agency were satisfied with the substitution. And the bridal couple had their June wedding and honeymoon.

Some weeks later, while the bride was out of town visiting her ailing mother, the groom was invited to a party. As he entered the apartment, the hostess greeted him and in the course of introductions, who should he come upon but the very same Miss Rose.

As the hostess began introducing them to each other, the young husband stopped her—and the entire party as well—by declaring:

"Oh yes, I know Miss Rose. As a matter of fact, she substituted for my wife on our honeymoon!"

☻

Dave Schwartz, of Jonathan Logan, prefers this one:

After having an extremely profitable year, the wealthy dress manufacturer went to his Florida home.

While he was in Florida he met a buxom blonde beauty and immediately fell in love with her. Since he was somewhat older

than she, he knew that a little diplomacy and bribery were called for.

"Marry me," he told her, "and I'll buy you a new Cadillac convertible."

"I've got two already," she told him.

"How about a new diamond ring?" he offered.

"I've got a beautiful ring already," she said, lifting her hand and displaying a huge, shiny stone.

"I'll give you an exquisite mink coat."

"I've got a mink and a sable, too."

Confused, the manufacturer asked, "Well, what do you want?"

"Cash," she replied, "just cold, hard cash!"

"Sorry," came the reply, "that's one thing I can't get wholesale!"

Whenever I entertain in Miami, my old pal, Herb Kelly, of the Miami *Daily News*, usually attends at least one of my shows. Not too long ago, I noted that Herb was particularly impressed with this one:

A young man, who had recently graduated from Harvard, started out with a large silk firm as a stockroom boy. He was a bright lad, and within six months was made a salesman. In another six months he was upped to sales manager and shortly afterwards to general manager.

A few days after his last promotion, he was summoned by the president of the firm, who explained that he would retire soon and would turn the presidency over to the newcomer.

Overwhelmed, the young man said, "Thanks."

"Thanks!" growled the president. "You've been with this firm only a year. Is that all you can think of to say?"

"Well," said the young man, "thanks a lot, Dad."

And then there's the one broker Adolphus Roggenberg, of Newburger, Loeb & Co., tells about the two garment manufacturers who were seated on the beach in Miami when an old Garment Center acquaintance passed by. "You see, Max, over there," said one to the other. "He must have had a bad year."

"How do you know?"

"Because he's staying at last year's hotel!"

The Lerner Boys of Philadelphia's Celebrity Room knew a thrifty fellow who came to Miami for the first time. Having heard about the prices of rooms in the gay resort, he decided to check with the desk clerk of the hotel before he signed the register. He walked up to the clerk and asked, "How much is a room?"

"A dollar a day," came the business-like reply.

"A dollar a day! Why that's wonderful! I heard that it was so expensive down here and—"

"And if you'd like a double occupancy room," continued the clerk, "it'll cost you a dollar and a half a day."

"Wonderful! Wonderful!" exclaimed the tourist. "At these rates, I'll be able to stay here for a month."

"I doubt it," answered the clerk.

"Why not?"

"The place is on fire!"

And Miami *Herald's* George Bourke tells the one about the silk salesman who was on the first rocket ship to the Moon.

When he arrived, he immediately began a tour of the places to see how the Moon men did things. During his travels he entered a huge factory and asked a Moon man what was manufactured there.

"This is a baby factory," explained the man from outer space. "Our babies come off an assembly line."

Then the salesman, who was amazed by this phenomenon, gave the Moon man a detailed description of how babies are conceived on Earth.

"What do you know!" exclaimed the listener. "That's just how we make automobiles up here!"

Dr. William Hitzig, the great diagnostician, who has always cared for my aches and pains, advised a Madison Avenue sportsman to take his ailing wife to Miami. The warm weather, he felt, would do her good.

When they arrived in the tourist town, the wife took a turn for the worse and the husband had to employ a full-time nurse. It just so happened that the nurse was a raven-haired beauty and the sportsman took an immediate liking to her.

The couple remained in Florida throughout the winter and when May came, they returned to New York.

About two weeks after their return, the husband received a letter. As he read the contents, a worried look came over his face. His wife, noticing his gloom, asked what the trouble was.

"Oh," he shrugged, "it's really nothing serious."

"But you seem so worried," she replied. "Won't you tell me what's wrong? After all, as man and wife we should share our sorrows and our joys. We're a team, you and I. We must share responsibilities. So tell me, darling, what's troubling you?"

"Well," he began, "since you put it that way, this letter is from the nurse."

"Yes?"

"It seems she's learned that she's in trouble, and she blames . . . us!"

Sammy Citron, of Barbara Dance Frocks, shares my Miami fans' enthusiasm for this one:

The bride greeted her husband with a big kiss when he returned home from work.

Anxious to please, she asked, "Had a hard day? I bet you're tired and hungry. How would you like a nice, thick steak with french fries, a big tossed salad and strawberry shortcake?"

"No, dear, let's just have dinner at home."

☺

Professors don't have a monopoly on absent-mindedness, agent Johnny Pransky tells me. He knew a businessman who returned from his honeymoon in Miami and spent days going through his files to refresh his memory as to what his own business was all about. He came across names on his calendar that he couldn't place for the life of him. One, in particular, bothered him because it looked familiar. Fearing that the name might belong to a business contact he couldn't afford to neglect, he decided to phone the number and find out who the man was.

"Hello," he said, "I'm sorry to trouble you, but I ran across your name on my desk. Is there anything I'm supposed to do for you?"

"You have already have," answered the voice on the phone. I'm your wife's first husband."

☺

**AND BEFORE WE LEAVE MIAMI
REMEMBER WHAT CONFUCIUS COHEN SAYS:
A HONEYMOON IS WHAT MAN GOES ON
BEFORE WORKING FOR NEW BOSS.**

THE BEST FROM TEX

Have you ever been to Texas? Well, if you have, you know that it's nothing but miles and miles of miles and miles . . . and by the time you get around to seeing it . . . you're too old to enjoy it.

When I was in Texas, I played at the Statler Hilton and the Shamrock Hilton. Hilton, you know who he is. He's the guy who builds hotels all over the world. He's even got one in Egypt. In fact, he's so progressive that he's got his architects working on the plans for a hotel that's simply out of this world . . . the Mars Hilton.

Speaking about Hilton, I wonder if Houston columnist, Paul Hochuli was kidding when he told me the following story:

A big game hunter, who wanted to add to his already impressive collection of trophies, induced a native of darkest Africa to lead him into dangerous territory never before explored by man.

After trudging through swamps and jungles, they came to a clearing. Turning around to the big game hunter, the native announced, "Me go now."

"But you can't leave me here!" pleaded the hunter. "I'll never be able to find my way back."

"You no worry," assured the native, "just sit down here, and before you know it, Hilton come and build hotel around you!"

☺

Getting back to Texas . . . and there's a lot to get back to, Texans as a group are probably the proudest people in this country . . . and the richest, too.

In Texas, they celebrate three holidays: Sam Houston Day, The Alamo Day, and December 15—that's the day the new Cadillacs come out.

I know one Texan who has two Cadillacs—one for red lights, and the other for green ones. But his neighbor has outdone him. He has *four* Cadillacs—one for each direction.

Texas is also the place where the men proudly proclaim: "Remember the Alamo," while the women counter, "Remember the Alimony!"

☺

Judge Abraham Lincoln Marovitz tells about a Texas wife who was suing her mate on the grounds of mental cruelty. As luck would have it, the judge was a life-long friend of the soon-to-be-shedded spouse.

"You will pay your wife $1,000 a week in alimony," the judge informed his friend.

"But Judge," pleaded the husband, "have a heart." Then he went into a long dissertation about how he had helped the judge attain his present position. He reminded him of how he had loaned him his assignments in high school and helped him maintain high grades.

"Well, I guess we can lower it to $500 a week," reflected the judge.

"And remember how I helped you with your math problems and your chemistry course," his friend continued.

"Make it $350."

"I even loaned you money to pay your tuition in law school."

"Three hundred it is," declared the judge.

Still not satisfied, his friend added, "And even after you grad-

uated, I was the one who fixed you up with a date for the homecoming dance, with the girl who was later to become your wife."

"So it was you!" roared the judge. He pounded his gavel and growled, "Case closed at $1,000 a week."

Texans are famous for their prosperity. And some of them go to ridiculous lengths to point it out. Like the man who couldn't find a parking space, so he bought downtown Dallas.

Dallas columnist Tony Zoppi says that gold-digging girls are always seeking to latch on to wealthy Texans.

He cites the case of the ambitious playgirl who ambled into a Texas bar and walked over to a prosperous-looking chap seated at the bar. In no time at all, they were deeply engrossed in conversation. In the middle of it all, the playgirl asked huskily, "Pardon me, but how much did you say your name was?"

☺

Danton Walker, the New York *Daily News* columnist who's a whiz on every subject, told me about another Texan who hadn't been feeling well for some time.

The rich rancher went to see his doctor, and after a thorough examination, the physician told him, "My advice to you is to take a trip to France. A rest in that climate will do you a world of good."

"Why go there?" asked the Texan. "I'll just send for it!"

☺

A Bostonian and Texan met on a plane headed for New York. Naturally, the cowpoke steered the conversation around to his native state.

"There's no place like Texas," he boasted. "Even our heroes are the bravest men in the world. Did Boston ever have anyone to match Sam Houston?"

"Well," countered the easterner confidently, "you've heard of Paul Revere."

"Paul Revere?" repeated the Texan. "Isn't he the guy who had to run for help?"

☺

A pair of Texans were taking a train trip across their native state. During a stop, they went into the station diner for a bite. When they reboarded the train, they noticed that a city dude had got on and taken one of their seats.

"That's my seat, son," one of the cowboys told him.

"It *was* your seat," corrected the new passenger.

Without blinking an eye, the Texan whipped out his six-shooter and shot the dude between the eyes. The conductor and a pair of porters carried out the limp form.

"You know, Clem," the sharpshooter told his friend as he re-holstered his gun, "it's people like that who give Texas a bad name."

☺

Even Texas doctors believe that there is no place in the world like Texas. Consequently, they think Texans are better in every respect than men from other places.

Willie Kolmar, of Kolmar-Marcus, the fellow who sells me my suits and never pulls any wool over my eyes, tells the one about the salesman who was down in Texas putting over a big deal with Neiman-Marcus.

One night he left his overcoat in his hotel room and caught a terrible cold. Try as he would, he couldn't shake it. In desperation he went to see a doctor.

Once inside the office, the doctor told him to take off his shirt.

"Ha," sneered the medico as he took it off, "you call that a chest? Texan men have hair on their chests as thick as wool." Then the sawbones looked at his arms. "And you call those arms," the M.D. sneered. "Texan men have hair under their arms as thick as wool."

Then the salesman, who was almost reaching the boiling point, removed his trousers.

"You call those legs!" the Doc shouted. "Texan men have hair on their legs as thick as wool."

The salesman had had enough. "Look, Doc," he exploded, "I came here for an examination—not to knit a sweater!"

☺

Texans have their troubles, though—at least this story Benny Papell tells proves that ranchers do.

The worried man called the vet. "I don't know what's the matter with my prize bull," he complained. "It's time for him to get together with the cows, but the listless critter hasn't made a move yet."

The vet said he'd be right over. And so he was, with a bag full of hormones, vitamins, and remedies designed to perk up bulls. He worked over the animal for an hour and assured the rancher he could expect results in 24 hours.

Two days later the cow man called the vet. He was not satisfied.

"Aren't you being a bit foolish?" asked the vet. "What did you expect—a calf overnight?"

"Look, Doc," said the rancher. "Last night I put him in the barn with two cows. The least I could expect was a couple of happy faces!"

Ben Mankin knew a traveling salesman who was swept off his feet by one of those tall, torrid Dallas models when he was traveling through Texas. After a whirlwind courtship, they were married and set off for a lavish honeymoon in Europe. For a month they really lived it up.

Trouble was that the salesman, at 62, was not the man he once was, while his bride, at 23, was in full bloom. By the time they returned to the groom's home in Brooklyn, he was worn down and out.

The first morning after their arrival, the salesman found he didn't have the strength to rise from his bed. A doctor was called. He examined the patient and found him suffering from acute physical exhaustion. As he was jotting down a prescription, the bride sauntered into the bedroom. Naturally, the doctor took note of her beauty and youth.

"Doctor," the patient called weakly. "Don't leave without telling me what's the matter with me. Come here."

The doc walked over to the patient's bedside. "Tell me the truth," whispered the aging salesman hoarsely. "Am I underweight?"

"Not dangerously," replied the doc, with a glance at the energetic bride. "Just undersexed."

Golf courses are the same the world over. I know one pair of Texans who were in the midst of a hot game when they were forced to halt by two women who were conversing in front of the 8th hole. Since they were some distance away, one of the men was appointed to approach the gossipy pair and ask them to move away.

He came back in a few moments, his face brick red. "Hank," he advised his friend, "I reckon you'd better be the one to talk to them gals. One of 'em's my wife and the other one's my girlfriend."

"Okay, partner," agreed his pal. "I reckon I can do that all right."

He started off across the links, but got no farther than the first man had. He was mopping his brow when he returned to the side of his friend.

"Tarnation," he muttered. "Small world, isn't it?"

☺

A Texas girl was telling her friend about her fiancé, an elderly Texan twenty years her senior.

"Jasper's a wonderful fellow," enthused the engaged girl. "I'm sure we'll be very happy."

"But he's so much older than you are," pointed out her friend. "He won't enjoy the same things you do."

"That's unimportant," insisted the betrothed. "I love Jasper for what he is—president of a bank!"

☺

A Wall Street financier asked a Texas oil tycoon, "How's business holding up in your part of the world?"

"Son," drawled the oil man, "in Texas we do more business by accident than you do on Wall Street on purpose."

☺

Top lawyer Moses Polakoff had a client, an automobile salesman, who visited his cousin in Texas during a vacation. While there, he decided to combine business with pleasure.

"Ken," said the salesman to his relative, "you've got a big place here, and from all indications, you do all right. But every time I look at that broken-down jalopy of yours, I start wondering about you, and I bet a lot of other people do, too. A fellow with your holdings should be riding around in a new car."

The old farmer regarded his younger cousin thoughtfully. "Frank," he began, "I don't need a new car. That there old one takes me where I want to go. Besides, I'd rather spend that same money on a good cow."

"Now, wouldn't you look silly riding to town on a cow!" taunted the salesman.

"Reckon I would," agreed the farmer. "But not as foolish as I'd look milkin' a car."

Funnyman Al Kelly says: "When you find a pair of boots on the floor with a big ten gallon hat on top of them, what have you got? ... A Texan with all the hot air let out of him."

The story is told of a quick-tempered Texan named Luke who was sentenced to twenty years in prison when he drilled a fellow full of lead during a poker game.

Of course, he was lonely in his solitary confinement—no one to talk to—no one to pass the time of day with. But one day, an ant crawled into his cell.

At first, Luke merely studied the actions of the ant, and then he discovered what scientists have always known—the ant is quite a remarkable little fellow: In fact, the ant is capable of almost anything.

And so, with the aid of a small matchstick, the prisoner set about experimenting with a few tricks for the ant. At the end of the year the ant could perform somersaults. At the end of five years the ant could do a back flip. At the end of ten years it could rear up and walk around on its two hind legs.

Time passed. Two more years, and the ant could walk five feet on two legs; one more, and it could hop; another, and it could waltz to a tune whistled by the prisoner.

Still Luke persisted with his little insect friend. He taught it to play hide and seek, obey commands, such as "trot-walk-dance-hop" all in sequence. And then, finally, the day came when the prisoner was released from jail.

With the ant in his pocket, Luke went out into the world, confident that his talented pet would make him a fortune. Accordingly, he stepped into a bar and ordered a drink. Then he put his little trained ant—the only one of its kind on the earth—on the bar and called the bartender.

"Bartender," he began proudly, "see this ant?"

The bartender took a look. "Oh," he said, "I'm sorry, sir!" And down came a huge, hairy paw with a splat.

A New York man who was vacationing in Texas, hired an old western guide to take him on an overnight camping trip.

"That's rattlesnake country, you know," the old cowboy informed him.

"There's a cure for snakebites, isn't there?" inquired the tourist.

"Out here when we get bitten by snakes we drink a jug of whiskey."

"Isn't there any other cure?"

The westerner gave him a quizzical look and drawled, "Who cares, son? Who cares?"

And then there was the Texan who was telling an easterner about the eating habits of the rough and ready Texas ranchers.

"A real meal consists of two jugs of liquor, a couple of thick juicy steaks and a hound dog."

"A hound dog? What's he for?"

"Tarnation!" bellowed the Texan, "Who the devil do you think is going to eat all that steak?"

☻

Did you hear about the Texan who received a statement from his bank pertaining to a check he had recently deposited. The note read: INSUFFICIENT FUNDS . . . NOT YOURS. OURS!

☻

No, all Texans are not wealthy. There was the poor Texas peddler who happened to be selling his wares in front of a house of ill repute when the police raided the place. Just for good measure, they arrested him, too.

The night court judge, notoriously intolerant of untruths, barked at the first girl, "Well, what do you have to say for yourself?"

The girl wept bitter tears and cried, "Your Honor, this is a miscarriage of justice. I'm not at all what you think I am."

"Oh?" asked the judge, "and what are you?"

"I'm a dressmaker, Your Honor."

The judge's brow darkened and he roared, "Lies are one thing I will not tolerate! Thirty days!"

The second girl, too, wept. "Your Honor," she whimpered, "I've been wrongly accused. I'm not at all like my friend. I'm a milliner."

The judge became nearly apoplectic and raged, "I will not stand untruths! Thirty days!"

The third girl before him took an entirely different tack. She faced him squarely and declared, "Your Honor, I might as well confess. I'm not a dressmaker or a milliner. I've led a wrong life

and I'm sorry for what I've done. Your Honor, I'm a streetwalker."

A silence fell over the courtroom. Finally the judge nodded benignly and told the girl, "Young lady, your honesty must be rewarded. Sentence suspended."

The judge then glowered at the next case—the aged, wizened peddler—and snapped, "Well what's your story?"

The man stood up straight, bit his lip, faced the judge, and replied in a clear tone, "Your honor, I'm a streetwalker, too."

AND BEFORE WE LEAVE TEXAS
REMEMBER WHAT CONFUCIUS COHEN SAYS:
THE ONLY THING BIGGER THAN TEXAS IS TAXES

GAY AT THE CHEZ

Chicago is the Windy City. And when one goes to the midwestern metropolis, one can always separate the natives from the tourists. In Chicago, when the wind blows, visiting females hold onto their skirts. Hometown gals hold onto their hats.

When I was in Chicago I appeared at the Chez Paree. The Chez is owned by Dave Halper. Dave is quite a wonderful guy and whenever we meet he greets me with a gag. During our last meeting he tossed this one at me:

A fire broke out in the girl's dressing room of a burlesque house. It took the firemen two hours to put the fire out . . . and it took three days to put the firemen out!

Nate Gross, who writes the clever quips for the Chicago *American*, is another who loves to exchange funny ones with me. Recently Nate told me the one about the temperance lecturer who was telling the good people of Chicago about the evils of liquor. In no uncertain terms, he blasted John Barleycorn.

"Who has the most money to spend?" he bellowed. "Who has the biggest house? . . . the saloon keeper! Who has the finest fur coats and the most jewelry . . . the saloon keeper's wife! And who pays for all this? . . . You do, my friends, you do!"

A few days later, a couple who had been in the audience met the booze-baiter on the street and congratulated him on the wonderful speech.

"I'm pleased to see that you've given up drinking," the lecturer said.

"Well, not exactly," admitted the man. "We bought a saloon."

Charlie Dawn, also of the Chicago *American,* appreciated the one about the wife who told her friend, "I gave my husband a bottle of scotch, and he took it as an insult."

"So what did he do?" asked the friend.
"What could he do? He swallowed the insult!"

Agent Charles Rapp likes this one:
The dress manufacturer confronted his sales staff. "Which of you has been taking my model out after hours?"

"Boss," owned up one, "I didn't think you'd mind. I mean, I didn't mean any harm," but he was interrupted by the confession of another. So it went, each employee admitting that he, too, had not been immune to the charms of the model. Except for the youngest salesman.

"I'm happy to say," he announced self-righteously, "that I've indulged in no extracurricular activities with the young lady in question."

"You're just the man we're looking for," boomed the manufacturer. "Get right outside and fire her!"

☻

Nat Sheinman, the dress manufacturer, swears that this happened in a Chicago dress house.

Every Friday was payday. Consequently, on that day there was more than $15,000 in the company safe.

During the lunch hour one Friday, the payroll clerk was alone in the office when two masked robbers entered.

"This is a stick-up," informed one of the pair, pointing a gun at the clerk. "Make a move and I'll drill you. Just open the safe and you won't get hurt."

Fearing for his life, the clerk obeyed, and the bandits scooped up all the money and put it in their pockets.

As they made for the door, the clerk shouted, "Just a minute!"

"Whadaya want?" barked one of the masked men, fixing his gun again on the clerk.

"Please take the payroll books, too! The auditors are coming tomorrow!"

☻

Jack Eigen, the famed Chicago disc-jockey, tells of a housewife who complained to her husband, "Just look at me! My clothes are so shabby that if anyone came to the door they'd think I was the cook."

To which the husband retorted, "Not if they stayed for dinner!"

☻

Waiving economy, a young miss bought a new pair of shoes in the most fashionable and expensive shoe store in Chicago. After several days she returned to the store and complained that the shoes weren't comfortable.

"I just can't walk in these shoes," she groaned.

"Madam," said the manager haughtily, "people who have to walk don't buy shoes in this store!"

☻

Louis Zahn, of the Zahn Drug Co. in Chicago, admitted that this could have happened in his town:

The motorcycle cop was right behind the lady driver when it happened. She suddenly pulled over in front of the motorcycle, turned sharply, and he smacked right into her.

Cursing, the cop jumped off his cycle. "Why didn't you signal?" he demanded.

"Why should I?" she asked innocently. "I always turn off here!"

☻

Irv Kupcinet, of the Chicago *Sun-Times,* liked the one I told him about the wealthy New York dress manufacturer who died and tried to get into heaven.

"Who are you?" asked an assistant angel.

"I'm a dress manufacturer."

"Well, what have you done to deserve a place in heaven?"

"Why, just the other day, I saw a blind man on Times Square and gave him fifteen cents."

"Is that all?"

"Oh, no! Last week when I was walking on Riverside Drive I met a shoe shine boy who was half frozen to death. I gave him a dime."

"Is that in the records?" the assistant angel asked the bookkeeper.

The bookkeeper thumbed through the pages of his ledger and confirmed the claim.

"What else have you done?" continued the heavenly interrogator.

"Well, er—that's all I can think of."

"What do you think we ought to do with this guy?" the angel asked the bookkeeper.

"Give him back his quarter and tell him to go to hell!"

An imaginative member of a Chicago finance company sent the following letter to one of his delinquent accounts:

"Dear Sir:

"After checking our records, we note that we have done more for you than your mother did—we've carried you for fifteen months!"

Bentley Stegner, the Chicago *Sun-Times* scribe, roared at this one:

The tycoon barked, "Send the accountant into my office at once!"

The accountant, a young, debonair chap, stepped into his office. "You want to see me?"

"Now, listen here, you," began the big boss, "I will not tolerate your behavior a moment longer. A year ago you forged two checks in my name. Six months ago you sold our business secrets to a rival firm and three months ago you took advantage of my daughter. Now the poor girl is going to have a baby. I'm warning you, the next least little thing you do—out you go!"

☺

Yes, this is a woman's world. When a man is born, the first question people ask is: "How is the mother?" When he marries, people say, "What a lovely bride!" And when he dies, they ask, "How much did he leave her?"

☺

Ann Marsters, the Chicago *American* columnist, tells of having lunch next to two young wives who were discussing the pitfalls of love and marriage. Ann couldn't help but overhear their conversation as they railed against their husbands and men in general. One of the chief complaints was the improvidence of their respective mates.

"If only I were the wife of a millionaire," moaned one.

"You mean, of course, if only you were the widow of a millionaire," corrected the other.

☺

Ira Arkin, of Ira L. Arkin Co., in the Windy City, loved this one:

Three old men were seated in Wrigley Field discussing their inevitable fate while they waited for the game to begin.

"When I die," said one, aged 76, "I want to be buried with John McGraw. He was a great manager and brilliant strategist."

"Me," said the second, aged 83, "I'd like to be buried with Abe Lincoln. Abe was a great man and all the people loved him."

"I," said the third, aged 92, "I'd like to be buried with Gina Lollobrigida."

"But she isn't dead yet," pointed out one of his companions.

"Neither am I!" cackled the old man. "Neither am I!"

☺

A husband was going about his usual daily routine on the morning of their 25th wedding anniversary, and his wife was rather peeved.

"Don't you know what day this is?" she scolded.

"Of course I do," he replied.

"Well, then, let's go to the Pump Room or something and celebrate. Let's do something unusual."

"All right," said her husband. "How about two minutes of silence?"

And if you're one of those who thinks that women do sometimes shut up, you'd do well to meet the fellow who would only go to a woman dentist. He claimed that it made him happy to hear a lady tell him to open his mouth instead of shut it.

And Jack Wasserman, the dress manufacturer, claims that the old theory that every woman has a price is *false*. He says he's never heard of a fellow who could find a buyer for his mother-in-law.

Which reminds me of the story Lee Sullivan, the Irish tenor,

told me about the big game hunter who went to Africa with his wife and his mother-in-law. They hired a guide and he took them on a safari into the wilds of the jungle.

One night, about a week after they were out, the husband and his wife awoke and discovered that Mama was missing. Naturally, they began searching for her. An hour later, they were shocked to see her cowering in a clearing with a huge lion standing over her.

"Oh, what are we going to do?" the horrified wife asked.

"Nothing," answered the husband quickly. "The lion got himself into that fix. Now let him get out of it!"

A Chicago school teacher asked, "Billy, if your father borrowed two hundred dollars and promised to give his benefactor $10 a week, how much would he owe at the end of eight weeks?"

"Two hundred dollars," came the quick reply.

"I'm afraid you don't know your lesson very well," scolded the teacher.

"I may not know my lesson," answered Billy, "but I know my father!"

And speaking about Billy's father, his wife recently brought him to court.

"Judge," she told the man on the bench, "my husband gets up every morning and immediately begins hitting me over the head with a frying pan. When he leaves for work, he punches me in the nose for good luck. Instead of eating lunch he kicks me in the teeth, and when he comes home at night he slugs me with a baseball bat and knocks me unconscious. Your honor, I think he should be put in jail for the rest of his life."

"Don't believe a word she says," said her husband. "She's punch drunk."

☻

Harry Katz, the Chicago packer, used to deal with a salesman who was quite a *bon vivant*. However, as he got older, the years of carousing began to take their toll, and he finally consulted a doctor.

"We can add thirty years to your life if you'll give up wine, women and song," the sawbones told him.

The salesman thought it over for a few minutes, and then said, "I'll settle for ten years, Doc. I never could carry a tune."

☻

Ed McGee, a native New Yorker, had married and moved to Chicago. The reason for his relocation: He wanted to be far away from his mother-in-law.

However, not two weeks after he moved into his new home, he walked in the front door and saw the old girl standing there surrounded by suitcases and trunks.

Naturally, he was taken aback, and while Mama was upstairs unpacking, the angry husband strode into the kitchen.

"As you know, my mother-in-law is here, and I've made out a list of her favorite dishes," he told the cook.

"I understand, sir," nodded the cook as she took the list from him.

"I'm afraid you don't," said Ed. "The first time you serve one of them . . . you're fired!"

☻

While eating at Carl's in Chicago, I overheard the fellow seated in the next booth call the waiter over.

"Why does this chicken have a leg missing?" he demanded.

"It was in a fight sir," kidded the waiter.

"Well then," cracked the diner, "take it back and bring me the winner."

☺

And then there was the buyer from Marshall Fields who had this to say: "You never know where your next break is coming from. All you can do is pray that it won't be a compound fracture."

☺

I knew one Chicago fellow who was so suspicious of his wife that when she gave birth to twins, he insisted that one looked like the iceman and the other looked like the milkman.

☺

Judge Ben Shalleck tells of a colleague who once tried a case involving a traveling salesman who had sent his wife a telegram informing her that he was returning home to Chicago a day earlier than he'd originally planned. On his arrival, the salesman found her in a fond embrace with another man. Enraged, he tore out of the house, checked into a downtown hotel, and the next morning started divorce proceedings.

When the case came before the court, the judge asked, "Why do you want to divorce your wife?"

The salesman told him the whole story.

The judge turned to the wife. "Is this true?" he asked her.

"Yes, Your Honor," she admitted. "It's all true."

"In that case you ought to be ashamed of yourself!"

"But Judge! It wasn't my fault."

"What!" exclaimed the jurist. "How can you make such a ridiculous statement?"

"Can I help it if I never received the telegram?"

The subject of girls who love loosely reminds me of the Chicago "sporting house" that was raided. Inside, the police found a parrot, which they turned over to the local pet shop. The parrot was a garrulous old bird who swore a blue streak whenever it opened its mouth.

The pet shop owner finally sold it to a rich old society matron, who put the bird in a gorgeous cage, threw a cover over it and left it alone.

One night, about three weeks later, the matron had a big swanky party in her house attended by only the best people. When the affair was in full swing, the hostess suddenly decided to take the cover off Polly's cage. The old bird looked around, displaying a great deal of interest.

First he looked at the surroundings. "Brand new House" he croaked.

Then he looked at the woman. "Brand new women," cackled the parrot.

Then he looked at the men, "Ah—but the same old customers!"

My old Garment Center pal Teddy Brown likes this one:

The pretty, but distraught, Chicago girl took her troubles to a psychiatrist.

"Doctor, you must help me," she pleaded. "It's got so every time a boy takes me out, I always end up saying 'yes.' And then afterwards I feel guilty and depressed all day long."

"I see," nodded the analyst. "And you want me to strengthen your will power."

"Heavens, no! exclaimed the disturbed girl. "I want you to weaken my conscience!"

☺

Diamond merchant Aaron Perkis knew a Chicago man who bought a farm out west. The ex-urbanite, however, wasn't much of a farmer and nearly all the heavy work fell to his wife.

For years he scarcely turned a hand. Finally his conscience caught up with him. One day, as he was napping next to the cook stove in the kitchen, he was roused by the entrance of his wife from the cellar. She was carrying a heavy load of coal.

"This has to stop," he cried. "For years I've been watching you carry that heavy load of coal up those stairs. From now on, there'll be no more of that, no sir! . . . I'm going to get you a smaller pail so you can make it in two trips!"

☺

AND BEFORE WE LEAVE CHICAGO
REMEMBER WHAT CONFUCIUS COHEN SAYS:
THE BEST WAY TO GET A JOB DONE
IS TO GIVE IT TO A BUSY MAN.
HE'LL HAVE HIS SECRETARY DO IT.

AMUSEMENT IN ATLANTIC CITY

Atlantic City is the scene of the Miss America beauty contest. Every year ambitious beauties flock to this seashore resort with hopes of attaining fame and fortune.

Many of these girls are very publicity minded. I knew one Miss America aspirant, for instance, who was caught sun-bathing in her birthday suit by a brash photographer who promptly took her picture. The infuriated miss chased him all around the patio.

"I'll teach you to play a trick like that," she shrilled. "You shot the wrong profile!"

Or as one fellow I know puts it . . . a beach is a place where a girl goes when she has nothing to wear.

Bob and Harry, two enterprising young Garment Center salesmen who work the same side of the street, are an astonishing pair. Neither of them was remarkable as a single, but since they teamed up, their record has been unbelievable.

Skinny D'Amato, of the "500 Club" in Atlantic City, tells a story about the legendary duo which might explain their success.

They were at a convention in Atlantic City. Hoping to combine pleasure with business they were standing behind a pillar, casing the joint, when they spied a striking model posing languorously on a sofa not far off.

Bob, the handsomer of the pair, strolled over and introduced himself while Harry remained hidden behind a pillar.

In ten minutes Bob had maneuvered the curvaceous lass up to his room. Safe from the prying eyes in the thronged lobby, Bob took the girl in his arms and whispered, "How about a little kiss?"

The girl was willing, but she had to think of her obligations, too, so reluctantly she held out for ten dollars.

"All right," said Bob, "ten dollars it is, but on one condition."

"Yes?"

"That you let me turn out the lights and kiss you as many times as I want to and for as long as I want."

The girl agreed.

Two hours later, she whispered in his ear, "Gee, you're kissing better than ever, Bob."

"Bob's at the Turkish bath," chuckled Harry, "but he'll be taking over again in ten minutes."

Murray Hamburger, who makes bridal gowns, tells the one about the garment salesman who was vacationing in Atlantic City with a colleague. During the vacation they spoke about many things, but inevitably the salesman got around to talking about his wife. "When I was first married," he began, "I was the happiest man in the world. When I came home at night my wife would get my slippers, and my dog would run around the room barking at me. And now, after ten years of married life, everything has changed. Now the dog brings me my slippers and it's my wife who runs around the room barking at me!"

"So what are you complaining about?" shrugged his friend. "You're still getting the same service."

And David Mankin tells the one about the salesman who suspected his wife was running around with other men. Just to make sure, the fellow hired a private detective to tail his spouse.

A week later the Sherlock reported and said, "You were right. Your wife *is* running around with another man." Then he submitted his bill. "And what are my next instructions?" asked the detective.

"I want you to follow my wife and that bum. Keep on their trail night and day—even if you have to track them the length of Europe and back. And then I want a complete report on what he sees in her."

Joe Leventhal, the dress manufacturer, is a good listener to a good gag. I cornered him recently and sprang this one on him:

Max was one of those men who was a born optimist. No matter what happened his philosophy would be: "It could've been worse."

One day a tragedy took place in the neighborhood. Ben, his next door neighbor, who was a traveling salesman and spent a good deal of his time away from home, returned unexpectedly one night and found his wife in the arms of another man. In a blind rage, Ben ran to a drawer, seized his pistol, and shot and killed both his wife and the stranger. The district attorney charged him with double murder.

Naturally, the whole neighborhood was abuzz with talk about the calamity. But every time the tragedy was discussed in Max's presence, he'd simply say: "Oh, well, it could've been worse."

"Are you crazy, Max?" one of the neighbors jumped on him. "What could possibly be worse? Two people are dead and a wonderful fellow like Ben will probably be executed!"

"Nevertheless, I still claim it could've been worse. If Ben had come home Wednesday instead of Thursday, you'd be sending *me* flowers."

☻

The aged salesman who had attended more than 50 Atlantic City Conventions left the dining room right after dinner. His younger associates had invited him to accompany them on some fun and frolic, but he refused. "I'm not as young as I used to be," he apologized. "I think I'll just turn in."

When he was upstairs, he undressed slowly and then crawled into bed. But no sooner had he turned off the light, than a gorgeous blonde model opened the door and slinked in.

Puzzled, the old salesman switched on the light and looked up at the dazzling damsel.

"Oh, I'm terribly sorry," said the girl," I guess I'm in the wrong room."

"Oh no," sighed the salesman, "you're in the right room—but you're about 40 years too late!"

☻

Sam Love tells of a publicity man who was showing a promoter around the new stage for the Miss America contest in Atlantic City. "That girl," he said pointing to one of the entrants, "is wearing a $15,000 bathing suit."

"That might be true," agreed the promoter eyeing her carefully, "but her heart isn't in it!"

"Roast Beach is our favorite sport," the Atlantic City lad told his friend from New York.

"Roast Beach?" asked his pal, "why I never heard of that game. How do you play it?"

"Every day," explained the young native, "we go down to the beach and see who's cooking!"

Nat and Billy Rolfe were recently in Atlantic City. One afternoon while they were seated in the lobby of their hotel waiting for dinner to be served, they overheard a fellow telling his friend the following story:

A prominent manufacturer of women's panties was a little hard-pressed for money. Accordingly, he went to the nearest bank to ask for a loan. He was given all sorts of papers and forms to fill out, and finally, one of the bank executives interviewed him.

Looking over the forms, the banking man glanced up at the panties man and said, "I don't know if you're a good risk. How many pairs of panties have you in stock right now?"

"One hundred thousand," answered the manufacturer.

The executive pulled out a pad, jotted down a few memos and then said, "Well, in that case I guess we can give you the money."

One week later, the manufacturer returned to the bank and handed the banker the money he had borrowed along with the interest. "I sold my panties and made a big profit," he said.

"Well, that sounds wonderful," enthused the banker. "Now that you have all that extra money, why don't you bank it here?"

"I'd like to, but first I'd like to ask you one question."

"Yes, go right ahead."

"How many panties do *you* have in stock?"

The Latin Quarter's Ed Rissman tells about a dress manufacturer who staged a fashion show in association with a Miss America Beauty Contest. In the middle of everything, he discovered that one of his top models had disappeared.

Frantic with worry, the manufacturer told one of his salesmen, "I've got to find a pretty girl to fill in for her."

"It just so happens," the salesman told him, "that I know a model who can replace her."

"Can you lay your hands on her?" cried the excited boss.

"I'll thank you to leave my private life out of this!" retorted the salesman.

The curvaceous cutie bounced into an Atlantic City bank and placed a check before the teller.

"Do you have an account here?" asked the man in the cage.

"No."

"Well, I'm afraid I can't cash your check then unless you can provide me with some sort of identification."

"I'll find someone to vouch for me," said the girl and flounced out of the building. In a minute she returned with a cop.

"Hello, Clancy," greeted the teller. "Do you know this woman?"

"I most certainly do!"

Reassured, the teller cashed the check and the girl departed with a fistful of greenbacks.

"I'm glad you were on the corner," the teller told Clancy. "I couldn't cash her check without some sort of identification."

The policeman scratched his head thoughtfully. "Let's see, it's goin' on fifteen years Gert's been makin' the conventions here," he calculated. "That is, not countin' them three years in stir on that bad check charge...."

☺

Joey Gold & Jesse Berley were describing one of their unpopular associates to me.

"He's the kind of fellow," mused Joey, "who throws a drowning man both ends of a rope."

☺

Nat Tuman tells of the two old school pals who were seated in an Atlantic City bar reminiscing.

"I'll always remember my school days," said one, "I'd say they were the happiest days in my life."

As he was speaking he saw another fellow walk in to the bar.

"Charlie," he nudged his friend, "isn't that Mr. Berlin, our old principal?"

"It certainly looks a lot like him," agreed his associate, "but don't you think he'd be a little older?"

"Maybe not. He was a pretty young principal."

"Yeah, he was a real nice guy. I can't remember him ever so much as raising his voice. Everybody liked him."

"Why don't you go over and see if that's him?" suggested Charlie.

With this his friend walked over to the fellow and asked if he was their former principal.

"Why don't you get the hell out of here and stop bothering me," growled the man. "You got a lot of nerve!"

Unhappily, the fellow rejoined Charlie, "Now we'll never know if that's him," he said sadly.

Will Steinman knew an elderly couple who went to Atlantic City on their 50th anniversary. They took a lavish suite overlooking the ocean so that they could watch the tides.

One afternoon while they were seated near the window, the wife poked her spouse in the ribs and said, "Look, Irving, there's a mermaid!"

The husband was unimpressed, "A mermaid—what's that?"

"You don't know what a mermaid is? It's half woman and half fish."

"So?"

"So, nothing—I bet you'd be interested if it were half herring!"

Jimmy MacWhan, who handles special service for the Pennsylvania Railroad, likes this one:

The broke hobo approached the circus manager for a job. "What can you do?" the boss asked.

"I jump off a 50-foot tower and land in a tank of water five feet deep."

Impressed, the manager agreed to try out the act that night.

At eight sharp, the hobo was there. When the band began to play, he climbed to the top of the tower. Then, with the floodlights shining on him and the drums rolling, he dived into the tank.

The crowd went wild; and the manager, realizing he had a find, approached the daredevil. "You're great," he enthused. "I'm going to make you the star of the show. Can you sign a contract right now?"

"Nothing doing," replied the hobo. "Once is enough. A fellow could get himself hurt pulling a fool stunt like that."

☺

Returning home from Atlantic City, my dentist, Dr. Ira Landau, was stopped by a traffic cop.

"Can't you read, Bud?" asked the policeman sarcastically.

"Why, of course, officer."

"Well, you don't act it. The signs say 50 miles an hour and you were going 60."

"Sixty!" my dentist protested. "I wasn't even going 30!"

The officer merely glared.

"In fact," continued the doc, "I wasn't going 20, or even 10!"

So the officer gave him a ticket for illegal parking.

☺

A generous tipper at an Atlantic City hotel found a brand new waiter serving him one morning.

"Where's Charlie, my regular waiter?" he demanded.

"Well, I'll tell you," explained the new man, "Charlie got himself involved in a little crap game last night."

"Aha!" chuckled the patron indulgently. "He struck it rich and he's taking a little vacation, eh? I get it."

"I'm afraid you don't," continued the new waiter. "Charlie lost. *I* won . . . you!"

AND BEFORE WE LEAVE ATLANTIC CITY
REMEMBER WHAT CONFUCIUS COHEN SAYS:
IN ATLANTIC CITY ONLY THING WORSE
THAN RAINING CATS AND DOGS
IS HAILING JITNEYS.

LAS VEGAS LAUGHS

Las Vegas is the place where they give you odds that you'll never get even.

In recent years, Las Vegas has become the gambling center of this country and the good citizens of that fair city have taken great pains to drive home this fact to visiting tourists.

Out in Las Vegas they have traffic lights that say—"STOP"—"GO" and "6 TO 5 YOU'LL NEVER MAKE IT." And all the motels have three types of towels: "His" . . . "Hers" and "You Wanna Bet!"

Las Vegas is a scenic town replete with many of the nicest hotels in the country. Some of the better hotels are "The Sands," "El Rancho Vegas," "The Thunderbird," "The Flamingo," "The Royal Nevada" and "The Dunes." The owners of these hotels are all wonderful people. They pay you your salary and then invite you to go into the gambling room and double it . . . or lose it.

They even have dice made from Ivory Soap so that you can have floating crap games in the swimming pools . . . and after you play . . . you're really washed up.

Yes, everyone in Las Vegas is betting conscious. I know one fellow who walked into a Las Vegas diner and ordered a plate of pancakes. When he got them, he looked them over and screamed to the waiter, "Take them back! They're marked!"

And once when I passed a funeral parlor, I noticed the undertaker standing outside his mortuary. "How's business?" I asked.

"Not too good," he answered sadly.

Peering inside, I noticed four coffins with bodies in them. "But, you have four customers," I said. "Don't you consider that a good day's work?"

"Only one," he corrected. "Three of them are shills!"

Agent Mark Leddy says Las Vegas is the only place in the world where they play the show "You Bet Your Life" . . . for real.

Jack Entratter, the gay blade of The Sands, recently told me about a fellow who used to come to his hotel every night and beg the guests for money.

"Please," he'd ask anyone who would listen, "just loan me $100. I'll double it in no time and pay you right back."

But night after night, people would shake their heads and walk away. However, one night, he ran into a generous oil man from Texas who handed him a crisp C-note and told him, "Here, Boy, enjoy yourself!"

After thanking his generous benefactor, he walked over to the Black Jack table and blew the money in five minutes. The next night when he saw the Texan, he again asked him for some money, and again a hundred-dollar bill was forthcoming. But that, too, was gone within a matter of minutes.

This continued for more than three weeks. Every night the Texan would give him money, and every night it would be gone almost before he had it.

Finally, in desperation, the unhappy fellow told one of his friends about his experience with the generous Texan.

"There's only one thing to do," his friend told him. "Lose the bum—he's bad luck for you!"

Frank Sinatra, who frequently entertains in Las Vegas, knew a young couple who went to the Nevada gambling town on their honeymoon.

Upon arriving at the resort town, the husband immediately became fascinated by the plush gambling rooms and started betting on all the attractions. And just four days after their arrival, as a result of continued bad luck, they had just $2 left between them.

"Let me go down to the gambling room alone," the husband told his wife. "I've got a feeling that today my luck will change."

Once downstairs, he walked over to the roulette table and put his last two dollars on number 14, black. Luckily, his number won. He continued betting and his luck was fabulous. Over and over again, his would be the winning number, and within one hour, he had run his winnings up to $50,000. Feeling that his luck was bound to change for the worse, he picked up his winnings and started walking toward the cashier's cage. But just before he reached it, he felt one final urge to bet. Taking his entire winnings, he walked back to the roulette table and placed it all on number 16, red.

The wheel began to spin round and round until it finally stopped on number 12, black. Heartbroken, the young fellow walked slowly to the elevator and went up to his room.

Upstairs, his wife, who was impatiently awaiting his return, asked anxiously, "Well, Harvey, how did you make out?"

"I lost the two dollars," he told her sadly.

And then there is the Joe E. Lewis story about the big gambler who went to Las Vegas to double his fortune. Checking into a hotel, the man wasted no time finding his way to the Black Jack tables.

But the gambler ran into a streak of bad luck, and in no time at all, lost all his money. Left without a penny to his name, the despondent chap decided to take his life.

He walked out of the gambling casino and looked for the nearest cliff. He was just about to jump when he heard a mysterious voice behind him say, "Don't jump off the cliff."

Startled, he asked, "Why not?"

"Go back to the casino, borrow two dollars, go over to the roulette wheel and bet on 10, black."

The fellow did as he was told. Naturally, he won. "Now bet on 12, red," the voice instructed.

And again he won. This went on for more than an hour. Each time he did as the voice told him, and each time he won. When he counted his winnings, he found that he had more than $25,000 in chips.

"Stop gambling now," the voice told him, "I can't help you any more."

But the fellow disregarded the advice and put his entire fortune on 11, black. The wheel spun around, and his number lost.

"Oh, I'm broke again," moaned the broken-hearted gambler. "What am I going to do now?"

"Jump off a cliff!" the voice from behind him said.

Las Vegas is the only town in the world where you get tanned and faded at the same time. But don't get me wrong, some people do make big killings in the gambler's paradise.

Two fellows I know were speaking about a friend of theirs who had just left Las Vegas with a bundle of money.

"Joe," said one, "left Las Vegas with $50,000."

"I know," said the other, "but he went there with $100,000!"

Talent representative Eddie Rio says Las Vegas is Monte Carlo with Cowboys. I heard about two westerners, who at the end of a particularly torrid card game, surprised each other by announcing, "I've got five aces!"

"Well then, who wins?" asked an onlooker.
"The one who draws first!"

☺

"In Las Vegas," says insurance man, Gerson Geizler, "people are always kind to animals . . . that's why they're always giving money to the kitty."

☺

Speaking about animals, Beldon Katleman, the shining light at El Rancho Vegas, likes the one about the Las Vegas bookmaker who was given a parrot in lieu of a cash payment by one of his clients. And to tell the truth, the parrot was truly a talented bird. Not only did he speak English perfectly, but French and Spanish as well.

Being a whimsical sort, the bookie took his bird with him one night when he went to "El Rancho."

While standing at the bar, the bookie got into a conversation with the bartender, and in a few moments was raving about his new bird.

Having heard such claims before, the bartender was not impressed. Irritated, the bookie offered to bet the bartender $50 that

his parrot could speak to him in three different languages. The bet was made quickly.

"*Parlez-vous français?*" said the bookie to the parrot.

There was no response.

Nor did the parrot respond to questions in English or Spanish, and the bartender pocketed the $50.

When they were outside, the bookie screamed at his bird, "What a stupid parrot you are! You just cost me $50 because you turned temperamental."

"Don't be a jerk," replied the parrot. "Just think of the odds you'll be able to get in that joint tomorrow!"

☻

Another of Beldon's favorites deals with the farmer who asked the clerk in the town sporting goods store to show him a shotgun.

Naturally, the clerk reached for the most expensive rifle in the place and handed it to him.

"This is our finest model," the man behind the counter told him. "Notice the craftsmanship. It's a bargain at $250."

"Oh, that's too expensive. What else have you got?"

Then the clerk took out another model and told him that it was a steal at $175.

"Too much," grunted the farmer, "I'd like to see another one."

The clerk took another weapon from the shelf. "This is the cheapest one we carry," he sneered, "no special features, factory produced. It costs $12."

"That'll be good enough," agreed the farmer. "After all, it's only a small wedding."

☻

Arranger and talent manager, Harry Brent, knew a couple who decided to take their second honeymoon in Las Vegas. The husband was a big card player and every night he made his way to the black jack tables. His wife always remained in the room.

One night, while he was in the midst of a hot game, a bellhop came running over and hissed, "Mr. Fenton, your wife is upstairs making love to your best friend."

Enraged, the husband shouted at the dealer: "Hurry up and deal! This is positively my last hand!"

☺

Stan Irwin, the bright boy of the Sahara, recently received a letter from a fellow who asked Stan's advice about the best way to handle his landlord. Stan wrote the fellow and told him which would be the best course to follow.

Not one week later, Stan received the following reply:
"Stan:
"I wrote you about my troubles with my landlord. You advised me and I took your advice. Now I'm not having any more trouble with that dirty bum.
      Sincerely,
      JOE MUGG
      Sing Sing Cell 110421"

☺

"How far is Reno?" a tourist asked a native of Virginia City, the headquarters of Café Society expatriate Lucius Beebe.

"Oh, it's 25,540 miles the way you're heading," the native told him, "but about 20 miles if you turn around!"

☺

Sophie Tucker, the grand old lady of show business who frequently appears at El Rancho Vegas, has a great sense of humor. Whenever we meet, I always spring the latest gags on her—I love to listen to that hearty laugh of hers.

Among her favorites is the one about Jack Goldberg, who left a small upstate New York town and came to New York to seek fame and fortune.

In his ten years in New York, Jack realized both his ambitions. He became a prominent member of the Garment Center and lived in a fashionable Fifth Avenue apartment.

One day, Jack got an uncontrollable urge to visit his old home town. He wanted to impress his friends with his great success and wealth.

The next morning, he was on the train. When it stopped at his birthplace, Jack picked up his suitcase and walked proudly through the depot. As he emerged from the depot, he was feeling a little disappointed, because he hadn't come across any of his old friends. But upon hitting the street, he was immediately stopped by Artie Flowers.

"Hey, Jack," shouted Artie, "what're you doing? Leaving town?"

Everyone who goes to Las Vegas isn't prosperous. Recently, while I was standing in the lobby of El Rancho Vegas, I spotted an odd-looking cowboy walking into the hotel.

Completely oblivious to everything going on around him, he strutted up to the desk and signed the register with a big "X."

The desk clerk noticed that the new guest had left muddy tracks clear across the new rug. "Sir," he admonished the cowboy, "when you patronize a hotel which prides itself on its cleanliness, you might at least wipe half the mud of Texas off your shoes."

The Texan eyed the room clerk with honest amazement and asked softly, "What shoes?"

While a guest on a small yacht cruising around Nevada's huge Lake Tahoe, a has-been movie actor accidentally slipped over the side. Immediately the crew went into action, sweeping the water with the ship's spotlight until it illuminated the figure of the actor. He was threshing about wildly—his stuntman had always done his swimming for him.

"Don't panic," admonished one of the crew. "We'll be with you in just a minute."

"Just throw me a life preserver," gurgled the actor, "and then take your time. It's been so long since I've been in the spotlight!"

Coat Manufacturer Willie Cornet overheard the following conversation in Las Vegas:

MARILYN: How can I have beautiful hands?
DIAMOND JIM: Deal yourself plenty of aces.

And there's "Music Man" Jack Kahner's favorite about the young couple who checked into a Las Vegas hotel. When the bellhop took them to their room, they nodded approval. The boy was given a generous tip, and as he was about to leave, he asked, "Will there be anything else, sir?"

"No thanks," said the man.

"Anything for your wife, sir?" the boy asked.

The man meditated for a moment, then looked up and said, "Why yes, come to think of it. Bring me a post card to send her."

☺

In Las Vegas, everything is wonderful:
You can't beat the weather . . .
You can't beat the hotels . . .
And you can't beat the crap tables!

☺

In the great gambling town, says Choreographer Boots McKenna, they have a drink called the Lottery Cocktail . . . one drink and BINGO!

☺

They were married in New York and went to Las Vegas for their honeymoon. They checked in at The Sands, and were having a wonderful time until their first spat three days later.

"I've had all I can take from you already!" threatened the disillusioned bride. "In fact, I'm through! I'm getting out of here. You'll be sorry when I become a big star. I'm going to Hollywood, or else back to New York—alone! I'll become a famous model or a big name in television. But wherever I go or whatever I do, I'm leaving you!"

With that, she marched out the door, slamming it angrily behind her. Hardly five minutes had passed before she was back.

"I thought you were leaving," said the bridegroom mildly.

She began to unpack huffily. "Lucky for you it was raining," said she.

☺

Jack Squire's favorite concerns a 92-year-old grandfather who returned from a Las Vegas vacation and announced to his family that he'd met his future wife.

"You! Married!" they exclaimed in unison. "Who is she? How old is she?"

"Her name is Sara Cohen," said Grandpa, "and she's 18."

"Eighteen!" repeated his grandson incredulously. "How can you consider marrying a girl of 18!"

"Why not?" asked Grandpa calmly. "She's exactly the same age as my first wife when I married her."

AND BEFORE WE LEAVE LAS VEGAS
REMEMBER WHAT CONFUCIUS COHEN SAYS:
THE ONLY WAY TO DOUBLE YOUR MONEY
IN LAS VEGAS
IS TO FOLD IT AND
PUT IT IN YOUR POCKET.

CATSKILL CAPERS

Ranging from Monticello to Liberty, the Catskills is one of the most popular resort areas in this country. When a proud patriot like Patrick Henry can say "GIVE ME LIBERTY OR GIVE ME DEATH!" and a great statesman like Thomas Jefferson confesses that he likes to: "SPEND MY SPARE TIME IN MONTICELLO," you just know that these places are something special.

The fellow who called the Catskills the Derma Road knew what he was talking about.

And if you're ever in the Catskills and you see a white line on the road . . . *Remember!* . . . that's not paint . . . it's *sour cream!*

I've played in the Catskills many times and for such fine people as Jenny Grossinger of Grossinger's, Arthur Winarick of the Concord and Jack Paul of Paul's.

And although I didn't get my start in the great resort area, such famous showfolk as Red Buttons, Phil Silvers, Danny Kaye,

Eddie Fisher, Jan Murray, Sid Caesar, Jerry Lewis and many, many others graduated from the Catskills to the top of the entertainment world.

If you've ever been to the Catskills, you know that a large portion of the hotel guests spend almost their entire vacations sitting on the hotel lawn talking about themselves.

And during these "sitting sessions" it is not uncommon for the guests to exaggerate a little.

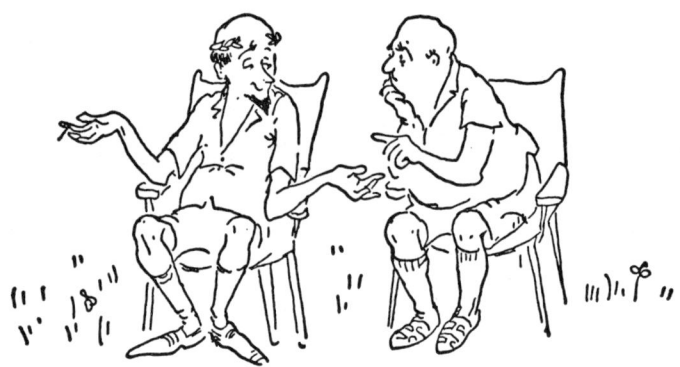

Thus, on a hotel lawn, a cutter becomes a manufacturer; a teller becomes a bank president; and a hospital orderly becomes a surgeon.

I'm thinking specifically of an old friend of mine who believed he was the greatest writer of his time.

One day while he was seated on a hotel lawn he struck up a conversation with a fellow seated next to him.

"What do you do?" the fellow asked.

"I'm a writer," my friend said proudly.

"Have you written anything recently?"

"As a matter of fact, I have. I've just completed the greatest play of the century."

"Is that right? What did you call it?"

"I've entitled it *Hamlet*."

"*Hamlet!* You must be joking. Didn't you ever hear of a fellow named Shakespeare?"

"Isn't that strange," smiled my friend, "they asked me the same question when I finished *Macbeth*."

☺

After working like a slave for more than a year, the shy cutter approached his boss.

"I'd like to remind you, that when I came to work for you, you told me that I could expect a substantial increase within twelve months," he began.

"So I did," smiled the top man. "Well, starting next month there'll be an extra two dollars in your pay envelope—even though I think you still have a lot to learn."

"You're so right," grunted the unhappy employee, "for years I thought substantial was a ten dollar word."

A top garment center salesman went to the Catskills for a well-earned vacation. However, while he was there tragedy struck. He overexerted himself on the golf course, had a heart attack, and passed away.

When his boss heard of his untimely demise, he was beside himself. Immediately, he wired the hotel:

ARRANGE BEST FUNERAL MONEY CAN BUY. BUT FIRST SEND BACK JACK'S SAMPLES!

☺

Fabrics man Nat Marcus tells of a fellow who was in such a hurry to get to the Concord to spend his annual two-week vacation that he lost control of his car just outside Monticello, and ran into a telephone pole.

When he regained his senses he found himself lying atop several phone wires.

"Thank goodness," he sighed. "It's a harp!"

☻

Murray Oliphant knew an eccentric old fellow who was going to the Catskills for his two-week vacation. Not being a member of the monied class, the old gentleman didn't own a car, so he had to travel by bus. But he was a jolly sort and this didn't bother him. Besides, this was his first trip to the Borscht Belt and he was as excited as a small boy. Even the fact that there were no seats available when he boarded the bus at Jerome Avenue in the Bronx didn't faze him. He simply planted himself in the middle of the aisle and proceeded to sing brightly: "I'm going to the Catskills; I'm going to the Catskills."

The bus driver noticed the lone standee and called out, "Move to the back of the bus, Pop."

But the gay old blade continued to sing out his ditty as the driver pulled away from the curb.

In a few minutes, the driver, visibly annoyed, turned around and snarled, "Hey, you, I told you to get to the back. Now, move!"

Unperturbed, the old gentleman repeated the musical: "I'm going to the Catskills; I'm going to the Catskills."

A couple of miles later, the bus driver was nearing the end of his patience. "Listen, you," he shouted, "either you get back there where you belong or I'm going to stop the bus and personally throw your valise out the window!"

Still there was no response from the preoccupied old codger whose tuneful chant continued uninterrupted.

The driver managed to contain himself for a mile or two more, but his temper was nearing the breaking point.

"I told you I'd throw your valise out the window," he yelled at the rear-view mirror, "and in two more minutes, Dad, that's just where it's going if you don't make tracks."

"I'm going to the Catskills; I'm going to the Catskills," sang the old man happily in reply.

The bus driver could stand no more. Fuming with rage, he slammed his foot down on the brake, pulled the bus over to the side of the road, and stormed back to where the troublesome passenger was standing. He picked up the valise and tossed it out the nearest window.

Still the old guy was undisturbed. After a brief pause, his song began anew: "I'm going to the Catskills; I'm going to the Catskills . . . I won't call up the police; I didn't bring a valise . . . I'm going to the Catskills. . . ."

☻

Phil Greenwald, who books acts at the Concord, roared when I told him this one:

The father, who had been approached by his daughter's steady, told the young man, "I see no reason why you shouldn't marry my daughter—if you can support a family."

"I'm prepared to do that, sir."

"Good," replied the patriarch, holding out his hand. "Counting my daughter, there are seven of us."

☻

Advertising executive Milton Blackstone tells about the two cellmates who whiled away their sentences bragging about the criminal "firsts" in their respective families.

"When they invented the pay telephone," boasted one, "my grandfather was the first guy to use a slug."

"That's nothing," scoffed the other. "My grandmother was the first woman—and there wasn't any man ahead of her either—to get ten years for petty larceny."

"Ten years! What did she steal?"

"A coat hanger at Grossinger's."

"A coat hanger! You mean to tell me your grandmother got ten years for stealing a coat hanger! She must have polished off the cop who arrested her to get that kind of a stretch."

"No-o-o," admitted the braggart, "the coat hanger happened to be attached to a mink coat."

In the same prison, according to Morty Curtis of Grossinger's, there was a thief who was none too bright. It seems he had broken into a Monticello dress shop three times.

"What did you steal that took three break-ins?" asked a fellow prisoner. "Three burglaries in one place . . . crazy!"

"I was only after one dress for my wife," explained the naive thief, "and she kept making me change it."

If you've ever been to the Catskills, you know that the staffs of many hotels are made up entirely of college students who are trying to save up a little money for next year's tuition. Thus, almost every season the turnover in these hotels is almost 100 per cent.

Gus Feldman, of Sanjo Dresses, likes the one about Herb Schier, an old Catskill waiter, who returned to a hotel where he had worked a few years before. He walked into the help's quarters and knocked at the door of his old room.

"Yes?" queried the occupant of the room as he opened the door.

"This was my room when I worked here," Herb explained, "do you mind if I come in and look around?"

"Oh not at all," replied the current tenant.

As he entered the room, Herb glanced around and smiled nostalgically. "Same old room, same old windows and same old furniture," he mused. Then he looked at the closet and his smile broadened. "And same old closet." He walked over and opened the door. There stood a girl, rigid with terror.

"This is my sister," explained the young waiter.

"Yes, sir," said Herb, "same old story!"

☺

There's no doubt about it. The story is the same, but the girls are different. "Every summer," says agent Al Perry, "the girls go to the Catskills to look for husbands . . . and the husbands go to look for girls."

☺

When a husband and wife go to the mountains, each takes special pains to keep an eye on the other.

A married couple was seated in the dining room of the Con-

cord. While they were eating, a shapely lass passed by.

"That's an attractive woman," commented the husband.

"You mean the one with the dyed red hair and the cheap-looking platform shoes?"

"Yes, she does have red hair."

"With her complexion she should never wear that purplish color," remarked the wife. "Her dress is badly cut through the middle and hangs unevenly in the back. She shouldn't wear such light stockings, and I hate green nail polish."

"I still say she's attractive," said the husband.

"Of course, I can't say for sure," answered the wife, "I really didn't take a good look at her!"

☺

Bert Roth and Al Rappoport of D.R.A. Dresses, once employed a terrific salesman whose name was Murray. Murray was well-liked by all the customers and continually outsold all the other salesmen. Since he always made a lot of money, he really should have been quite a happy fellow. However, he wasn't. It seems that Murray looked exactly like Mario Lanza.

At first it didn't bother him too much. Total strangers would stop him in the street and ask for his autograph. Others would slap him on the back and say, "Hi, Mario, what's new?"

And to all of them Murray would answer politely. "There's been a mistake. You've got the wrong guy. I'm not Mario Lanza."

But, try as he would, Murray continually ran up against this situation until finally it got completely out of hand. He had no privacy and he was being pestered to death.

Noticing that Murray was upset, Bert Roth suggested that he take a vacation in the Catskills and forget about the whole thing.

So Murray went to the mountains. He checked into Paul's, but before he could sign his name, the desk clerk extended his hand and said, "This sure is an honor. I've always wanted to meet you, Mr. Lanza."

Murray had had enough. "I'm not Mario Lanza!" he screamed,

and I don't want you to call me that! My name is Murray: M-U-R-R-A-Y . . . do you hear me!"

And with that he grabbed his key and stomped up to his room. He turned the key, walked in, and what do you think he saw? There, seated on a chair, was the most beautiful girl he had ever seen in his whole life.

"Oh," she sighed, "I've wanted to meet you all my life, Mario. You're wonderful! I've waited so long for this moment."

And Murray threw back his head and began to sing loudly, "BE MY LOVE!"

Mark Wachs, the witty New York gag-writer, tells about an-another Catskill romeo.

This one had just stepped into the lobby of a Catskill hotel when he spotted a gorgeous redhead. They exchanged significant looks and smiles. In a moment they were at the desk together registering as "Mr. and Mrs. Max Cohen."

The next morning Max was the picture of contentment as he checked out. But the smiles disappeared quickly when his bill was announced.

"Five hundred dollars!" he repeated incredulously. "Why, I've only been here one night!"

"I know," replied the clerk. "But your wife has been here for three months."

Every Catskill resort has a pool. Generally, that's the place where the boys and girls meet and plan for the rest of the day . . . and sometimes for the rest of their lives!

George and Abe Mitchell, of Mitchell Paper Stock, laughed when I told them this Mrs. Finster yarn.

Mrs. F. was vacationing in the Catskills. She had gone for

her health, but so it shouldn't be a total loss, she was keeping an eye peeled for a young man for Rosie, her eldest.

One afternoon she was seated by the pool when it occurred to her that the handsome young lifeguard might be a likely prospect.

"Young man," she called, "come and talk to an old lady." When he was standing by her chair, she said, "Sit down, you look like a nice young man. I'd like you to meet my daughter."

"What does she look like?" asked the youth.

"She's a wonderful girl," gushed Mrs. Finster, "and very intelligent. She graduated from Hunter with honors."

"Oh, yes? And is she good-looking?"

"And now she's got a job teaching on Long Island. She makes all her own clothes and she can cook better than her own mother."

"She sounds like a nice girl. But is she pretty?"

"Her uncle in the clothing business gave her $25,000 when she graduated, and . . ."

"Is she here with you now, Mother?"

And how about the recent conversation United Audit accountant, Sam Mandelbaum, overheard at another Catskill pool?

"Helen shouldn't go in the water alone. She almost drowned yesterday and that handsome young lifeguard had to use artificial respiration," said one.

To which the other answered: "You mean Helen had to use artificial drowning."

William Bass and Jack Feit, of Bass-Feit, were seated at the edge of the pool at the Concord when they heard a fellow scream, "Help! Save me! I'm the father of 15 children!"

The lifeguard dived into the water and shouted, "Okay, mister, I'll save you, but you sure picked a fine time to brag!"

And not too far away were seated a husband and a wife. The wife suspected her husband was carrying on with one of the waitresses at the hotel.

"I'm warning you!" she bawled, "If you don't stop drinking and running after women, I'm going to throw myself into the pool and drown myself."

"Promises, promises," sneered the husband, "that's all I ever get—promises."

Judy Gibbs, of Judy Formals, had a very homely girl-friend who was finding it extremely difficult to hook a man.

"Let's go up to the Concord," suggested her father. "There are a lot of eligible young men up there."

But after three days at the famous resort, the poor girl hadn't even had a nibble even though there were plenty of fish available.

Finally, the father hatched a scheme. Though Rosalie was an excellent swimmer, her father advised her to forget it for the purposes of the plan. She should wait at the pool for Papa's signal to fall in accidentally on purpose.

That afternoon they were strolling by the pool, and Papa said, "Now."

Dutifully Rosalie toppled into the water and began flailing about helplessly. In a few moments a handsome young man was pulling her to safety.

"My boy," beamed Papa, "that was a very courageous act indeed. There's too little heroism in the modern world, and I believe in rewarding a hero. I'm going to give you a check for $300, young man. And not only that—though it pains me to lose her, I'm going to give you the hand of this fragile flower you've rescued from the deep—my daughter Rosalie . . ."

"Never mind the hearts and flowers, mister," retorted the youthful hero. "But I'll take your money. It's the least you can do for pushing me in the pool."

Harry Rosen, ad boss of the New York *Post*, knows another father who took his daughter to the Catskills to get a man. He pointed out an old fellow to his daughter.

"There's a good catch," said father.

"But Dad," she complained, don't you think he's a little too old to be considered eligible?"

"My dear girl," said her father, "he's a little too eligible to be considered old."

Although most people think of the Catskills as exclusively a resort area, there are still many farms scattered throughout the area.

Joe Gordon, of Petite Lady Dresses, knew a woman whose husband had recently passed away. Since they had been a devoted couple, the wife was completely broken up by his passing.

"Why don't you go to a farm in the Catskills," a friend advised. "The fresh air and sunshine will do you good, and maybe you won't think about Seymour so much."

The wife agreed, and the next day she headed toward the Borscht Belt. Once on the farm, she was in much better spirits. She ate good wholesome food, got plenty of sleep, and for exercise she took long walks.

One afternoon while she was walking through the pasture, she heard her departed husband's voice.

"Sara," he called, "this is me, Seymour."

"Oh, my darling," she called, "how are you?"

"Well," he began, "I've come back to life. Right now, I'm standing in a pasture, not far from where you are, surrounded by 500 big healthy cows."

"Oh," moaned his wife, "it must be terrible with all those cows around."

"It's not really so bad," soothed her husband, "because you see dear, I've come back as a bull!"

Paul Grossinger, of the famed resort, knew a famous world traveler who, being of the Jewish faith, always made it a point to spend Yom Kippur at Grossinger's.

For years the traveler had mapped out his schedule and always made sure that when that day rolled around he would be praying at the temple of the famed hotel.

But one year, due to a very important assignment, he was unable to make it, and when the high holy day rolled around, he found himself in China.

Truly disturbed by his inability to be at the hotel for the

holiday, the traveler walked unhappily down the streets of Nanking brooding over the turn of events.

While he was walking, he happened to look up, and was amazed to see a temple with a Jewish star in front. He walked in, and was really astonished to see a Chinese rabbi conducting the services. He walked over to the side of the room, picked up a prayer shawl, and joined in the services.

Several minutes after he was seated, the rabbi walked over to him, stared, and then asked, "Are you Jewish?"

"Well, er—yes I am," said the traveler.

The rabbi eyed him again and then said, "Well, you certainly don't look it!"

AND BEFORE WE LEAVE THE CATSKILLS
REMEMBER WHAT CONFUCIUS COHEN SAYS:
MEN BETTER START LAUGHING
AT GIRL'S BATHING SUITS
BECAUSE SOON THERE WILL BE
NOTHING TO LAUGH AT

IT'S A PLEASURE TO MEET THE PRESS

Of all the people I've known during the years I've been in show business, none have been as warm and receptive as the many columnists and reporters I've met and dealt with.

I remember when I was making the transition from a Garment Center gagster to a night club entertainer how these guys and gals encouraged me. Since the beginning of my career, I've always been warmly appreciative of the wonderful treatment accorded me by all the members of the Fourth Estate. As a small token of gratitude, I devote this chapter to them.

Since ladies come first, it seems only fitting that I start off with the female members of the press:

Muriel Fischer, the gal who gets all those scoops for the New York *World-Telegram*, always finds time to listen to my latest stories. At our last meeting, Muriel applauded when I told her the one about the rather obnoxious woman who was boasting to her friend about the wonderful achievements of her ancestors.

127

"My great-great-great-great grandfather fought with Washington," she said proudly.

"Is that right?"

"And my great-great-great grandfather fought with Jackson."

"Really?"

"Not only that, my great-great grandfather fought with Grant."

"No kidding."

"And my grandfather fought with Pershing and my husband fought with Eisenhower."

"Say," said her friend, "your family didn't get along with anybody, did they?"

☻

The New York *Herald Tribune*'s Marie Torre loves the one about the fellow who was awakened by a burglar. Grabbing his shotgun, the house owner raced downstairs and confronted the crook.

"Okay, you," he threatened, "put all that stuff back in the safe."

"But I can't," protested the bandit, "half of it belongs next door!"

☻

Pretty Atra Baer, the clever TV critic of the New York *Journal-American*, likes the one about the vain young woman who was taking her first driving lesson.

"Richard," she told her husband, "that little mirror up here isn't set right."

"Why sure it is, dear," replied her spouse.

"Oh, no, it isn't," insisted his wife. "I can't see myself in it. All I can see is the cars behind me!"

☻

TV critic Harriet Van Horne is a wonderful girl with a terrific sense of humor. Her favorite story deals with the henpecked husband who was spending an infrequent night out with the boys. However, while the other fellows were relaxing and playing cards, the little fellow seemed tense and worried. Presently, he told them that it was getting late and that he had to go home.
"Why are you leaving so early, Bob?" one fellow asked.
"Well, er—you see, er—I don't like to leave my wife..."
"Why are you so afraid of her? What are you, a man or a mouse?"
"Why, I'm a man of course," the husband answered quickly.
"Really? What makes you so sure of that?"
"Because my wife is afraid of mice."

Hedda Hopper, who writes about Hollywood for the New York *Daily News* and other papers, attended a very exclusive Beverly Hills party and happened to overhear the following conversation between two catty females:
FIRST GIRL: (who is showing an expensive pearl necklace she received from an admirer to her friend) "Darling, they're genuine pearls... in case you've never seen the real thing before."

SECOND GIRL: "Oh, I know real pearls when I see them . . . no matter how small they are."

☺

And Louella Parsons claims that the trouble with most newly-married girls is their lack of understanding of their husbands' salaries. The way they handle the budget, usually there's too much month left over at the end of the money.

☺

The New York *Daily Mirror*'s Frances Merron tells of the Garment Center manufacturer who died and went to heaven.

When he arrived, he was greeted by St. Peter who began showing him around. The heavenly gate-keeper showed him the beautiful scenery, the wonderful facilities, and the people, who all appeared extremely happy.

After showing the newcomer the entire layout, St. Peter was hurt because the chap seemed completely unimpressed. Finally, he asked, "You mean you don't like it up here?"

"It's not that," answered the man from 38th Street, "but Miami's got better hotels."

☺

Frank Farrell of the *New York World Telegram & Sun* has a psychologist friend who told him the following story:

Two silk manufacturers requiring a private secretary called in a psychologist. After testing more than 30 applicants, the psychologist eliminated all but three of them.

In the final test, the first girl was called in: "How much is three and three?" the dome prober asked.

"Six," she replied.

The second girl was asked the same question and replied, "It could be thirty-three."

The third one answered, "It could be six and it could be thirty-three."

When the girls left the room, the psychologist turned proudly to the partners and said, "That's logic for you. You noted that the first girl gave the obvious answer, the second girl showed more imagination, and the third showed both practicality and imagination. Now which girl will you hire?"

The partners moved over to the opposite corner of the room, conferred briefly and then announced their decision, "We'll take the blonde in the sweater."

Earl Wilson, who's always telling those gay girlie gags, loves the one about the middle-aged woman who was having trouble falling asleep. She tried aspirin, sleeping pills, and every other known remedy in an attempt to rid herself of her insomnia. How-

ever, none did any good. Finally, as a last resort, she went to see a psychiatrist.

"Tell me," asked the head shrinker, "do you dream frequently?"

"Why, yes," she blushed. "I have the same dream every night."

"Really?" asked the psychiatrist with interest. "Tell me about it."

"Well, in this dream I'm always being pursued by the same handsome young man, and he always wants to make love to me."

"I see," mused the doc, inwardly pleased that he'd arrived at the crux of her problem so quickly. He reached into a drawer of his desk and took out two dozen pills, which he slipped into an envelope.

"Take two of these every night before retiring," he told her. "Then come back to see me in two weeks."

Two weeks later she returned to his office, her features less cheerful than before.

"What's wrong?" he asked. "Didn't the pills take effect?"

"Oh yes," she replied. "They worked fine. As a matter of fact, I haven't felt so rested in years." Then, after a moment's hesitation, she added coyly, "But frankly, doctor, I miss that young man!"

Leonard Lyons, Earl's colleague at the New York *Post*, was walking down Madison Avenue the other morning. During his stroll, he passed a pair of odd-looking fellows and overheard the pair discussing a cute little cocker spaniel one of them was taking for its morning walk.

"Oh, what a cute little pup," commented one.

"I got it for my wife," beamed the other.

"How'd you ever make a trade like that?"

Lee Mortimer, columnist, commentator, author and critic, tells about the two killers who were hired to assassinate a leading political figure of a foreign country who was touring the U.S. The pair checked his habits and learned that every evening before he dressed for dinner the foreign bigwig went to his hotel barber shop and took a shave. This occurred at exactly six o'clock every evening. Accordingly, the hoods decided to knock him off just before he took his shave.

That night, the pair strategically seated themselves in front of the barber shop at five-thirty and took up their vigil. At six, they put their hands on their pistols and watched the door anxiously. But the statesman didn't come.

"He'll be here any minute," one assured the other.

Six-thirty came and went, and there was still no sign of the diplomat.

The crooks were beginning to worry, "Do you think he'll show?" whispered one to the other.

To which his nervous associate answered, "Gee, I hope nothing happened to him."

Ed Sullivan, TV M.C., columnist and former sportswriter, recalls the days when he used to cover all the top sporting events.

He specifically remembers the time when he was covering an important game at the Yankee Stadium.

A small boy was lost in the crowd and kept annoying all the fans by screaming, "Where's my mother? I'm lost!"

Distracted by the little boy's cries, people would give him nickels, dimes and quarters in an effort to keep him quiet until his mother returned. But as soon as he collected, he would start bawling again, "Where's my mother! I'm lost! I'm lost!"

Seeing the little fellow's plight, a kindly old gentleman approached him and said, "Stop crying, little fellow, I know where your mother is."

"So do I," whispered the kid. "But keep it quiet, will ya! Keep it quiet!"

☻

Hy Gardner of the New York *Herald Tribune,* who is also a TV celebrity, was discussing grandmothers with John Crosby, the radio-TV columnist for the same paper.

"No one is prouder than a grandmother," Hy was saying. "They have forgotten all the wet diapers and hard work associated with bringing up a baby. All they notice is how many steps their little darlings can take, the cute words of wisdom that come out of the mouths of the little angels, and how many times the sweet little things kissed grandma on her last visit."

"I know exactly what you mean, Hy," answered John. "Last week, while I was walking through the park, I met a neighbor of mine who was taking her two little grandsons for a walk. I waved to her and said, 'You have very nice looking grandchildren, Mrs. Brown. How old are they?'

"Smiling proudly, she said, 'The lawyer is four and the doctor is six.'"

☻

Bob Sylvester, who writes those comical columns for the New York *Daily News*, recently visited a friend who owns a chain of hardware stores.

The fellow lives on Riverside Drive, and when Bob walked into the house, he was very impressed by the layout and furnishings. But when he stepped into the living room, he was shocked to see the fellow's little three-year-old son holding a hammer in his hand and knocking nails into the piano, the chairs, tables, and even the floor.

"That seems like an expensive way for your son to play," he told his host.

"Oh, not at all," his friend assured him. "You see, I don't pay for the nails!"

☻

Sid Fields, who writes the ever popular "Only Human" column for the New York *Daily Mirror* loves the one about the prominent psychiatrist who was vacationing in Las Vegas. Although the head shrinker wasn't a gambling man, he would go to the gambling casino every night in order to study the reactions of the people who were betting in the various games of chance. However, no matter where he'd begin, the psychiatrist would always wind up watching the poker players.

Noticing the doctor's fascination for the poker games, one player asked him about it.

"Well, let's put it this way," said the medical man, "I've come to the conclusion that a good poker player is the type who could hold down any kind of job."

"But doc," replied the card shark, "what would a good poker player want with a job!"

☻

Marty Burden of the New York *Post* recently told me about a young college student who was called into his English professor's office.

"Young man," began the learned man, "who wrote that excellent essay you submitted to me yesterday?"

"I did," replied the student quickly.

"Is that so?" smiled the professor. Then, in a voice dripping with sarcasm, he added, "To think that in my lifetime I'd come face to face with Ralph Waldo Emerson!"

Nick Kenny, who writes those pearls of wisdom for the New York *Daily Mirror*, once knew a comedian who was asked to entertain at a policemen's benefit ball. Being a charitable guy, the comic agreed. On the night before the show, the Police Commissioner called the comic aside. "I'll have to audition you before you go on," the top cop told him.

"Is that so?" asked the comedian innocently. He gazed thoughtfully at the floor for a moment and then added, "I wonder if you'd mind waiting here for a minute. I won't be long."

"Where are you going?"

"Out to audition the nearest burglar alarm. I want to see how good you are!"

Lovable Louis Sobol, dean of the New York *Journal American* staff overheard the following conversation between two unhappy husbands.

"Does your wife listen to you?" asked one.

"The only time my wife shows the slightest interest in my conversation," his friend answered sadly, "is when I'm talking to another woman."

When I was breaking into show business, Lee Mortimer of the New York *Daily Mirror*, was one of my greatest boosters. I've never forgotten this, and every time we meet, we both break into big, broad smiles. Then we exchange the stories we've collected since our last meeting. Recently, I broke Lee up with the tale about the young mother who was called to school because her little Melvin's deportment was not all that it should be. It just so happened that Melvin's mother had graduated from Barnard and had majored in—you guessed it—psychology. Not only that—she had read all the latest books on the subject. When Mom arrived in school she wasn't at all what the teacher had expected.

"Your son is very noisy and disrupts my class," said the teacher severely.

"Let me warn you," began the mother quickly, "you must never raise your hand to Melvin. He is a very sensitive child and physical punishment directed against him may cause a trauma. The poor boy, I'm afraid, has paranoic tendencies. He's always suspecting people of plotting against him. So if you are convinced he needs discipline . . . hit him while he's looking."

Harold's mother—Harold was a classmate of Melvin—dealt with a similar problem a bit differently. She, too, had received reports that her boy's conduct was troublesome. But she hadn't read any psychology books.

When she came to visit the teacher, she, too, explained that her Harold was sensitive. However, she was perfectly aware that he could be a behavior problem.

The question was: how to discipline Harold without scarring his sensitive nature.

"The thing to do is scare him," she advised the teacher. "If he acts up and you just can't stand it anymore, hit the boy in front of him."

☺

Ben Gross and Sid Shalit, radio and TV critics for the New York *Daily News* recently asked a 12-year-old boy his opinion of the romantic programs as compared to the rip-roaring westerns.

"I can't stand that mushy stuff," came the expected response. "But I got a system. Whenever my mother and father watch one of those pictures with a lot of huggin' and kissin', I just pretend the guy is chokin' the dame to death."

☺

Danton Walker, one of the long-time top Broadway columnists, likes the one about the two New Yorkers who went on a hunting trip. One took a quart of liquor and the other brought a jug of coffee. Both drank heartily. Then they found the right spot and waited for their prey.

After waiting about two hours, a lone duck appeared 50 feet away. Lifting up his rifle, the coffee drinker shot, and missed. From further back, the liquor drinker shot and hit the bird right between the eyes.

"Good shooting," said the coffee man.

"It wash nothin'" answered his inebriated pal. "With a flock like that, I should have brought down 10 or 12!"

☺

Abel Green, the beloved editor of *Variety*, is one of the most popular guys in show business. Everyone agrees that Abel's got talent and wit to burn. Not too long ago, I ran into him on Broadway and he told me about the southern politican who boarded the train in Raleigh, North Carolina, and told the porter, "Ah'm to be sworn in as a membah of Congress in Washington tomorrow morning. Listen to what Ah tell you, boy. When we get to Washington, even if Ah'm *sound asleep*, you put me off this train."

Of course, the porter promised to do as the Representative-elect wished. But the next morning when the train pulled into Penn Station in New York, the politician was fast asleep in his berth. As the train jogged to a halt, he woke up and gazed, baffled, out the window. When he realized where he was, he hit the ceiling. He scrambled out of his berth and raced up the aisle, bellowing: "Where's that porter! Let me at him! Ah'll tear him limb from limb!"

Meanwhile, the porter had wisely hidden behind a seat. Another porter discovered his friend where he was crouching and asked, "What's the matter with that man running around and screaming like that? Boy, is he mad! He looking for you?"

"He's looking for me, all right," said the guilty porter, "and he sure *is* mad, but nothing compared to the man I put off in Washington."

The A.P.'s Hal Boyle likes to tell the one about the press agent who was forever pestering a certain columnist. The drum beater had a new client and wanted to get an item in the paper to impress him. Finally, after several calls, the persistent fellow got through to his man.

"I've been trying to see you for almost a month. Can I set an appointment for sometime next week?" he asked.

"Well," stalled the columnist, "why don't you get in touch with my secretary?"

And the p.a. quickly replied, "I did. So last night we had a wonderful time. But I still want to see you!"

Ted Green, of *Radio Daily*, was standing on Broadway when he witnessed the following scene. It seems that a cute little blonde was standing in front of the Paramount waiting for her beau. While she was standing there, a middle-aged wolf walked

up to her, smiled, and said, "Say, you're a doll. Where've you been all my life?"

The girl looked him up and down and said drily, "Well, for the first half of it, I wasn't even born."

Clark Kinnaird, author and columnist, for King Features, while seated at his desk, overheard one copy boy tell another about the haughty career woman who was forced to travel by a devious route in order to reach Chicago where she had an important business appointment. Getting off the train late at night at the little village which was a transfer point on the railroad, she was dismayed to learn she had missed the mainliner. There wouldn't be another until morning.

Since there was nothing else to do but to spend the night in this one horse town, she asked the aged baggage master about hotels.

"Ain't got no hotel in this town," he informed her.

"Oh come now, my good man, where am I going to sleep tonight?"

"With the station master, I guess," said the old man slyly.

"How dare you!" came the indignant reply. "I'll have you know I'm a lady!"

"So's the station master, ma'am," chuckled the old man.

Bob Williams, the radio and TV columnist for the New York *Post*, tells about Ed Brown, a stubborn old man, who simply refused to carry an umbrella, wear rubbers on a rainy day, or otherwise cooperate with his wife's efforts to reform him.

"You never listen to advice for your own good," she nagged.

"Darn good thing for you I don't," he snorted, "or you'd still be an old maid."

Meyer Berger, who writes those wonderful pieces about New York in the *Times* once had a friend who was one of the most prominent lawyers in the country. This man had a Park Avenue office which was always packed with clients. Being so successful, he was naturally in demand as a speaker at law schools and legal gatherings.

One day, the president of the university from which he had graduated called and asked him to conduct an informal round-table discussion with the members of the current graduating class. Inasmuch as he was the idol of many of these students, he felt it was his duty to go.

When they were seated around the table, one student asked the famous attorney how he happened to choose law as his calling.

"When I was a young fellow," he told them, "all I wanted to do was dance. I wanted to become another Fred Astaire and Arthur Murray wrapped into one. Every time I'd get a spare moment,

I'd call some girl and go dancing, and when I did I would forget everything. However, my parents wouldn't allow me to forget. Every chance they got they'd pull the phone from my hand and hand me a law book. Naturally, my dancing suffered. Instead of dancing, I'd spend all my time reading law books. And that gentlemen, is the reason why I am what I am today . . ."

". . . one of the world's greatest lawyers," murmured a student enviously.

"Oh, no!" snapped the great man. "One of the world's lousiest dancers."

☺

Leo Shull, editor and publisher of *Show Business*, once took a vacation at a dude ranch. It was a nice place and Leo enjoyed all the activities. But the incident which stands out most in his mind occurred the day before he was going to leave. While standing near the corral he suddenly saw a big rattlesnake wriggling toward him. He didn't know what to do but he'd heard somewhere that if you stand still the snake will go away. While he was standing thus, a cowboy shouted from the corral, "Hey, you! Get away from there! That's a rattler. If you go near it, it will strike."

"Good Lord!" yelped Leo, "Do these things have unions too!"

Jack Gould, TV editor of the *New York Times*, reviewed a recent program in which the owner of a luggage shop told his friend, "I guess I've seen everything now."

"What do you mean by that?" asked his friend.

"Yesterday I looked up and there standing in my store was a gigantic elephant who said to me, 'I'd like to see something new in trunks.'"

☺

Hobe Morrison, one of the top men at *Variety*, was seated with Jack Hellman in one of the better New York night spots recently, when they, as well as all the other patrons, were shocked to see an elephant walk in. He wasn't a self-conscious elephant, either. Just as if it were an everyday occurrence, the elephant sauntered up to the bar and ordered a scotch and soda.

The proprietor, fearing the reactions of his customers, sidled up to the beast and tapped him on the shank. But the elephant ignored him. Finally, the owner said, "It's been a long time since we've seen an elephant in here."

Still the elephant ignored him and looked up at the price list. Suddenly, with a toss of his trunk, he made his way to the door. When he reached it, he trumpeted, "And it'll be a long time before you'll see another one at these prices!"

Ben Rosenberg, Amusement Editor of the New York *Post*, knew an ambitious cub reporter whose first assignment might have been his last.

"There's been a bank robbery at Bayshore, Long Island," the editor barked. "Get out there and get all the facts. And hurry."

The cub raced down to his car and headed for Long Island. After he had driven through the Midtown Tunnel he jammed his foot down on the accelerator and the speedometer shot up to 90 miles an hour. In his haste, the eager reporter drove right through a house.

Jumping out of his auto, he asked the woman of the house, "How do I get to Bayshore?"

Pointing, she said, "Straight past the kitchen table and turn right at the TV set in the study!"

Sidney Skolsky, the fellow who says, "But don't get me wrong, I love Hollywood," tells of a noted star who applied for a passport to go to Europe. When she came to the question asking whether she was married, she paused for a moment and then quickly wrote: "OCCASIONALLY."

☺

Columnist Bugs Baer, who writes those clever quips for the *Journal-American*, recently met an old friend whom he hadn't seen for several years.

"How's your wife?" Bugs asked, "has she changed much?"

"Plenty," answered his friend ruefully. "My habits, my clothes and my friends."

☺

Columnist Irving Hoffman has a friend who believes the American way of judging a movie is as follows: condemning it for being immoral; attending it to see if it's as shocking as advertised; and then kicking because the spicy parts have been cut out.

☺

Bennett Cerf, the author-columnist-humorist, knew a railroad claim agent who was teaching his wife to drive. Suddenly, the brakes failed on a steep downhill grade.

"I can't stop!" she screamed. "What shall I do?"

"Brace yourself," advised her spouse, "and try to hit something cheap."

☺

Jim O'Connor, the popular drama critic of the *Journal-American* tells of the teenager who explained why he preferred to sit in the last seat in the classroom.

"Sitting there I get last chance at a question," the youngster said. "By then it's almost impossible to guess wrong."

Robert Dana, of the *World Telegram & Sun* knew a young bride who told her spouse, "Darling, I'm afraid your dinner is a little burned tonight."

"The hell you say!" exclaimed her husband. "Don't tell me they had a fire at the delicatessen!"

The *Daily Mirror*'s Frank Quinn was lunching in the Pen & Pencil when he overheard the following heart-to-heart talk between a boss and his employee:

"Bill, how is it you never come to work on time anymore?"

"Well, boss, it's like this," explained Bill. "You've done such a thorough job of educating me not to be a clock-watcher during office hours that I've lost the habit of watching it at home too!"

Hinson Styles, also of the New York *Daily Mirror*, always has a good story for me whenever we meet. Recently he told me about two business partners who had never had an argument in thirty years. However, one weekend one of the pair came down with the flu and missed a few days at the office.

About the third day, the partner at work phoned his ailing friend and announced, "I just found $10,000 missing from the safe. What shall I do?"

To which his ailing friend quickly replied, "Put it back!"

Statistics cannot always be relied upon, reports writer Paul Denis.

For instance, he cites an item to the effect that in the United States there are only 87 women who are hunters and trappers.

☺

Mel Heimer, who writes those witty columns for King Features, has a friend whose son is a freshman at college. The boy, it seems, is deeply interested in the theater.

Recently the proud papa received a letter from his son in which the lad enthusiastically announced that he'd landed a part in a school play. "I play a man who's been married for twenty years," the boy wrote.

"Good luck, son," his old man wrote back. "Keep up the good work and before you know it they'll be giving you a speaking part."

☺

Frank Coniff, the *Journal-American* columnist, has a wonderful sense of humor. Not too long ago he told me about the football player and his girl who were standing on the sidelines watching the rest of the team scrimmage. It was obvious that a tall end was the star of the team.

"Next year," said the fellow to his girl, "Jim is going to be our best man."

"Oh darling," the girl trilled, giving him a quick kiss on the cheek, "what a nice way to ask me!"

☺

Marvin Kirsch and Joe Morris, two of the top men at *Radio Daily*, once employed a reporter who had a knack for coming up with the best stories. However, in the love department the guy batted .000. He rarely went out with girls and whenever he did get up enough nerve to ask one, the evening generally turned out to be a disaster.

This went on for many years, until finally the timid Lothario met a middle-aged spinster he liked. He dated her several times, and he was sure she shared his feelings. He decided to ask her to marry him and he stayed awake nights planning his approach. But, plot and scheme as he might, once they were together, his

courage would fail him. Finally, he decided that the only way he could untie his tongue would be by calling and asking her over the phone. Resolutely, he dialed her number.

"Is this Alma?" he demanded.

"This is Alma."

"Look here, will you marry me?"

"Why, of course," answered Alma quickly. "Who is this, please?"

Harry Hershfield, who has been making humor headlines these many years, had a conscientious bookkeeper who showed up at his office one morning looking completely worn-out.

"You must have had a big evening," said one of his associates.

"It isn't that," yawned the bookkeeper. "I couldn't get to

sleep so I started counting sheep. But I made a mistake, and it took me all night to find it."

AND BEFORE WE GO TO THE NEXT CHAPTER
REMEMBER WHAT CONFUCIUS COHEN SAYS:
NEWSPAPER WHICH PRINTS PICTURE
OF GIRL WEARING FALSIES
IS GUILTY OF TOPOGRAPHICAL ERROR.

THERE'S NO PEOPLE LIKE SHOW PEOPLE

There's no people like show people. They're gay, they're talented and they're lovable. Even more important, they're generous.

Almost daily, one reads or hears about a forthcoming marathon at which a name star will devote his time to raising money for the unfortunate and afflicted.

Such stars as Dean Martin, Jerry Lewis, Milton Berle, Martha Raye, Eddie Cantor, Joey Adams, Danny Kaye, George Jessel, Harry Hershfield and many others have unselfishly given their time and energies to helping the sick and needy.

Walter Winchell is another; he has devoted a tremendous amount of time and energy to creating and guiding the Damon Runyon Cancer Fund.

Dean Martin, who used to team up with Jerry Lewis on those Muscular Dystrophy Marathons, acts as a double threat now that he's a single. Besides singing, Dean keeps the audience in stitches with his stories.

One of Dean's favorites deals with a hobo who walked up to the front door of a large mansion.

"Well?" asked the housekeeper, "what can I do for you?"

"Oh nothin' much, ma'am," he assured her, "I just wondered whether I could cut your grass for my dinner?"

"Of course," replied the understanding housekeeper, "but you don't have to cut it. Eat it just as it is."

☻

On a marathon, Jerry Lewis jumps, yells, mugs, mimics, and tells jokes like this one:

A husband and wife were arguing outside the Latin Quarter.

"What do you mean by coming home at 4 A.M. the other night? If I've told you once, I've told you a hundred times . . ."

"All right, dear," her spouse answered meekly, "I won't come home that early again."

☻

Milton Berle, the wonderful Mr. Television who's currently leaving them laughing at the better night spots around the country, recently told me about a very exclusive eatery in Las Vegas.

The place is so fancy that when somebody orders Russian dressing, the waiter puts on Russian clothes to serve the dish. And when a customer orders Hungarian goulash, the waiter puts on a Hungarian costume.

"But after I ate there," says Miltie sorrowfully, "the cops closed the place down. I never should have ordered that salad without dressing."

☻

Martha Raye, who owned Miami's "Five O'Clock Club" when I worked there, knew a girl who registered at a Miami employment bureau.

"How would you like a job as an airline stewardess?" asked the interviewer.

"Sure," she agreed, "it will give me a chance to meet men."

"But that's silly," chided the interviewer, "you can meet men on practically any job."

"Strapped down?"

Eddie Cantor likes the one about the old man who was confronted by the conductor.

"Where's your ticket?" asked the conductor.

"To tell the truth," the old codger began, "I haven't got a ticket. My daughter is getting married in New York today, and it wouldn't look good if I'm not there. Look at me. I'm an old man. What would you gain by throwing me off this train? Please, let me go to the wedding."

The conductor looked at him for a few moments and then said, "Okay buddy, I'll give you a break. But keep very quiet so that nobody notices you."

"Oh, thank you," answered the old man. He sank into his chair and the conductor moved along.

As he was walking, he suddenly spied another stowaway behind a chair. Yanking the fellow out by the collar, the conductor shouted, "What's going on here, anyway? Where's your ticket?"

The second fellow was obviously frightened. He pointed down the car to the first stowaway. "*I* don't know anything about any tickets, but he invited me to the wedding!"

☻

Joey Adams, the prosperous author, scholar and comedian, has a friend whose little boy shows considerable promise. One day after school he told his father that he'd decided he wanted to enter politics when he grew up.

"That sounds like a fine ambition," said the father. Then he told the lad that they would take a trip to Washington the following weekend and see how things were done in the capital.

First they took a tour of all the famous sights—from the Lincoln Memorial to the FBI building—and then they went to the Senate building to watch the goings-on from the gallery. As they walked in, the boy spotted a chaplain seated in a far corner of the chamber. "Daddy," said the little boy, "is the chaplain there to pray for the Senators?"

"As a matter of fact," his elder answered, "the chaplain looks at the Senators and then prays for the country!"

☻

Danny Kaye frequently entertains at the Palladium in London where he draws standing-room-only crowds. On free afternoons he loves to roam around the city or take in matinees.

On one such afternoon he took in a play that was being received with the reserve we've come to associate with the British (which has never been in evidence among Danny's audiences).

As the play was letting out, Danny overheard the play being

discussed by three British army officers who were standing stiffly to one side:

"Ghastly," said one.

"Beastly," agreed the second.

The third was even more tight-lipped. He didn't say a word.

One of the vocal ones turned to him. "And what was your opinion, Colonel?" he asked.

"Came on a pass," he explained. "Hardly cricket to speak out under the circumstances, you know. But if you gentlemen will excuse me...." and with that he strode to the box office a few feet away and bought a ticket.

He was back in a moment, his ticket held gingerly between thumb and forefinger.

"A stinker, gentlemen," he said tersely.

George Jessel, known as the Toastmaster General, has probably appeared at more banquets than any other American. George, who's got a story for every occasion, likes the one about the well-dressed fellow who walked into a Seventh Avenue bar, demanded a double shot of rye, downed it in one gulp, tossed a five-dollar bill on the counter, and walked out. In all that time, he didn't say a word.

The bartender picked up the bill, folded it and put it in his pocket. "Can you beat a guy like that?" he remarked to the other fellows in the bar. "He comes in here, laps up a double rye, leaves a five-dollar tip, and then beats it without paying!"

Hy Gardner, who is not only a clever columnist but a great raconteur as well, likes the one about the much-married Hollywood star who ran out of women to marry. In fact, he actually married one of his former wives for the second time without realizing it. But in the morning, when he came down for breakfast he recognized his mother-in-law.

☺

Harry Ritz's specialties often have a Yiddish flavor:

Irving Cohen (no relation) was sent to an insane asylum by his relatives. When the first meal was served him in the institution, he refused to eat it and yelled hysterically:

"I'm kosher—I won't eat this food—I want kosher meals!"

In order to calm Irving, the director hired a special Yiddish cook to serve him strictly kosher meals. Naturally, he had the best meals in the place. However, the director kept a keen eye on Irving.

It seems that every evening after his meal, the cracked Cohen would pull out a big cigar and smoke it. When Friday night came around, Irving again pulled out a big stogie and began puffing it.

The director confronted him. "Listen, Cohen, you can't expect to get away with that kind of stuff. You came here and demanded kosher food because you said you were religious. We went to the expense of getting you a special Yiddish cook. And now on Friday night, when it's against your religion, you smoke a cigar. What's the big idea?"

"Listen," countered Irving, "what's the use of arguing with me? I'm crazy, ain't I?"

☻

Morey Amsterdam likes the one about the rich old uncle who was attempting to induce his young nephew to come into his dress business with him. "But don't think you're coming in here and starting at the top," his uncle told him. "You'll begin as a partner, just like all the rest of us did."

☻

Harry Hershfield often tells the one about the grouchy wife who spent twice as much as her husband earned. She also constantly nagged the poor fellow and continually compared him with all their friends.

"Ben has a new car and Phil just bought Mary a new mink," she complained. Another one of her pet gripes was the apartment they rented. "All our friends live ten times better than we do," she whined. "They'll all laugh at us if we don't move into a more expensive neighborhood."

One night her long-suffering mate came home and told her, "Well, we won't have to move to live luxuriously. The landlord just doubled our rent."

☻

Henny Youngman tells of the well-known actress who was crazy about Swiss cheese. She had it for breakfast, lunch and supper and often in between meals. An interviewer, who had heard about her strange eating habits, decided to have some fun with her.

"Tell me," he asked her, "why do you like Swiss cheese?"

To which question the charming star quipped, "I'll tell you

if you can tell me why they put holes in Swiss cheese when it is limburger that needs the ventilation."

☻

Groucho Marx knew a slightly simple-minded foreigner who immediately headed for Reno when he got off the boat in New York. According to Groucho, the fellow said he'd heard that Reno was the place where women were made free.

☻

Barry Gray, writer, columnist, broadcaster and humanitarian, often comes up with some of the funniest I've ever heard. Typical of Barry's humor:

At a huge gathering, a female psychology student was rebuked when she stated that men were much vainer than women. Naturally, she was immediately challenged by a fellow standing near her. In order to prove her statement, she said in a clear voice that carried through the room, "It's a shame that most intelligent and sensitive men attach so little importance to the way they dress. Why, right this minute, the most cultivated man in this room is wearing the most clumsily knotted tie."

Whereupon, as if on cue, every man in the room immediately put his hand to his tie.

☻

My boy Danny Thomas always gets the audience in the mood with ones like this:

MOTHER: "Don't worry, dear. Mother will tell you everything you should know before you get married."

DAUGHTER: "That's wonderful! Then I'll be able to get as much alimony as you did."

☻

Bob Hope tells of the elderly spinster who passed a red light and paid no heed to the loud blasts from the traffic cop's whistle. He finally caught her attention and she pulled over to the side.

"Didn't you hear me whistle?" he demanded.

"Certainly I did," she answered, "but I never flirt when I'm driving."

Buddy Hackett always seems to be hungry. Consequently, many of his stories deal with food.

One of his favorites is about the playboy who purchased a farm in Iowa.

"What are you going to plant?" asked a friend at his farewell party.

"Razor blades and cabbages," he answered, without blinking an eye.

"Razor blades and cabbages!" echoed the stunned guest. "What do you expect to get out of that?"

"Cole slaw."

And Jack E. Leonard is another who loves to tell stories about food.

Jack often tells the one about the little old man whose doctor put him on a diet of fresh vegetables. The fellow, a bachelor, would eat his meals at a small restaurant right off Seventh Avenue. Every day he would sit at the same table and order a vegetable plate with whole wheat bread. But every day, the waitress would bring him white bread with his meal. This went on for three weeks, until one day the fellow decided he'd outwit the waitress.

"Bring me a plate of mixed vegetables with white bread," he told her.

Instead of going to the kitchen and placing the order, the girl just stood there staring at him.

"What's the matter?" he asked. "Is there something wrong?"

"Oh no, sir," answered the puzzled girl, "but aren't you the fellow who always orders whole wheat?"

Steve Allen, who is a philosopher as well as a comedian and author, contends that the best way to give advice to your children is to find out what they want and then tell them to do it.

And Jimmy Durante likes the one about the boss who walked into his office one day and asked his assistant, "Is my daughter here?"

"Yes sir," came the reply, "I saw the salesman try to kiss her."

"Did he succeed?" asked the boss.

"Oh, no, sir. She slapped his face."

"Then that wasn't my daughter!"

Jokester Jan Murray knew a prosperous garment manufacturer who fell in love with a night club singer and hired a private detective to check up on her. Two weeks later, he received the following note: "The girl in question has a good reputation. She comes from an excellent family, has many friends of high social standing, and was spoken of most highly until a few weeks ago. At that time she began running around with a garment manufacturer of questionable character."

☻

Rowdy Red Skelton's repertoire includes the impersonation of several different characters—ranging from a punch drunk fighter to a hill-billy farmer.
When Red's a punchy pugilist he prefers this one:
DRIVER: "You walk as if you owned the street!"
RED: "Yeah—and you drive as if you owned the sidewalk!"

☻

And when he's portraying a half-witted hill-billy, Red's apt to tell this one:
The minister reproved the husband for spending so much time tinkering with his new car.
"If I were you," asserted the clergyman, "I'd put my wife before my car."
"I'd sure like to," he sighed, "but I'm afraid someone might catch me at it."

☻

Jack Benny, of course, likes to tell jokes dealing with money. He fractured an audience with this one:
A prosperous silk manufacturer took an out-of-town client to his home for dinner. When the meal was over, the host took

his business associate into the study and they began talking about various topics. While they were talking, the manufacturer's three young sons came running into the room. They ran around and around and made a fearful racket.

"Be good," warned the mother from the kitchen, "or you won't have any ice cream for lunch."

But the boys took no heed of their mother's warning.

"My system is better," the father told his associate. "I give Tom, my oldest son—he's seven—a dollar, and he keeps still." He handed the boy the bill, and sure enough he shut up. "And," continued the father, "I give Bob—he's five—a half-dollar and he quiets down."

"Sounds interesting," said the guest, "but what about your youngest son?"

"Oh, him," came the mother's voice from the kitchen, "he's like his father—good for nothing!"

Jackie Gleason wows any audience when he tells the one about the small-time entertainer applying for a job in a night club. "I'm the greatest entertainer in the world!" he told the owner.

"Well, what do you do?" asked the boss.

"I imitate all the big stars. I'm a mimic." Then, the fellow went into his act, impersonating everyone from James Cagney to Lassie.

Impressed, the bistro boss said, "Okay, you start on Monday night at $200 a week."

When the week was over, the boss handed the mimic a check for $50.

Amazed, the fellow went over to the owner and said, "But you promised me $200. How come I only got $50?"

"You're a mimic."

"Yes, but . . ."
"All right, then. So make like Rockefeller!"

Sid Caesar's favorite goes like this:
Two old friends met in front of the Paramount Theatre on Broadway. It was a cold, wintry day with the temperature three below zero. One of the pair wore a heavy winter coat, a thick woolen muffler and a warm hat. The other had on a light top coat and wore neither hat nor scarf.

"Sam," asked his friend, "how come you go around dressed like that in weather like this? What do you want to do, catch pneumonia?"

" Oh no," assured Sam, "it's not that at all. It's just that I don't feel cold."

"You don't feel cold!"

"No, let me explain it to you. I just bought my wife a new mink coat, and when I think of how much it costs . . . I start perspiring."

Red Buttons, who recently made a name for himself in Hollywood, has been telling a lot of film funnies lately. For instance:

Walking out of a theatre after the movie debut of a famous actor's son, a critic summed up his opinion tersely with: "Just a slice off the old ham."

Lucille Ball and Desi Arnaz favor this one:
In Washington, a guide was asked by a tourist about the top man's preference in food and drink.

"The President's tastes are quite simple," explained the guide. "He is easily pleased with the best of everything."

☻

Phil Silvers loves to start off with the one about the small dress shop owner who was bemoaning his fate to a friend who was visiting him.

"Oh, Benny," he complained, "at this rate I'll be out of business in no time."

"Is it that bad?"

"Just to give you an example," he began, "yesterday I sold only one dress, and today business is even worse."

"Worse? How could it be worse?"

"The woman who bought that dress yesterday, . . . well, she returned it today!"

☻

Recently I heard comedian Phil Foster delight an audience with the one about the housewife who went into a drug store and told the clerk, "Give me two packs of invisible hairpins."

"Yes, Ma'am," answered the fellow behind the counter, and began to wrap up a package for her.

"Tell me," asked the woman as he was wrapping them, "are you sure they're invisible?"

"I'll say they are," came the prompt reply. "I sold $8 worth this morning and we've been out of them for two weeks!"

☻

Joe E. Lewis, the carefree comic, loves the one about the death of a stingy, penny-pinching boss. Despite his parsimonious habits, his partner and other associates decided to give him a big funeral. On the day of the burial, the deceased was taking his final ride in a big black Cadillac. Directly behind him in the next car was his partner of 30 years.

Just before they reached the cemetery, a big coal truck pulled out from a side road into an opening between the two cars and joined the procession.

Upon seeing the coal truck in front of him, the partner commented sadly, "I knew where Harry was going, but I didn't know he had to furnish his own coal!"

The last comedian just loves to play at benefits. And the reason why I call him the last comedian is that he's the last one anybody invites. The guy I'm talking about is my brother, Phil Cohen, who is currently the leading comedian in the Garment Center. Whenever Phil appears at a benefit he tells the best jokes because he steals them from one of the best comedians in the business . . . me.

Phil's favorite deals with the Garment Center manufacturer who, after many years of scrimping and saving, had a fabulous season. Being the thrifty sort, the fellow invested his money in government bonds. When the bonds matured, he took out all the money and bought a beautiful mansion in Southampton, a very exclusive section of Long Island.

Soon after the happy man and his wife moved into their new house, they began to mingle with the other residents of the town. They were invited to everyone's home, and in turn they, too, invited their neighbors over for a pleasant social evening.

After dinner, everybody went into the drawing room. In no time at all, the guests were engrossed in a conversation about the great names in music and their wonderful contributions. Such names as Beethoven, Brahms, Bach, Tschaikowsky and Mozart were mentioned. And when Mozart's name was mentioned, the hostess commented loudly so all her guests might hear, "Mozart!

I know him well. In fact, I saw him on the red bus going to the beach this morning."

At this there was a sudden hush. All the guests looked up and stared at her. However, they were all too discreet to say anything.

Late that night, when all his guests were gone, the host confronted his wife: "You had to be such a smart aleck! You had to show off your brains! Do you know you made a fool out of yourself tonight? You ought to know that the red bus doesn't go to the beach!"

AND BEFORE WE GO TO THE NEXT CHAPTER
REMEMBER WHAT CONFUCIUS COHEN SAYS:
HE WHO GO INTO SHOW BUSINESS
OFTEN HAVE TO LIVE
FROM HAM TO MOUTH.

GAGS FOR GOURMETS

Entertaining at one of the New York niteries is fun because it gives me an opportunity to drop into some of my favorite eating places and see some of my favorite people.

These genial restaurateurs can serve up feasts of mirth as well as delectable dishes.

All who know Toots Shor feel that he is one of the greatest guys on Broadway. He's always ready to give a helping hand to a struggling performer or athlete. And his sense of humor never fails him.

His favorite joke deals with the hotel guest who was a real pain in the neck. While this fellow was at the hotel, none of the help had a moment's rest. No matter what he got, he wasn't satisfied. Needless to say, when it came time for him to check out, no one was sorry. However, the entire staff was concerned about the size of the tips this fellow would leave.

One bellhop, who didn't like to leave anything to chance, decided to give the guest a tactful reminder about tipping.

"You won't forget me, sir, will you?" he asked.

"Of course not," smiled the guest. "I'll write you every day."

☺

Danny Stradella, the lovable host of Danny's Hide-A-Way, is another fellow I'd like to see more often. Danny's favorite is about a crude fellow's first visit to a fancy restaurant. His worst habit was tucking his napkin under his chin. Naturally, this

caused the entire staff to stare at him. The *maître de* quickly ran over to the waiter who was serving the fellow and said, "Inform that man that he shouldn't wear a bib in here. But remember, do it very tactfully."

With this, the waiter walked over to the fellow and asked, "Would you like a shave and a haircut also?"

☺

Once, when I was in Danny's Hide-A-Way, I met Danny Davis. Danny's a glib guy who just loves to tell funny stories on or off stage.

One of his favorites deals with the scion of one of our wealthiest families who was a petty officer on a submarine during the last war.

"Torpedoes are expensive," the captain warned the crew. "Before you release one, make sure you're going to hit the target."

Shortly after this lecture, the million-dollar officer spotted a destroyer coming toward the sub. "Destroyer spotted on the portside," he yelled into the megaphone.

There was no answer.

"Destroyer 400 yards away!" he bellowed.

Pause.

"Two hundred yards away!" shouted the rich boy.

Still no answer, and no action.

"One hundred yards away!"

No answer; no action.

"Fifty yards away!"

Nothing.

"Fire!" bawled the playboy. "I'll pay for it!"

The last time I visited his fine eatery, George Mitchell, of the Assembly Restaurant, was talking to C.B.S. producer Marlo Lewis. Both boys were in great spirits, and when they saw me the jokes began to fly.

"Did you hear the one about the manufacturer's wife who told her friend, 'I had such a wonderful time with my husband . . . he thought I was his secretary?'" asked George.

"No," I answered, "but I heard the one about the manufacturer who said there would be a lot of changes in women's styles . . . but none in men's pockets!"

Then Marlo told the one about the wool cutters' convention at which Bob Hope was scheduled to appear as guest star.

When Bob walked into the place, everyone ran over to him and shook his hand. Everyone, that is, except one fellow.

"That's Bob Hope over there," his friend told him. "Don't you want to meet him?"

"Why should I want to meet him? Who's Bob Hope?" he asked.

"You never heard of Bob Hope who's in radio and television?" his friend asked in total disbelief.

"No. What's he in? Wholesale or retail?"

At the Spindletop that night, I saw Alfred Bloomingdale, president of the Diners' Club, and his two associates, Ralph E. Schneider and Matty Simmons. I joined the group long enough to exchange a few funnies. For instance, there was the one about the young lover who was shopping for a gift for his latest flame. He tried an exclusive Fifth Avenue shop and pointed to a bottle of Arpège in the case. "How much?" he asked.

"Fifty dollars, sir," she smiled.

The customer emitted a long, incredulous whistle and gestured toward another bottle on the counter. "And how much is that?" he asked the saleslady.

"That," she replied crisply, "will cost you two whistles."

Whenever I dine in Lindy's, I always exchange stories with the wonderful staff. Managers Ben Epton and Christopher Rudd once told me about two back country boys who walked into a very exclusive restaurant and ordered spare ribs.

After they had finished their meal, the waiter brought finger bowls and placed them before the two diners.

"I never seen glasses like that before," Clem told his friend.

"I guess we're supposed to drink from them."

"Maybe we oughta ask the waiter what they're for?"

With this they called over the man in the white jacket and asked him about the finger bowls.

"They're finger bowls," he told them. "You use them to clean your hands."

The two country boys looked at each other, and when the waiter walked away, Clem whispered to his buddy, "You see, Zeke, when you ask a silly question, you get a silly answer!"

☺

Lindy's waiters also are known for their wit. On many occasions, I've heard Sam Jaeger, Irving Weintraub, Frank Pepitone and Mickey Marks come up with real gems.

Sam once told me about a fellow who, upon leaving a restaurant, asked a waiter who hadn't served him, "Is it raining outside?"

"How would I know," sniffed the waiter, "that's not my table!"

☺

Captains of Lindy's waiters are Dave Bass, Louis Barin, Wesher Berger, and Chris Cassapoglou. These guys all believe in mind over platter and always come up with culinary chuckles.

Chris tells about the Jewish couple who dined out one evening in the neighborhood kosher delicatessen. They were amazed when a Chinese waiter approached them to take their order. But their surprise turned to shock when the suave Oriental addressed them in perfect Yiddish.

As soon as he had gone into the kitchen they motioned to the proprietor. "A Chinese waiter in a Jewish delicatessen!" exclaimed the man. "And not only that, but he talks Yiddish. How come?"

The proprietor looked around quickly and put his finger to

his lips. "Shhhh," he whispered, "he thinks I'm teaching him English!"

☻

Lindy's cashiers, Irving Areloff, Charles Dewland and Philip Davis like this one:

The two men had just dined together. Outside the restaurant, one turned to the other. "Jack," he said, "how come you left the hatcheck girl a two-dollar tip?"

"Listen," explained his friend, "isn't this new coat she gave me worth two dollars!"

(When hatcheck girl, Billy DeAngeles heard this story, she swore she wasn't the girl.)

☻

Once while lunching in Lindy's, I met Paul Waldman, the advertising genius, who told me about a psychiatrist who was so modern that he got rid of his old-fashioned couch and got a Castro convertible.

One day, a complete stranger walked into his office, opened up the Castro, and went to sleep.

Slightly annoyed, the doc woke the fellow up and asked him what he was up to.

"It's cold outside and I have nowhere to sleep," the man explained, "so I thought I'd come in here and take a quick nap."

"Oh," said the doc. "Well, the least you could do is say goodnight."

Once while I was entertaining at the Latin Quarter, I invited the wonderful Tisch family to catch my act. Mr. and Mrs. Al Tisch were present as were Bob and Larry Tisch. Two of their better known hotels are the Traymore in Atlantic City and the Americana in Florida. E. M. Loewe, the popular Latin Quarter host, was seated at their table.

They all enjoyed the one about the woman who walked into a millinery store and instructed the salesgirl: "That lavender felt hat with the black plume and thick band—would you take it out of the window for me, please?"

"Of course, Ma'am," agreed the clerk, "I'd be glad to."

"Thanks so much," smiled the woman as she walked toward the exit. "That horror was giving me a turn every time I passed by."

While dining recently at the Old Homestead, I bumped into Al Albert of Albert Decorators on the Grand Concourse. Al decorated my home for me.

As soon as he saw me, he asked, "Myron, did you hear about the fellow who was so rich that he served mixed greens for lunch . . . shredded fives and tens?"

"No," I retorted, "but I heard about the native who loved his fellow men . . . medium-rare."

Also, at the Steak Pit that night was Mr. Yasky of the Hotel Fourteen, which is located across the street from the Copa.

He liked the one about the man who complained to the owner of a super market about the behavior of a certain clerk.

"I'll talk to him," the manager assured the customer. "After all, we aim to please."

To which the piqued customer replied, "Then why don't you close up for a day and get in some target practice?"

☻

Before dining one night, I stopped off at Victor's barber shop at 1400 Broadway. After giving me a quick haircut and shave, he remarked, "There's one thing you can say for baldness—it's neat!"

☻

My two other favorite barbers are Angelo and Eddie of the Dawn Patrol Barber Shop. Like all barbers, both boys are always full of stories. However, the last time I was there I pulled a switch and told them this one:

A retired millionaire was talking to his lazy son. "You lazy bum! Why don't you go out and find a job? When I was your age, I was working for five dollars a week in a store, and at the end of the year, I owned the place."

"Yeah?" tossed off the young one, "you wouldn't get away with that today . . . they have cash registers."

☻

I was dining in Shine's one evening with Ralph Snider and Al Taxier of Boston's Bradford Hotel, when Nat Berkowitz, of Bienen-Davis, the handbag firm, walked in. As soon as he spotted me, he came dashing over and the jokes began to fly.

First he told the one about the couple who had been married for more than 30 years and had never stopped battling. Finally, they could stand no more. She sued him for divorce and they went before the judge.

They both told their stories, and when they had finished the judge spoke: "Madam, I have decided to find for you. I'm giving you fifty dollars a week."

Hearing this, the husband spoke up: "That's handsome of you, judge—I think I'll throw in a few dollars myself."

And I came back with the one about the wife who went in front of a judge and said, "All I'm asking is that my husband should leave me the way he found me."

Slightly taken aback, the judge said, "But lady, that's impossible."

"Why impossible?" she persisted. "He found me a widow, didn't he?"

My tenpercental manager, Henri Giné of Artists Corp. of America, agent Nat Dunn, and two of my other associates, Myron H. Cohen, the Equitable Life agent, and agent Charles Rapp, were dining with me at Gross's Dairy Restaurant on Broadway and 37th Street. We were all in high spirits that evening and I began the festivities with the story about the strict, old-fashioned boss who was becoming irritated with his untidy secretary. One morning he called her into his office after noting how sloppy her desk was. He had noticed all the old slips and memos piled high upon her desk and decided to give her a pointer or two on cleanliness.

"Miss Jones," he asked, "what do you do with the slips you are through with?"

"Usually," said Miss Jones, "I give them to the Salvation Army."

Then Nat countered with the tale of the handsome personnel director who, one Friday afternoon, went over to the desk of a pretty young secretary and asked, "Miss Brown, are you doing anything Sunday night?"

"Well, no," answered the girl, blushing.

"Then I suggest you get a good night's sleep and try to get to the office on time Monday morning."

Seymour Klein, of the Gem Garage on 54th Street, was standing on Seventh Avenue talking to Nick Giovanna, of Chrysler-Manhattan cars. When I walked over to say hello, I noticed that Nick looked particularly unhappy.

"How's business, Nick?" I asked.

"To tell you the truth, Myron, it could be better."

"How come?" I asked.

"It's those small foreign cars. They've really made an impression," he explained. "New York is so full of them that, whenever you cross the street, you have to look left, right and down!"

AND BEFORE WE LEAVE THIS CHAPTER
REMEMBER WHAT CONFUCIUS COHEN SAYS:
PEOPLE WHO EAT LOTS OF SWEETS
WILL SOON DEVELOP LARGER SEATS.

CoHEn AT HoME

I am what is called a gentleman farmer. If you're not quite sure what that is, let me explain it to you. A gentleman farmer is a fellow, who, when walking through his garden, tips his hat to all the tomatoes.

I wasn't always a farmer. Before I had my home in New City, New York, I lived on Davidson Avenue in the Bronx. *I loved the Bronx!* When I lived there, I used to go to work in the morning and come home at night and relax. But a farmer can never relax!

I go to sleep with the chickens, get up with the roosters, work like a horse, eat like a pig, and get treated like a dog.

Let me tell you something else—the fellow who said, "A farm is where you can make a living from dirt," must have been out of his mind! Believe me, I've tried!

When I first bought the place, I didn't know a thing about farming. I read all the latest books on modern methods of planting, milking and taking care of a home. Still, I felt I didn't know enough, so I decided to seek the advice of a few of my neighbors, all of whom seemed to be prosperous and to know what they were doing.

The fellow next door seemed to be especially rich. When he started showing me around his place I was amazed at the revolutionary methods he used. This fellow even tried crossing tomatoes with scotch . . . he wanted stewed tomatoes!

"I once had a hen," he told me, "that was really great. She won dozens of awards. When I put a red quilt in front of her, she would lay red eggs, when I put a green quilt before her—green eggs. A blue quilt—blue eggs. But one day someone accidentally put a plaid quilt in front of her . . . and the poor bird died trying to deliver the goods!"

Then he showed me the cows in his barn. "See that one over there," he said pointing to a healthy looking specimen. "She's a real character. I used to milk her at five o'clock every morning for more'n a year. But the morning that daylight saving time began, I got up to milk her at four o'clock. It must have given her quite a turn when I walked in at that time because when she saw me, she gave a sigh of relief and said, 'Thank God, it's you. I thought I was being robbed.'"

Seriously, though, I love my home in the country. Bill Robbins, my friend and adviser, thought it was a wonderful idea; a place for me to spend my idle hours relaxing.

About a week after I moved in, Bill pulled up in front with a small trailer attached to his car. "I brought you a little housewarming present," he smiled.

When I looked in the trailer, I was shocked to see a great big cow.

"But Bill," I protested.

"Isn't she beautiful?" he sighed. "She's a real Holstein. But to make her feel more at home, maybe we'd better change her name to Goldstein."

Jeanne Sager, my very imaginative press agent, warned, "Remember, Myron, it takes a lot of hard work before a house is completely decorated and furnished."

"That's right," added her husband, Jerry, who is a top public relations man. "A house is not a home."

☺

And Eleanor Malisoff, my pretty and very efficient secretary kidded, "Now you don't need any more writers—you can get all the spice from your garden!" But if I become a silk salesman again, will I be able to get that kind of material from my garden? Of course, I can always raise silk worms!

☺

I will always be grateful to Eddie Davis, of the famed "Leon and Eddie's," who did so much in furthering my career. Whenever Eddie, who is now in retirement in Florida, comes to the big town I always invite him to my home. The last time he came, Eddie told some of the funniest stories I've ever heard.

"Myron," he asked, "did you hear the one about the fellow who went to an art museum. . . ?"

It seems that in one room there were three statues in a row. One was posed with his arms folded and the second was pointing his finger in the direction of the third, whose arms were outstretched.

The tourist wondered if there was any connection between the statues and asked the guide for an explanation.

"Well, I'll tell you, mister," said the guide. "So many people asked me that question that I've had cards printed up explaining it."

He handed the fellow one of the cards. This was the dialogue printed there:

First Statue: Who threw that cigar butt on the floor?

Second Statue: He did!
Third Statue: Who, me?

My New City neighbors—the Norbitzes to the east, and the Jukes to the west—have done a wonderful job of helping me adjust to the life of a country squire. Whenever they drop over, I always try to get a laugh out of them. The last time they visited, I used this one:

A timid office boy walked into his employer's office and announced, "I think you're wanted on the phone."

"You think!" barked the boss. "Don't you know?"

"Well sir," replied the boy, "the voice on the other end said, 'Hello, is that you, you old goat?'"

My two nephews, Burton and Mitchell Cohen, always greet me with gags whenever we meet.

Burton's favorite is about the two cocker spaniels who met on the street.

One said: "Have I got problems! I think I'm headed for a nervous breakdown."

"Why don't you see a psychiatrist?" his pal suggested.

"I can't," mourned the spaniel, "I'm not allowed on the couch."

And Mitchell says, "With the price of meat what it is, lamb chops should come with two pair of pants."

☻

Recently I had the honor of entertaining Judge Jonah Goldstein, who, among other things, is a life member of the Grand Street Boys' Club. That evening, Morris Landsburg, owner of Florida's Sans Souci; Herb Fine, of Goldman's, in Pleasantdale, New Jersey, and Happy Waters, of Green's, which is also in Pleasantdale; were also my guests.

The best story told that night dealt with a new employee of a dress house, who was stopped by his boss as he entered the office.

"You're twenty minutes late again!" barked the head man. "Don't you know what time we start work in this office?"

"Well, er—no, sir," stammered the new man. "They're always working when I get here."

☻

On another occasion, I entertained several of my out-of-town friends. Included in that group were: Jay Isaacson, of the Toledo Tire Company, Toledo, Ohio; Max Ackerman, an insurance man from Springfield, Massachusetts; Harry Drake, the Boston agent; and Allan Bregman, the TV and radio man from "Soupy Sales" in Detroit.

Harry Drake's story about the two wise guys who visited a nudist colony broke everyone up.

While canvassing the grounds, one of the pair, upon seeing an extremely beautiful and shapely nude stroll by, commented to his pal:

"Some doll, eh Bob? Boy, wouldn't you like to see *that* in a bathing suit!"

☻

A frequent guest at my home is Dr. Alex Rosen, the noted dentist who is responsible for the care and capping of dozens of celebrities' teeth. Alex is a great one for daffynitions. For instance, he claims that a pessimist is a guy who stops himself as he's reaching down to pick a four-leaf clover for fear he'll be bitten by a snake.

☻

Milton and Carl Shapiro and Moni Avedon of Kay Windsor dropped by one night. We got to talking and swapping stories and I told them this one:
The young fellow had just been brought before the desk sergeant for questioning.
"Have you ever been arrested before?" asked the presiding officer.
"Oh, no, sir," answered the culprit. "And I must say there's been some misunderstanding here. Oh, I know I shouldn't have done it. But pilfering my little brother's bank hardly deserves the attention of the police."
"Pilfering your little brother's bank!" repeated the desk sergeant. "What is this anyway!" And he was about to dismiss the prisoner and chew out the arresting officer when said cop intervened.
"Just a minute, just a minute," interrupted the flatfoot. "The prisoner neglected to mention that his brother happens to be a teller in the First National Bank on Pine and 20th Street."

☻

One afternoon, Kate Smith and Ted Collins, who had been busily preparing for an upcoming radio show, dropped by for a little chatter and relaxation.
No sooner had he sat down, than Ted sprung this one on me:
The rich old man, who knew that his time was running out,

had a new will drawn up. It provided that his wife would receive $5,000 a year if she remained single—and $25,000 a year if she remarried.

"That's a strange twist," said his lawyer, "how come?"

"If he marries my wife, whoever he is," said the old man. "he'll need the money—and he'll deserve it."

☻

And Kate countered with the one about the small businessman in upstate New York who after six months of valiantly trying to make ends meet decided to call it quits. He posted the following sign in his window:

OPENED BY MISTAKE.

☻

One of the reasons that I'm so fond of my New City home is that it's so convenient. Besides being so close to New York, it's also a stone's throw from Philadelphia.

Harvey and Tillie Lockman from Philadelphia's Harvey House often drop by to spend the day. Sometimes we lounge around the house and tell stories and often we have a bite to eat at Jerry Carnegie's in New City.

Jerry is a wonderful host and knows even more about food than Jack E. Leonard. The last time we were there, he tried this one on us:

The president of a prosperous Philadelphia bank was making a speech at a banquet in his honor.

"Friends," he began, "when I came to this town fifty years ago, I was a complete unknown. All I had were the clothes on my back, and a yellow handkerchief in my pocket. The balance of my worldly possessions were wrapped up in that handkerchief.

"Today I am the president of a bank. I own three department

stores, a filling station, four movie houses, and a beautiful home."

When he sat down his friends gathered around him and patted him on the back. One of them asked, "Ben, what did you have in that yellow handkerchief?"

"Well," smiled the oldster, "as I remember it, I had three hundred thousand dollars in cash and one hundred thousand in bonds!"

Ed Mitchell, of Mitchell's Restaurant in Philly, is another who frequently drives up from the city of brotherly love. On his last visit I took him to New City's Dellwood Country Club where we had a fabulous time with host Bernie Nemeroff. As soon as we walked in the door, Bernie spotted us and came over. He asked us if we'd heard about the advertising executive who suffered such a severe shock that his hair turned charcoal gray.

"That's nothing compared to the woman who didn't want to read the 'Kinsey Report' because she was waiting for the picture to come out," countered Ed.

I added, "And what about the psychiatrist who told his wrestler patient, 'Get a grip on yourself!'"

Philly real estate man, Richard I. Rubin and his son Ronnie, get a kick out of this one:

The tycoon found the attitude of his youthful associate not all that it might be. The junior lacked ambition and get-up-and-go according to the boss.

"You've got to get in there and pitch all the time," remonstrated the seasoned big shot. "Why, when I was your age I had already inherited my second million!"

And Frankie Bradley, of Bradley's in the same city, claims a wedding ring is like a tourniquet—it stops the circulation.

☻

Ending a book of gags like this one is not an easy thing to do. I could go on and on until I'd find myself with an encyclopedia, but still there'd be the problem of ending it—both because the yarns just keep right on spinning themselves, and because it's hard to decide which to end with. I suppose one should sign off with The Favorite, but every day I've got a new one. That's the reason I hit on the idea of wrapping up this volume with the chapter, "Cohen At Home."

You know, when I moved out to my rural shack, I must admit I was afraid I might be lonesome. During those first few days of getting settled I felt awfully far from Manhattan. I *was* lonesome. But I hadn't reckoned on that old tradition, the housewarming.

My wife and I were unpacking boxes late one night when there came a knock at the door.

"Whoever could it be?" wondered my wife.

"It must be a salesman," I told her. "Who else would have the gall to come calling this hour of the night?"

Before I could answer the door, it flew open and there was a salesman on the threshold, all right. Not one, but dozens. Salesmen of laughs, that is—my buddies from the Friars Club.

Led by Carl Timin, they piled in like a football team in a scrimmage. When fat Jack Leonard and Jackie Gleason barreled through the door, I found myself with a sunken living room. I never did measure how far it sank, but I remember through the blur noticing a couple of miners raiding the icebox.

The neighborhood and house were still strange, and the sudden, unexpected gathering of the clan was too much for me. I kept thinking it was an all-star benefit show and got to worrying about being onstage without having rehearsed my act. And I couldn't retreat into the wings, because they hadn't been built yet. You would have thought it was a benefit, too—though, like me, you might have wondered for whom—if you could have seen the all-star cast. In one corner alone there were Georgie Jessel, Milton Berle, Jack Carter, Ted Lewis, Alan King, Gene Baylos, Jackie Gleason, Sammy Davis Jr., Dick Shawn, and Lou Holtz—

each competing for the floor to share their latest funnies. As I passed this group on my way to another, I dropped a plate of cold cuts on Jackie Gleason's lap. No harm done, though. In five minutes even the spots were gone. Jackie wasn't on a diet then.

I managed to sandwich in a gag here, too. It went like this:

The aging movie producer had just divorced his fifth wife and was determined to stay out of trouble for a while when he met a movie starlet who had what it took. I don't mean she was a great actress—she had what it took to make a sixty-year-old Lothario feel like a young colt instead of a jackass.

Anyway, the producer found he was too old to change his habits, so he proposed to the young girl.

Now, there are obvious advantages in combining career and marriage when the guy happens to be a producer, and our girl wasn't blind to them. But this guy was rumored to be impossible to live with. "I hardly know what to say," hesitated the girl. "I've heard so many stories about you, and if any of them are true, I—"

"Don't listen to that gossip," interrupted the producer. "Nothing but old wives' tales."

☻

"That reminds me," ad libbed Jackie, "of the madam who squelched the gossip about her reportedly coming from a former 'girl' of hers with, 'You wouldn't listen to that old roomer!'"

☻

Between a helpless chuckle and a groan, I moved to another corner of the room where Bing Crosby, Eddie Fisher, Joey Bishop, Jerry Lester, Harry Rose, Frank Ross, Alan Gale, Eddie Schaffer, Morty Gunty and Eddie Cantor were holding forth.

Old Banjo Eyes hasn't lost his touch. He drew the biggest laugh with this one:

Two psychiatrists were talking shop. Inevitably, the conversation got down to specific cases.

"You think you got problems," said one after listening to his colleague's tale of woe. "I've been conducting a testing program among my patients. You should live so long!"

"What sort of test?" asked his friend.

"Well, I'll try out a few questions on you. What would you say if I asked you what wears a skirt and employs the lips to give pleasure?"

"I'd say a Scotch bagpiper."

"And you'd be right. Next question: what has streamlined curves and arouses the most basic instincts in man?"

"A roller coaster?"

"Of course. Now, what's warm and soft and a pleasure to share a bed with?"

"A hot water bottle, of course."

"What else? But you should hear some of the crazy answers I get from my patients!"

In the far corner of the room there was another all-star huddle. The circumference of this circle was composed of Joe E. Lewis, Ray Bloch, Cy Reeves, Lenny Kenty, Joey Adams, Benny Fields, Jackie Kannon, Ken Kling, Sidney and Harold Gary, Phil Spitalny, Harry Hershfield, Carl Timin, Harry Delf and Danny Thomas. I poked my head in long enough to tell them this one:

The scholarly-looking little man seemed out of place in night court. Charged with being a Peeping Tom, the hapless fellow had been caught red-handed with a pair of binoculars trained on a window across the court.

"You have been charged with spying on the girls at the Emerson Residence Hall. How do you plead?" the magistrate challenged.

"Not guilty, Your Honor."

"Just a minute," interrupted the arresting officer. "We caught this guy with a pair of binoculars focussed right on a window where a girl was undressing. He can't pretend he's innocent!"

"I was simply indulging in my hobby," countered the accused self-righteously.

"Hobby, is it?" sneered the man on the bench. "Well, I suppose counterfeiting could be called a hobby, but it's still against the law."

"My avocation happens to be ornithology," sniffed the defendant. "I am a bird-watcher."

"That's a new one!" roared the judge. "And your binoculars slipped, I suppose, and accidentally got focussed on the bedroom of a semi-nude blonde?"

"Not at all," replied the accused haughtily. "The blonde you mention is a very ordinary example of her species. But, now, you take her parakeet . . . !"

☻

I had no sooner delivered the punch line than Milton Berle, the abbot of the Friars, sneaked up from behind and grabbed me by the arm.

"Surprise, surprise," he giggled, as he led me to the door followed by the gang of suddenly-silenced jokesters.

He gestured toward a brand-new Cadillac parked in front of the house. "Myron, the boys of the Friars decided you should have a beautiful car to match your lovely new home," said he solemnly.

"Gee, fellows," I muttered, all choked up, "I hardly know what to say."

"Don't try, old man, don't try," said Dean of the Friars Harry Delf, patting me gently on the shoulder. He handed me a small book. "This goes with the car," he explained.

"What's it about?" I asked, touched. "I suppose it tells how to take care of the car?"

"Sort of," piped up Jack Leonard. "Every time you make a payment, they'll tear a coupon out of it."

And so it went. It was a housewarming that really lived up to its name, what with all the hot ones that scorched the air between midnight and dawn. Yes, the Friars are a great bunch. I was only sorry all the boys couldn't make it that night. Oh, I did have one small complaint: what with all those familiar Friar

faces, plus the effect of the "refreshments" they brought with them, and the old school feeling of the scene, I got a little confused about time and place. Maybe it was my conscience for putting it off, or the sentimentality that oozed from my pores—but whatever it was, I kept insisting on paying my dues. I don't know if it was three or four, five or six, or even twenty times. And I paid in cash . . . so I'll never know. . . .

As I've said before, *seriously*, I liked the job of selling silk, but selling laughs isn't work to me. It's still hard for me to realize that I can make a living on humor after those years of giving it away. Now those customers who wouldn't give me orders after they'd laughed at my jokes have to pay to see me perform. What bliss! Meanwhile, I hope you've enjoyed all this; and if you smiled and chuckled as you read, you'll howl when you see me in person. After all, even my mother did the first time she looked me in the face. It's the only one of its kind.

Volume Two

More Laughing Out Loud

**Volume Two
More Laughing Out Loud**

**by
Myron Cohen**

with drawings by Sheila Greenwald

Dedication

TO THE MEMBERS OF THE BOARD OF THE MYRON COHEN FOUNDATION, WHOSE HELP IS SO GREATLY APPRECIATED

PREFACE

I began telling stories when I was a silk salesman in the Garment Center and as my friends and associates will attest, I enjoyed it so much that I never stopped.

I told stories to customers, competitors, and cutters, and soon it got to a point where I had a story for every occasion. If someone started talking about his wife, I'd get a gleam in my eye and smile, "Wife ... Did you hear the one about the new bride who asked her spouse, 'If someone asks me what I see in you, what should I tell him?'" And I'd go on and on and on....

Before long, everyone in the Garment Center began encouraging me to become a professional. My boss said, "You're a wonderful story teller and you ought to get paid for telling them. But not by me!"

And when I left the silk business to become a full-time comedian, there were even more opportunities for me to tell my stories. I told them in night clubs, on TV, at conventions, and I even got around to telling them in print. Writing my first book, *Laughing Out Loud*, was a pleasurable experience, but unfortunately there were too many stories I could not include because of lack of space.

When my publisher suggested that I write a sequel, I welcomed the opportunity to share more of my favorite stories with you.

CONTENTS

Once a Salesman . . .	17
Strictly from Hunger	41
Do Not Disturb	60
Calling All Cards	67
The Cocktail Hour	85
No Place Like Home	107
Caught in the Sports Whirl	132
Tales of Salesmen	151
Katleman's Kapers	173
Hurray for the Irish	186
One for the Road	196

More Laughing Out Loud

ONCE A SALESMAN...

Some of my most enjoyable afternoons are spent visiting my many friends in the Garment Center. Whenever I appear, I set off a chain reaction. "Hey, Myron," someone will say, "did you hear the one about..." and it'll start... the stories will begin to fly. Bosses, employees, models, and secretaries all have stories to tell and most of them are worth listening to.

Let's start off with the bosses.

A boss is a fellow who'll raise the roof before he'll raise your salary. He's the guy who shares the credit with the fellow who did the work and the one who watches the clock during the coffee break.

Two cutters were discussing their respective bosses.

"My boss is very cheap and is very unpopular with all his employees," said one.

"My boss," said the other, "you can't help liking him. If you don't, he fires you."

☺

"Do I detect the odor of liquor on your breath?" a stingy boss asked his sales manager.

"You do," admitted the sales manager. "I've just been celebrating the twentieth anniversary of the last raise you gave me."

☺

A guy who noticed that his boss looked pretty unhappy said, "You sure look worried."

"Listen," answered the boss. "I have so many worries that, if something happened today, I wouldn't have time to worry about it for another two weeks."

☺

A. E. Wullschleger, who was my last boss in the Garment Center, received a call from an employment agency about a fellow who worked for him.

"Was he a steady worker?" the fellow from the agency asked.

"Steady?" A. E. screamed. "He was motionless!"

☺

And A. E.'s former junior partner Henry Roth opines that a lot of guys who think their boss is dumb would be out of a job if he were any smarter.

☺

The eagle-eyed owner of a silk firm walked through his shipping department one day and noticed a boy lounging against a box reading a comic book.

"How much do you get a week?" he asked the boy grimly.

"Fifty dollars a week, sir."

The owner handed him fifty dollars out of his pocket and said, "Here's a week's pay. Now get out!"

As the boy left, the angry man turned to the head of the shipping department and snapped, "When did you hire him?"

"Never, sir," was the reply. "He just brought in some packages from another firm and was waiting for his receipt."

☻

If you work hard and keep both feet on the ground, you'll eventually reach a point at which you'll be able to keep both feet on a desk.

☻

A boss approached one of his most ambitious and competent men and told him, "I've had my eye on you. You're a hard worker, and you've put in long hours. You're very ambitious."

"Thank you," replied the employee.

"So, consequently," added the boss, "I'm going to fire you. It's men like you who start competing companies."

☻

A boss who was evaluating the worth of one of his employees said, "I'm overpaying him, but he's worth it."

☻

"Your salary is your personal business," a boss told his newest employee, " and it shouldn't be disclosed to anyone."

"I wouldn't think of mentioning it to anyone," came the reply. "I'm just as much ashamed of it as you are."

☻

My brother Milton of Kay Windsor asked me whether I heard about the nearsighted employee who almost worked himself to death. He never could see when the boss was coming so he had to keep working all the time.

☻

A guy who applied for a job as a resident buyer gave such a glowing account of himself that the boss got suspicious.
"How long did you work in the other place?" he asked.
"Twenty years."
"How old are you?"
"Thirty."
"Then how could you work for twenty years?"
"Overtime."

☻

"Who are you going to get to fill my vacancy?" queried a cutter who had just been fired.
"Sam," growled his erstwhile employer, "you're not leaving any vacancy!"

☻

"Ability," says Jack Silverman of The International, "is what will get you to the top if the boss has no daughter."

☻

PROSPECTIVE EMPLOYEE: Just why do you want a married man to work for you rather than a bachelor?
Boss: The married men don't get so upset if I yell at them.

☻

A boss's wife tiptoed silently into his office, sneaked behind him while his head was down, clasped her hands over his eyes, and said, "Guess who?"

"I told you there was no time for fooling around," he shouted. "Now get those letters out."

☻

Boss: This is the end. You're fired!
Worker: Fired? I always thought that slaves were sold.

☻

Sign on a Boss's Desk: THIS IS A NON-PROFIT ORGANIZATION PLEASE HELP US CHANGE

☻

Henny Youngman says his unemployed brother-in-law gave up his job because of illness. His boss got sick of him.

☻

The fiery-tempered boss of a silk firm returned to his office after a month's vacation in Florida and was approached by a timid bookkeeper.

"If you don't mind, Mr. Kramer," said the bookkeeper meekly, "I'd like to take my vacation now."

"I was away for four weeks," snarled Mr. Kramer. "Wasn't that enough?"

☻

"No man goes before his time," says New York *Mirror* scribe Frances Merron. "Unless, of course, the boss leaves early."

☻

A boss told his junior partner, "Quite a few people in this firm are already working a four-day week. The only trouble is that it takes them five days to do it."

☻

The prospective boss looked up at the job applicant and asked, "Tell me, what have you done?"

"Me?" answered the startled applicant. "About what?"

☻

A cutter was handed a pay envelope which, by error, contained a blank check. Astonished, he looked at it and moaned, "Just what I thought would happen. My deductions finally caught up with my salary!"

☻

When the firm's top buyer who happened to be a woman asked the boss for a raise, he objected.

"Your salary is already higher than any male buyer working here and they all have families with two and three kids."

"Look," she countered, "I thought we got paid for what we produce *here,* not for what we produce at home on our own time."

☻

Did you hear about the fellow who was so in love with his wife that he went home for all his coffee breaks?

☻

The fellow who said, "The surest way to get a thing done is to give it to the busiest man you know, and he'll have his secretary do it," knew what he was talking about. You can't underestimate the value of a good secretary. I knew one employer who spent three months looking for a suitable secretary because he knows it pays to have a good head on your shoulder.

☻

I like the story about the boss who told his new secretary, "Renee, always add a column of figures at least three times before you show me the result."

The next day she came in with a broad smile. "Mr. Drew," she said, "I added these figures ten times."

"Good," he said. "I like a girl to be thorough."

"And here," she said, "are the ten answers."

And then there was the girl who graduated from secretarial school with highest honors. She finished three laps ahead of her closest competition.

A businessman hired a new secretary, and the first morning she worked for him, he dictated a letter to his wife who was away on a trip. When she brought the letter back for his signature, it was perfect with one exception. She had omitted his final words which were, "I love you."

"Did you forget my last sentence?" he asked.

"Why, no," she replied. "I didn't think you were dictating."

A businessman had to fire his secretary because she lacked experience. All she knew was shorthand and typing.

A secretary who was leaving for her annual vacation told her replacement, "While I'm gone you'll continue what I was working on, but that doesn't include Mr. Franklin."

The personnel director who was checking the references of a prospective secretary called her former boss.

"How long did she work for you?" he questioned.

"About eight hours," said the former boss.

"But she told me she was with you for three years."

The ex-boss replied, "She was! She was!"

☺

"Most amazing," the boss said to his new secretary. "You've been with us only two weeks and already you're a month behind in your work."

☺

"Just why are you so suspicious of your husband's secretary?"

"Because I used to be a secretary."

☺

It's Jimmy Durante's story about the boss who dictated a difficult letter to his secretary. When she brought it back for his signature, he read a garbled version of his carefully thought-out remarks.

"Didn't you read this letter before you put it on my desk?" he screamed.

"Oh, no," she answered. "I thought it was confidential."

☺

A girl asked her friend, "How long did your sister work for her last boss?"

Her friend replied, "Until she got him."

☺

One afternoon the boss's wife met him at the office. As they were going down the elevator, it stopped, and a shapely and extremely pretty secretary got on. Poking the boss in the ribs, she said, "Hello, cutie pie!"

Without blinking an eyelash, the wife leaned over with a smile and said, "I'm Mrs. Pie."

☻

NEW SECRETARY: How long have you been working here?
OLD SECRETARY: Ever since the boss threatened to fire me.

☻

Phil Foster knew a very efficient secretary. She didn't miss a coffee break in twenty-five years.

☻

"The average secretary's life is divided into two parts," says King Features' columnist Mel Heimer. "The first part is spent

listening to a boss who dictates, and the second is spent dictating to a husband who listens."

☻

A boss called his new secretary into his office.

"Miss Handler," he said, "you're the best-looking girl we ever had working in this office."

A pleased look came into her eyes.

"You're a smart dresser. You have a pleasant voice, and you make a good impression on my customers," the boss continued.

"Oh, thank you," she said. "Your compliments are very pleasing."

"Enjoy them to the fullest," said the boss, "because now we're going to discuss your spelling, punctuation, and typing."

☺

A secretary was complaining to a friend, "If it weren't for the good salary, the air conditioning, the swimming pool, the free theatre tickets, the four-week vacations, and the generous pension and profit-sharing plans, I swear I'd quit this miserable job!"

☺

A boss told his secretary, "Congratulations, Miss Arnold. This is the earliest you've ever been late."

☺

Jim O'Connor, the popular night club editor of the New York *Journal-American*, likes the story of the harassed boss who told a friend at lunch, "My secretary has an unusual brain."

"Unusual brain?" asked his friend.

"Yes, it starts working the moment she gets up in the morning and doesn't stop 'til she gets to my office."

☺

Two secretaries were talking.

"How's your boss?" asked one.

"Oh, he's all right except he's kind of bigoted," said the other.

"Why?"

"He thinks words can only be spelled one way."

☻

A tardy secretary told her boss, "I'm really not late. I took my coffee break coming in."

☻

Charlie Dawn of the Chicago *American* tells of the young secretary who informed her boss she was quitting.
"But why?" he questioned.
"Because I don't like the surroundings," she replied.
"What exactly don't you like?" he asked.
"You!"

☻

Anyone who likes to listen to good stories knows that many of the funniest yarns deal with the lives and experiences of the Garment Center manufacturers.

I like the story of the unsuccessful manufacturer, known for his ill-fated ventures, who consulted a psychiatrist after having the same dream for twenty-five nights in succession.

"In my dream," he told the head doctor, "there are always two of me. We're seated in chairs facing each other, and one of me is giving advice to the other me. Doctor, am I losing my mind?"

"No," replied the psychiatrist. "As long as you just dream you're all right. But if you listen to that advice . . . you're *sunk!*"

☻

Two coat manufacturers were exchanging gripes.
"You should see my showroom," said one. "It's like a haunted house."
"Don't complain," said the other. "You're lucky to have ghosts."

☻

Jack Geizler, one of my former bosses, claims many manufacturers don't know where the next check is coming from or when the last one is coming back.

☻

A nouveau riche manufacturer hired a researcher to trace his pedigree. A few weeks later, a friend who knew about the researcher asked about the results. "He uncovered so much," the manufacturer said, "that now I'm paying him hush money."

☻

Claire Barry and husband Al Weinberg heard a prosperous man being discussed by two rivals.

"He claims he was born with a gold spoon in his mouth," said one.

"If he was," said the other nastily, "I'll bet there was somebody else's initials on it!"

☻

A manufacturer was reprimanding his son for being lazy. "Son," he said, "when I was your age, I worked sixteen hours a day learning the silk business."

"I'm very proud of you, father," replied the son. "If it hadn't been for your ambition and perseverance, I might have had to do something like that myself!"

☻

The story is told of the eighty-five-year-old manufacturer who was known for his penny pinching.

"Can't you persuade him," a friend told his wife, "that he can't take it with him?"

The wife replied, "Why, I can't even persuade him that someday he will have to go."

☻

A cutter who noticed that the head bookkeeper hadn't been to work for a few days asked a member of the bookkeeping department, "Has Mr. Lewis gone away to take a rest?"

"No," replied the bookkeeper. "He's gone away to avoid it."

☺

Did you hear about the wealthy Garment Center executive who was so ostentatious he told his wife to bury him in Miami when he died?

☺

Speaking about departed manufacturers, I like Harry Hershfield's tale of the owner of a silk business who insisted on having all his checks dated ahead. When he died his tombstone read: HERE LIES SAM JONES. DIED JUNE 5TH AS OF JULY 1ST.

☺

And then there's the story of the partners who arrived at a cemetery to bid good-bye to a competitor and couldn't find his grave.

"Maybe," said one, "he put it in his wife's name."

☺

A fellow who worked in the Garment Center met his ex-boss's wife. She looked very radiant and extremely happy.

"Mrs. Stein," he said, "you must have some good news. You seem to be bursting with it."

"Wonderful news!" she exclaimed. "Simply wonderful news. My husband's had a breakdown, and we have to go to Palm Springs for the next three months."

☺

In a similar vein, here's a conversation I recently overheard between two manufacturers. The first said, "I just spent a two-week vacation in Pallum Springs."

"Speak English for a change," the other said. "You mean Palm Springs."

"You're right," the first one replied. "It was my error. I had it confused with Pallum Beach."

☻

An efficiency expert was called in to see why a Seventh Avenue firm was losing money.

"What do you do around here?" he asked one fellow.

"Nothing," was the reply.

"And you?" he asked, directing his question at another member of the company.

"Nothing at all," the second man responded.

"Hmmmm," said the efficiency expert knowingly, "just as I thought. Too much duplication."

☻

And while we're on the subject, how about the one Monica Boyar told me of the woman who was explaining her husband's job to a friend? "My husband's an efficiency expert for a large company," she said.

"What's an efficiency expert?" her companion asked.

"Well, put it this way," the spouse explained. "If we women did it, they'd call it nagging."

☻

After ordering 15,000 dresses from a manufacturer, a buyer asked, "How long will it be before you deliver them?"

"Thirty days," said the manufacturer.

"Thirty days," protested the buyer. "Why the good Lord took only six days to create the entire world."

"That may be true," said the manufacturer, "but have you

taken a good look at it lately?"

☻

Sign on a shuttered Seventh Avenue store: WE UNDERSOLD EVERYONE.

☻

The nouveau riche manufacturer and his spouse were having difficulty adjusting to a life of elegance. After the first dinner in their new twenty-five room mansion, the husband turned to his wife and asked, "Do you want to have an after dinner drink in the library?"
"It's too late," she replied. "The library closes at six."

☻

While selling a friend a new suit, a Seventh Avenue clothier was raving about the garment. "It's beautiful," he said. "Even your best friends won't recognize you in that suit! Just take a walk outside for a minute and examine it in the light."
The customer friend went out and returned a moment later. The clothier rushed up to him with a smile.
"Good afternoon, stranger," he beamed. "What can I do for you?"

☻

Mike Durso related the story of a businessman who was telling his friend about the host of worries plaguing him, declaring, "They're beginning to smother me, dozens closing in from all sides."
"Thing for you to do," counseled the friend, "is to simplify them by lumping the related ones. That's what I did, and now I have only three problems—nagging creditors, a profitless business, and the fact I'm broke."

☻

A businessman told a friend, "I wanted my son to share in the business, but the government beat him to it."

☺

A successful, but illiterate manufacturer who had managed for years by signing his checks with two X's received a call from his bank.

"One of your checks came in today," a teller told him, "and it was signed with three X's. Is it yours or is it a forgery?"

"It's mine," explained the manufacturer. "You see, my wife has social ambitions and she thinks I ought to have a middle name."

☺

A teacher asked a Garment Center manufacturer's son, "How many seasons are there?"

The boy thought for a moment and then said, "Just two."

"What are they?" inquired the puzzled teacher.

"Slack and busy."

☺

Robert Dana, of the New York *World-Telegram and Sun* knew a very poor businessman. He went bankrupt twice and didn't make a cent either time.

☺

A guy described a pair of dishonest businessmen.

"They're so crooked that, if one stood at the top of a circular staircase and the other at the bottom, they could look each other in the eye."

☺

COLE (over the phone): Are you going to pay us?

Russell: Not just yet.

Cole: If you don't, I'll tell all your other creditors that you paid us.

☺

Bob and Phil decided to end their partnership and go their separate ways. Since each knew the other was planning to start a new business of his own, a bitter rivalry developed during the last days over who would retain the services of Stone the designer.

Bob returned from lunch one day and saw the designer and Phil talking in Phil's office. He waited outside until Stone walked out and then stopped him.

"How much did that cheap chiseler offer you?" Bob demanded.

"Why, nothing," replied the surprised Stone.

"Don't take it," roared Bob. "I'll give you double."

☺

"In the old days," observes Jack Benny, "a man was known by the company he kept. Nowadays, he's known by the one he merges."

☺

Seven prominent members of the Garment Center were named pallbearers in the will of a manufacturer who died penniless and owing them considerable sums. "They have been wonderful creditors," the will said, "and I would like to have them carry me to the end."

☺

A manufacturer told his newest employee, "All I had when I first faced the cold business world was youth, determination, and a will that left me a quarter of a million dollars."

☺

"On Seventh Avenue," notes writer Paul Denis, "when people don't care for something, they say, 'It's not my glass of tea.'"

☺

Fred and Jim were both wealthy. They were also business rivals and disliked each other intensely. At every opportunity each flaunted his wealth in the other's face.

One day when they met, Fred said, "Listen Jim, I can buy and sell you."

"Is that so," answered Jim. "I not only can buy you, but I can afford to keep you."

☺

Did you hear about the pickpocket who's reading the fashion pages because he wants to see where the pockets will be next season?

☺

A manufacturer stepped briskly up to the proprietor of a swank men's shop. "I just found out," he said, "that my son has owed you for a suit of clothes for three years."

"That's right," said the proprietor. "Did you come in to settle the account?"

"No," said the manufacturer. "I'd like a suit on the same terms."

☺

"It's not easy to get ahead in this world," a businessman assured a young friend. "As a lad I started out at the bottom. I struggled, worked, sweated, climbing the ladder of life hand over hand, rung by rung."

"And now," interposed the friend, "you are a great success?"

"Well, no," admitted the businessman, "but I'm getting good at climbing ladders!"

☺

There's a manufacturer who lost a fortune in the stock market and now won't even read a book with margins in it.

☺

A labor leader who was seeking a wife went to a matrimonial agency. "Is this a union shop?" he inquired. Assured that it was, he picked out a picture of a luscious twenty-three-year-old and said, "I'll take her."

"No, you have to take this lady," said the manager, showing a picture of a gray haired woman of sixty.

"Why do I have to take her?" thundered the labor leader.

"She," said the manager, "has seniority."

☺

"It won't be long until we all have money to burn," says Sidney Fields of the New York *Mirror*. "In fact, it's almost cheaper than fuel right now."

☺

A manufacturer who refused to give a buyer his price and lost a sale said, "He's the toughest buyer I have to deal with. He not only demands a tooth for a tooth, he expects yours to have gold in it."

Successful partners in business, Steve and Don spent most of their spare time trying to outdo each other. If one bought a $150 suit, the other bought one costing $200. If one bought a Cadillac, the other bought a Rolls Royce.

One day, Steve had a phone put in his car. Don was furious when he heard about it and immediately had one installed in his car. Then he called Steve and said nonchalantly, "This is Don. I'm phoning your car from my car."

"Would you mind holding on for a minute?" answered Steve briskly. "I've got a call on another wire."

☺

A holdup man entered a Seventh Avenue fabric house and ordered the bookkeeper to hand over the payroll.

"I'm very sorry," said the bookkeeper, "but I'm off duty and the union won't let me."

☺

Sid Edwards, the Maître d' at the International, was told of a psychiatrist who caters to the garment trade. He's experimenting with a new form of shock treatment for his wealthier patients.

He sends them his bill in advance.

☺

A wealthy manufacturer who was asked if he'd ever had ulcers replied, "I don't get ulcers. I give them!"

☺

Jackie Gleason tells the story about the businessman who went to a medical specialist, had a check up, and received a bill for $150.

"Your fee is entirely out of line," he complained to the doctor. "Anyway, business is so bad now that I just couldn't afford to pay you that amount."

"All right," said the M.D., "make it $100."

"That's still too much. Even though I'm not making so much now, I still have a wife and five kids to feed."

"Okay," said the doctor, "make it $50."

This went on until the fee was down to $5.

"Look," said the specialist, "you know I'm a leading specialist and have to charge high prices. Why did you come to me in the first place?"

"Where my health is concerned," replied the businessman, "I never stint on money."

☺

A manufacturer who was considering joining a lodge asked the president of one of them, "Does your lodge have any death benefits?"

"It certainly does," the lodge president replied. "When you die, you don't have to pay any more dues."

☺

Steve Allen tells of the spendthrift who was reprimanding his partner for being so frugal.

"Max," he said, "I think the practice of putting something away for a rainy day is foolish."

"That may be so," replied Max, "but that's exactly what Noah's neighbors used to say when he was building his ark."

☺

A manufacturer who wanted to borrow $250,000 went to his bank.

"That's a lot of money," said the bank president. "Can you give me a statement?"

"Yes," said the manufacturer. "I'm optimistic."

☺

"If it takes two to make a bargain," asks Frank Quinn, of the New York *Mirror*, "how come only one gets it?"

☺

Hal Boyle, the A.P. scribe, likes the story about the Garment Center manufacturer who died and went to heaven. When he arrived at the Holy Gate, he noticed a group of marching angels.

"Do you wish to enter?" asked the guard at the gate.

"I thought I did," replied the man from Seventh Avenue pointing to the marching angels, "but after seeing them, I'm not sure."

"Why?"

"In my entire lifetime I never passed a picket line, and I don't intend to start now."

☺

Georgia Gilly tells of two shady businessmen, known to do most anything for a buck, who were discussing their problems.

"Did the insurance company come up with the fire insurance you asked for?" questioned one.

"No," the other replied. "They offered to give me earthquake insurance instead, but I turned them down."

"I don't blame you," the first one agreed. "It's awfully hard to start a convincing earthquake."

☻

"Now, gentlemen," the owner of a big dress house said as he looked around the conference table at his staff. "I have a suggestion to make about a change in company policy for the coming year." Smiling paternally at the men, he continued, "I'd like your opinions, all of you. Those opposed to my little idea will signify by saying, 'I resign'."

☻

A businessman who was supposed to marry his pretty model told her, "Darling, I'm ruined. My business has failed and I'll have to declare bankruptcy. I don't have a cent."
The model replied, "Don't worry, sweetheart. I'll always love you, even if I never see you again."

☻

Speaking about models, I like the tale about the one who went to a cosmetic salon and asked for some advice on highlighting her face.
"If you want to highlight your face," she was advised, "don't wear such tight dresses."

☻

"I don't know the style or color of shoes, but I want low heels," the tall blonde model told the clerk.
"To wear with what?"
"A short, plump, elderly manufacturer."

☻

A manufacturer described his leading model: "She's got the kind of figure you give the once-over twice."

☺

A model was telling how embarrassing it was when her brassiere broke in the middle of a fashion show.

"It was a good thing for me," she said, "that another model was wearing it at the time."

☺

And as any businessman will tell you, we all know thousands of ways to spend money but only one way to make it.

STRICTLY FROM HUNGER

A balanced meal in a restaurant is one from which the diner has a fifty-fifty chance of recovery. I think this is a conservative figure because, when I began as a silk salesman, I ate in places where there was absolutely no chance of recovery.

I can recall one time when I was traveling down South and stopped off for a quick breakfast in an all-night diner.

"A couple of scrambled eggs," I said.

"Comin' right up," said the counterman.

"I'd appreciate it if they were fresh country eggs," I added.

"Yes, sir."

After a couple of mouthfuls I turned to him and said, "My good man! These eggs are terrible! I thought you said they came from the country."

"Yes, sir," he said, "the old country."

A little Jewish fellow entered a restaurant, studied the menu, and asked the waiter how much a roast beef sandwich cost. The waiter told him. Then he looked at the menu again and asked the price of a pastrami sandwich. Again, the waiter told him. Looking at the menu for a third time, the customer asked, "How much is a ham sandwich?"

Before the waiter could answer, the heavens let loose a tremendous clap of thunder and lightning. The little man fell to his knees and directed his terror-filled eyes to the sky. "All right! All right!" he pleaded. "I was only asking!"

☻

One of my favorite restaurants is the Stage Delicatessen. It's hosted by Max Asnas, a portly, good-natured, little man who is often referred to as the Cornbeef Confuscius.

Recently, a customer phoned Max and said, "I'd like to make reservations for six people and six fried herrings." Max replied, "Come right down. I can seat the herrings immediately, but the people will have to wait an hour."

Once, I asked Max why he didn't have a parking lot at his restaurant. He snorted, "If I had a parking lot, I wouldn't need a restaurant!"

☻

A fellow entered a restaurant and sat down at one of the tables. The waiter came and asked him what he would like.

The customer replied, "I'll have two bad eggs on a burnt piece of toast."

"But, sir," said the waiter, "you can't have that here. This is a highly respectable restaurant."

"I can't help that," the customer answered. "I've got worms and anything's good enough for them!"

☻

Mike Grieg of the San Francisco *Examiner* tells of a wealthy Texan who tipped a waiter $100 in a Chicago restaurant.

"Pardon me," gasped the astonished waiter, "I think you've made a mistake."

"That should teach you a lesson," barked the Texan. "Next time I come, I hope I'll get some better service."

☻

One of the women at the restaurant table was unable to finish the big steak she had ordered, so she got a bright idea.

Summoning the waiter, she asked if he would wrap the leftover piece for her dog, explaining to her companions when he had gone, "I haven't got a dog, but now I can have a steak sandwich for my lunch tomorrow."

A few minutes later the accommodating waiter returned with a big paper bag. "I found a lot of pieces of steak left over on other plates," he said, "so I just wrapped them all together."

☻

DINER: Why do you call this an enthusiastic stew?
WAITER: Because the cook put everything he had into it.

☻

Herb Caen of the San Francisco *Chronicle* tells the story of the wealthy Park Avenue socialite who was dining in a Broadway restaurant when it was held up. With methodical precision the stick-up men went from one table to another scooping up all the valuables belonging to the guests. When they reached the socialite's table, one of the crooks noticed her sparkling ring. He walked over, studied it for a moment, and then said, "It's a phony—a piece of glass." Furious, the socialite screamed, "You obviously don't know the first thing about jewelry. This ring costs $15,000." "O.K.," said the crook, "have it your way. Let's have the ring."

☻

A sea food restaurant was stuck with loads of lobster from the previous weeks. "Push lobster," ordered the manager. "No matter what the customers want, recommend lobster."

A few minutes later a man walked in. "What do you suggest?" he asked.

"Well," said the waiter, "the spoiled lobster is very good."

☻

I was dining in Lindy's one evening with my wife, Miriam, when I was introduced to another diner by a mutual friend. We became engrossed in conversation and when I mentioned how much traveling I do, he said, "Well, I, also, do quite a bit of traveling. In fact, I've moved seven times in the past nine years."

I thought for a moment and then said, "Well, I guess you must be either a minister or an army officer."

"No," he shook his head. "I'm neither. I'm a football coach."

☻

Once, when I had an appointment to meet a friend in Lindy's, I parked my car in front of a hydrant. After meeting my acquaintance, I told him that I might leave for a few minutes during the meal to find a safe parking place. After having a plate of soup, I excused myself and went out to my car. However, I was too late. When I arrived, a policeman was writing out a ticket. He looked up at me. "Hey," he said. "You're Myron Cohen. You're my wife's favorite comedian. She's been a big admirer of yours for years."

"Oh, really?" I said. "Does this mean you're not going to give me a ticket?"

"No, it doesn't," the cop said. "Yesterday, my wife sued me for divorce."

☻

A Hollywood agent was seated in a corner at Danny's Hide-A-Way bemoaning his fate.

"What's wrong?" asked a friend.

"It's that new client of mine," groaned the agent. "How'd you like to represent a client that sings like Crosby, wiggles like Presley, fights like John Wayne, and acts like Marlon Brando?"

"Are you crazy?" asked the friend. "You don't have any worries. You'll make a million with this guy."

"Guy nothing, you dope," griped the agent. "It's a girl."

☺

Two Garment Center manufacturers were dining at Sid Allen's Steak Pit and discussing their favorite subject.

"There are hundreds of ways to make a fortune," said one, "but there's only one honest way."

"And what's that?" demanded the other.

"Aha," smiled the first, "I thought you wouldn't know!"

☺

DINER: You call this creamed lobster your special? I can find neither cream nor lobster in it.

WAITER: Yes, sir. That's what makes it special.

☺

A fellow walked into a restaurant and ordered kidneys. While he was waiting for his order, he decided to go next door to a bar and have a few drinks. He forgot about his food and continued to drink. About a half hour later, the waiter from the restaurant came in and told him, "Your kidneys are spoiling."

The customer replied, "I've suspected that for years but I didn't realize it was visible to the naked eye."

☺

Sign in a Chinese restaurant: FORTUNE COOKIES! DIRE PREDICTIONS, 25¢ EXTRA!

☺

A rabbit and a lion entered a restaurant and parked themselves at the counter. "One head of lettuce," ordered the rabbit. "No dressing." The waiter pointed to the lion. "What'll your friend have?" he asked.

"Nothing."

"What's the matter? Isn't he hungry?"

The rabbit looked him squarely in the eye. "Look," he said, "if this lion was hungry, do you think I'd be sitting here?"

☺

Joey Bishop, the popular young comic, had a very unusual experience recently. He says he sat in the Four Seasons for ten minutes without hearing anyone remark, "This place is a gold mine."

☺

Gene DeForrest of the San Francisco *News-Call Bulletin* likes this one:

A friend called a Madison Avenue advertising executive one afternoon at one o'clock and was told by his secretary, "He's out to lunch, but I'll bet he'll be back soon."

"How do you know?"

"Because nobody took him."

☺

Ivan Paul of the San Francisco *Examiner* applauded when I told him this one:

A fellow who had been waiting over an hour for his lunch

called the waitress over and asked, "Must I sit here until I starve?"

"Oh no," replied the waitress. "We close at six o'clock."

☺

Sign in a restaurant: SPECIAL TODAY. WHAT WE COULDN'T GET RID OF YESTERDAY!

☺

I was seated in a restaurant recently when I heard a customer tell the proprietor, "That fellow who just left was wearing my new coat. Why didn't you say something?"

"As a matter of fact," said the owner, "I did comment to the cashier that the sleeves were too short."

☺

SALESMAN: When is the best time to see Mr. Brown?

RECEPTIONIST: Hard to say. Before lunch he's grouchy,, and after lunch he has indigestion.

☺

The story is told of the owner of a large chain of restaurants who went over his books and discovered that his most trusted employee had stolen over a million dollars from the firm.

"I want no scandal," the owner said. "I'll just fire you and forget about the entire matter."

The employee replied. "So you're going to fire me. True, I robbed your concern of quite a tidy sum. I now have yachts, a country mansion, a town house, jewelry, and every luxury you can think of. I don't need a thing, so why hire somebody else and have him start from scratch?"

☺

Merna Barry and husband Manny Pine overheard two women, seated in a restaurant, who were engrossed in a deep discussion about food.

"What is the opposite of a gourmet?" asked one.

The other replied, "Anyone who has had to live with one for years."

☺

Toots Shor, whose new restaurant may be open by the time this book is published, had a lot of free time when his first restaurant closed. A travel agent submitted an itinerary of a proposed trip around the world. At first Toots thought it a good idea but, when he took a look at the names, he reneged. "I can't pronounce the names of all those places," he said. "What's the use of goin' anywhere if I can't tell people where I've been."

☺

"We guarantee we can fill any order you ask for," boasted the sign outside the new restaurant, "or we'll give you $1,000."

Going inside a wily customer ordered walrus ears on a bun. Sure enough, after five minutes the waiter came back with a $1,000 bill.

"Aha," said the diner, "no walrus ears, you fraud. Take down your sign!"

The waiter slowly shook his head. "It's not the walrus ears. We have plenty of them. We just ran out of buns!"

☺

Jim Walls of the San Francisco *Chronicle* tells of the two diners who were talking. "I hear the owner of this restaurant has hired an ex-actor for cashier," said one.

"Why?" asked the other. "Is he good at juggling figures?"

"No, but he used to be a quick-change artist!"

☺

And at the next table, two men were discussing their wives. "If I had a wife like yours," said one, "I wouldn't go out at night."

"If you had a wife like mine," replied the other, "you wouldn't dare!"

☺

"Waiter," said the irate diner, "you have to take this hash back. It tastes funny."

"I wouldn't be surprised," replied the waiter. "You should have heard the cook laughing while he was making it."

☺

When he heard that a rival restaurant had burned down, a restaurant owner said, "I'm sorry to hear about it, but it's the first time the food's been hot in his place."

☺

I was dining in Lindy's when Harry Richman came in and told me he had just returned from a funeral.

"Oh, I'm sorry to hear that," I said. "Who died?"

"James Mason's cat."

"James Mason's cat?"

"Yes," Harry said tearfully. "Everybody was there and Georgie Jessel delivered a beautiful eulogy. You know, Myron, until I heard Georgie, I never realized how much a cat could do for Israel."

☺

WAITER: There hasn't been much stirring around this restaurant.
DINER: Why not?
WAITER: Somebody stole all the spoons.

☺

Charles Einstein of the San Francisco *Examiner* likes this one:

"I thought this place was under new management, but I see the same manager is still here."

"Yes, sir, but he got married yesterday."

☻

I was dining at Hy Kugler's Satellite Restaurant one evening when I spotted a guest who seemed to have an insatiable appetite.

"Who is that fellow?" I asked Hy.

"Why he's the Russian ambassador to the United States," Hy informed me.

"You know he eats like there's no tomorrow," I said.

"Maybe," said Hy, "he knows something."

☻

George Mitchell, of the Assembly Restaurant tells of the practical joker who sent a collect telegram to a friend which said: I AM PERFECTLY WELL.

About a week later the joker received a heavy package on which he was required to pay considerable charges. Upon opening it, he found a big block of concrete on which was pasted this message: THIS IS THE WEIGHT YOUR TELEGRAM LIFTED FROM MY MIND.

☻

Jerry Sager, Advertising and Publicity Director of the Moss Theatres, overheard this one:

"Waiter," said a diner who had just sampled his dinner, "these veal chops don't seem very tender to me."

"Sir," replied the waiter, "I used to be a butcher, and I can tell you that, less than a month ago, these chops were chasing after a cow."

"That may be," replied the man, "but not for milk!"

☺

DINER: Do you serve crabs?
WAITER: What'll you have? We serve everybody.

☺

American Weekly scribe Joe McCarthy likes this one:
A loudmouthed customer kept shouting at a pretty waitress. Another fellow, who was seated at the opposite end of the dining room, asked the girl, "Do you want me to take care of him for you?"
"Oh, no," she smiled. "He's my husband."
"Husband? But I don't understand."
"It's like this," she explained. "We've got it down to a science. He makes all the other customers feel sorry for me and they give extra large tips."

☺

I was leaving The Old Homestead one evening when I was stopped by a bum who said he needed carfare because he had lost all his money in a card game. "Are you a poker player?" I asked. "No," he said, "but I just left four guys who are."

☺

Charles Schlaifer claims he saw this sign in a restaurant:
OUR STEAKS ARE SO TENDER WE WONDER HOW THE COW EVER WALKED

☺

A restaurant patron demanded restitution for a topcoat that had been lifted.
"I'm sorry," said the cashier, "but you see the sign says we

are not responsible for coats unless checked."

"I know," said the customer, "but my coat was checked."

☻

Jack E. Leonard, the portly one, observes, "The man who reaches for the lunch check has many admirable qualities. He's generous, friendly, and on an expense account."

☻

When a pretty waitress came to work one night, the manager met her at the door.

"Betty," he said, "I want you to put on your cutest uniform,

fix your hair lovely, and see that your make-up is on neat."

"Something special on?" she asked.

"No," he said. "The beef's tough."

☻

A woman arranged a party for her daughter at a restaurant and asked the owner if the comedian who would perform had ever appeared on TV.

"No," he said.

"That's good," replied the woman. "My daughter knows all the TV comics' routines."

☺

Two women entered a restaurant, and one noticed a familiar face at the other end of the room.

"Do you see who I see sitting over there," she said looking where the other woman was sitting. "It's Helen. Tell me, do you believe that terrible story about her?"

"Yes," replied her friend eagerly. "What is it?"

☺

At a restaurant during the breakfast hour, a man asked a waitress for the lone piece of dried-up French toast left in the warming tray. She refused to give it to him, telling him that a fresh batch would be along in a minute. He replied that he would take it anyhow. The waitress, adamant, insisted that he wait for a fresh piece.

"Look lady," he shouted. "If I wanted to fight for breakfast I would have stayed home!"

☺

"How much are the cigars?" asked a customer.

"Two for a quarter," the girl behind the counter said.

"I'll take one."

"That'll be fifteen cents."

The customer paid the money and left. A man who had overheard the transaction came up to the counter. "Here's a dime," he said. "Give me the other one."

☻

Louis Sobol, the New York *Journal-American* columnist, was dining in a restaurant and told the waiter he wanted a baked apple.

"I'm sorry," said the waiter. "We don't have any."

Louis ate in the same restaurant the next three days and each time got the same reply. Finally, on the fourth day, he confronted the waiter and asked, "If you don't have baked apples why do you keep them on the menu?"

The waiter replied, "Would it be better if we left an empty space?"

☻

A pessimist explained why he always dines in restaurants where music is provided.

"Sometimes the music helps me forget the food. And sometimes the food helps me forget the music."

☻

When a restaurant patron complained that his breakfast sausages had meat at one end but bread crumbs at the other, the manager explained it was a matter of expediency. "In these times of rising costs, nobody can make both ends meat."

☻

After receiving a disappointing tip from an extremely crabby customer a waiter told him, "Now I'll give *you* a tip. Don't ever dare to sit at one of my tables again."

☻

A fellow named Ginsberg who was crossing the Atlantic for the first time was assigned to a table with a debonair Frenchman.

The first night out at dinner, the Frenchman rose, bowed politely, and said, "Bon appétit."

Ginsberg bowed politely and said, "Ginsberg."

The next morning at breakfast, the next noon at lunch, and the next evening at dinner, the ceremony was repeated, and Ginsberg felt his politeness wearing a little thin.

"It's getting on my nerves," he told a companion in the lounge. "He tells me his name, Bon Appétit. I tell him my name, Ginsberg. But at the next meal we start all over again."

His friend laughed. "The Frenchman isn't introducing himself. 'Bon appétit' is French for 'I hope you have a pleasant meal.'"

Ginsberg breathed a sigh of relief. The next morning when he appeared at breakfast, the Frenchman was already seated. Ginsberg bowed politely and said, "Bon appétit."

Whereupon the Frenchman rose, bowed, and answered, "Ginsberg."

☺

HOLDUP MAN TO CASHIER IN A CHINESE RESTAURANT: Give me all your money.

CASHIER: To take out?

☺

A waitress who became completely fed up with a patron's unreasonable demands told him, "If I were your wife, I'd give you poison."

"If you were my wife," he said, "I'd take it!"

☺

Sign in a restaurant. IT'S TOUGH TO PAY $2 FOR A STEAK AND IT'S TOUGHER WHEN YOU PAY $1.

☺

Al Kelly and his charming wife dropped into a neighborhood restaurant which both of them agreed was horrible.

"The food was so bad," Al reported later, "we might as well have eaten at home!"

☺

There's a waiter at a certain New York restaurant who is ready to commit suicide. For the last few weeks he's been throwing the tablecloth doodles of a steady customer into the laundry. The other day, the maitre d' pointed out the customer and said, "That's Salvador Dali, the artist."

☺

A fellow looked extremely unhappy when he came home from work one night.

"What's the matter with you?" asked his wife.

"I was in a restaurant this afternoon and I had an argument with a waiter. He got so mad that he called me a pig!"

"Listen," said his wife. "With the price of pork what it is today, you don't have to feel insulted."

☺

Six Sioux Chiefs, waiting for a luncheon table at a restaurant, were asked by the hostess, "Do you have a reservation?" "Yup," said one, "in South Dakota."

☺

A diner at a very exclusive restaurant was puzzled when he noticed that there was water in every ash tray.

"Do you put water in the ash trays to extinguish cigarets more easily?" he asked.

"Partly that, sir," replied the waiter. "But it also keeps people from pocketing them for souvenirs."

I was dining in Shine's one evening with Jim O'Connor, the popular New York *Journal-American* scribe when he told me this story.

An elderly, overweight man visited a doctor. He was examined and put on a strict diet. Two months later he returned for a check-up. He had followed the diet carefully and had shed a lot of weight. "I feel so young," he told the doctor, "that in

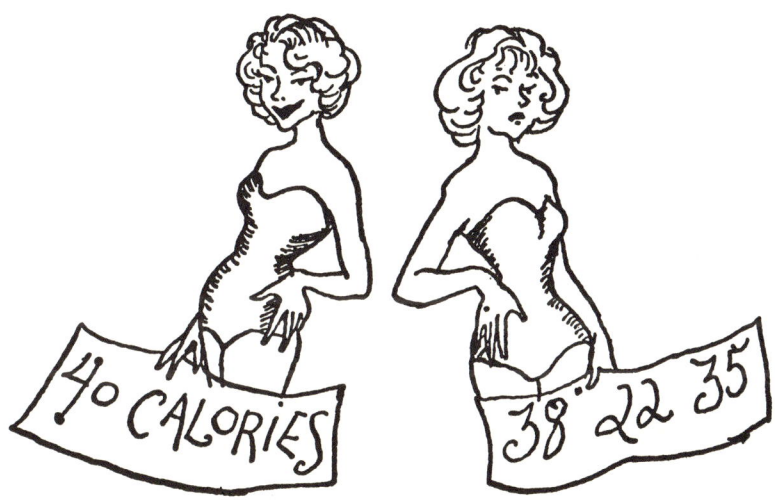

the elevator today I saw a girl bare her arm and I felt like biting it."

"You could have, you know," said the doctor. "It's only 40 calories."

Jack Wasserman and my friends at the New York Philanthropic League chose this story:

A rabbi and a pompous woman who were attending a luncheon were conversing.

"One of my ancestors," boasted the woman, "signed the Declaration of Independence."

"Is that so?" asked the rabbi. "One of mine wrote the Ten Commandments."

I am often called upon to act as toastmaster at luncheons; and as anyone can tell you, a toastmaster is a person who eats a meal he doesn't want so he can get up and tell a lot of stories he doesn't remember to people who've already heard them.

One of my favorite stories about after-dinner speakers concerns the toastmaster who spent nearly five minutes stressing the merits of the next speaker. He lauded his faithful service, eulogized his ability and the esteem in which he was held.

Somewhat overwhelmed, the speaker faced the audience and said, "After such an introduction, I can hardly wait to hear what I'm going to say."

☺

The Grand Street Boys Clubbers loved this one:

A beautiful movie queen was guest of honor at a football coaches' luncheon. One of the coaches remarked that although Hollywood was glamorous the life of a movie star was nowhere near as thought provoking as that of a football coach.

"I disagree with you," said the actress.

"How can you?" asked the coach.

"Because," she replied, "I have probably devised more defensive plays than the whole lot of you put together."

☺

A speaker who had bored his audience for almost a half hour said, "After partaking of such a meal I feel if I had eaten another bite I would be unable to continue speaking."

From the far end of the room came an order to the waiter, "Give him a sandwich."

☺

When toastmastering, George Jessel strives to introduce everybody on the dais to avert hurt feelings. Once, at a dinner for Eddie Cantor, Jessel introduced everybody but one man. He looked at the fellow for a few moments, realized he didn't know him, and then said, "That guy down at the end—frankly, I don't know who he is. But he must be somebody because we don't let any jerks sit at this table."

☺

A comic was invited to be toastmaster at a luncheon. At the end of the affair, the chairman of the entertainment committee came over and presented him with his check.

The comic who was doing exceptionally well in night clubs and on TV at the time said, "Why don't you give the money to some worthy cause."

"Would you mind," asked the chairman, "if we add it to our special fund?"

"Not at all," said the comic. "What is the special fund for?"

The chairman replied, "It's to enable us to get a better comedian next year."

☺

And before I pay my check, I'd like to say that I've come to an important conclusion. All waiters are cowards! I have yet to see one brave enough to lay a check face up on the table.

DO NOT DISTURB

A comedian is just like any other average American who stays up all night and sleeps 'til noon. I know this sounds glamorous to most people, especially those who have to get up in time to be at work by 9 A.M. However, it isn't as wonderful as it seems.

I don't know whether you'll believe it, but there are many comedians who never heard of oatmeal. I know one comic who never saw the morning sunlight until a few months ago when he played an engagement during the day season in Alaska.

Another thing that you have to remember is that a comic does a great deal of traveling in order to play night club dates all over the country. Consequently, on any given morning he can be sleeping in a hotel room anywhere from Hawaii to Alaska. This poses another problem. You never know who's in the next room. And you know what they say about hotel rooms. The walls are so thin when you try to sleep and so thick when you try to listen.

I remember one occasion when I was particularly tired after appearing at Chicago's Chez Paree. I went back to my hotel and instructed the desk clerk that I wasn't to be disturbed 'til noon.

After I closed my night light, I began to hear the fellow in the next room snoring loudly. I tried to ignore him but I found it impossible. "Sir," I screamed, "could you please stop snoring?" He didn't hear me. This went on all night. I kept pleading with him to stop snoring but it was to no avail. The next morning when I was leaving my room, I met him in the hallway. He eyed me suspiciously and took special notice of my bleary eyes. Then he said, "You know, fellow, you're a terrible guy to have a room next to. You talked in your sleep all night long!"

Speaking about insomniac comics, one of my favorite stories, told to me by my Chicago friend, Ira Arkin, deals with the one whose doctor gave him a box of colored pills and told him, "Take one of these pills before you go to bed tonight. You'll not only sleep but you'll take a trip. You'll wake up in Paris." Next morning, the comic called the medico and said, "Doc, I slept. But no trip. I'm right here at home." "What color pill did you take?" the doctor asked. "Yellow." "Darn," said the physician. "You made a mistake. You took the round-trip pill!"

Lou Wills, Jr. knew a funnyman who was even in worse shape. Lou met him on the street one day and the fellow looked awful. He had rings under his eyes. His shoulders drooped, and a listless air marked his every movement. Even his voice sounded tired. He told Lou, "I couldn't sleep a wink last night. It's that rotten insomnia again." Lou nodded sympathetically. "I can appreciate how you feel, but why don't you try the old remedy of counting sheep at night?" Angrily, the guy replied, "Lou, you know darn well I'm a vegetarian!"

Michel Rosenberg is another comic who likes to sleep late. However, he claims he hasn't had a good night's sleep in more than twenty-five years. I met him on Broadway once, and he looked completely fatigued. "What's the matter, Michel?" I asked. "Didn't you get any sleep last night?" "Yes, I slept," he answered, "but I dreamed that I didn't."

☻

And then there was the comic who stayed up all night and had daymares.

☻

When a comic sleeps late, and most of us do, the person who suffers most is his wife. She has to wait until her spouse arises before she can clean the bedroom and make breakfast. If she has something really important to do, like buying a new mink or playing mahjong, she may be held in the house 'til two or three in the afternoon because of a sleeping spouse. Recently, when Cindy Adams wanted to wake spouse Joey, she started screaming, "Brigitte Bardot! Brigitte Bardot!" Joey immediately leaped out of bed and raced into the kitchen. "Where is she?" he panted. "Oh, she's not here," Cindy pouted, "but I knew if I yelled 'breakfast! breakfast!' you would have never gotten out of bed."

☻

Sam Bramson, my representative at the William Morris office, heard a comic's wife tell him, "You need a self-starter to get you up in the morning." He replied. "Not when I have a crank like you to get me going."

☻

Milton Berle says he knows a great way to get comics out of bed. He's thinking of inventing an alarm clock that emits the

delicious odors of frying bacon and fragrant coffee. It's a novel idea, but is it kosher???

Another weapon that comedians' wives use to get them out of bed is a common household possession which can be found in almost every home—KIDS.

One of my favorite stories concerns the young son of a comic who walked into his father's bedroom, woke him up, and asked for a drink of water. "Let your mother get it for you," growled the funnyman. The kid left the room but was back again in five minutes. Once again his father sent him on his way. This continued at regular intervals for the next half hour. Finally, the father could take no more. "If you come in here once more," he barked, "I'll get up and spank you." Undaunted, the lad returned five minutes later and announced, "Daddy, when you get up to spank me, will you bring me a drink of water?"

☻

Jerry Lewis' wife Patti had to go shopping recently and left her three oldest sons home with Jerry who was trying to get some sleep. About an hour after she left, the three lads woke Jerry up and told him, "We did all the dishes, Dad." "That's wonderful," yawned Jerry. "How did you manage?" "I," said the oldest, "washed them." "And I," said the next, "dried them." "And I," said the youngest, "picked up the pieces!"

☻

Morey Amsterdam was awakened from a pleasant snooze when his son Gregory, who had a cold at the time, was sniffling in the next room. "Haven't you got a handkerchief?" Morey asked. "Yes," replied Gregory, "but mother told me not to lend it to anyone."

☻

A comic who was trying to get some sleep after an exceedingly difficult night club date (no one laughed at his jokes) was awakened by his young son who asked, "What did you do at the Copa last night?" "Nothing!" screamed the annoyed father. After a thoughtful pause, the boy inquired, "Pop, how do you know when your act is over?"

☻

The precocious son of a comedian, who prefers to remain nameless, constantly woke his father up. "The next time you wake me," hollered the sleepy one, "I'll spank you. I'm getting tired of your juvenility." "Well," answered the youngster in one of his rare rebellious moods, "I'm getting fed up with your adultery!"

☺

A Jack Paar slumber was interrupted when his cute little daughter Randy tapped him on the shoulder and showed him an adorable pup which she had found in the street. "What kind of a dog is that?" questioned Jack. "It's a police dog," Randy announced proudly. "A police dog? He doesn't look like one," said Jack. "Oh I know it," was Randy's answer, "but you see, daddy, he's in the secret service!"

☺

When Phil Silvers' little daughter woke him up, he scolded, "Didn't you promise to be a good girl and that you wouldn't make any noise." "Yes, father." "And didn't I promise you a spanking if you weren't." "Yes, daddy, but since I've broken my promise, you don't have to keep yours."

☺

When the son of a very talented but extremely homely comic made enough noise to wake Rip Van Winkle, the funnyman arose to find the kid staring into the mirror. "Daddy, did God make you?" the boy asked. "Certainly, he makes everybody." "That means he made me too, right?" "Of course, what makes you ask?" The lad replied, "Because, it seems to me that he's doing better work lately!"

☺

Comic (After his son woke him up): Now, Bobby, why don't you go play with your little friends?
Bobby: I have only one little friend, and I hate him.

☺

When Jan Murray's son Warren was a little lad, he came into his father's bedroom crying pitifully. "Mama doesn't want to give me a dark breakfast." "Dark breakfast?" asked the confused Jan. "What's that?" "Well," explained Warren, "last night she gave me a light supper, and I didn't like it!"

☺

Desi Arnez was jolted out of a sound snooze by the blast of a pair of six-shooters. As he picked himself off the floor, he came face to face with a rough shootin' tootin' hero of the old West—his son.

"Wass a matter?" asked Desi. "Where'd you get that outfit?"

"Mommy got it for me for school. Teacher said we're learning to draw tomorrow!"

☺

The young son of a night club comic came rushing home with his report card, raced into his father's bedroom, and screamed, "I got my report card today." His father who was completely worn out was more interested in getting some sleep at that particular moment. "Well," he humored, "just tell me if you were promoted?"

"Better than that, Dad," beamed the lad, "I was held over for another term."

☺

And as any comic will tell you, a sound sleep is the sleep you're in when it's time to get up.

CALLING ALL CARDS

A major portion of my afternoons are spent on the phone, and anyone who thinks talk is cheap need only look at my phone bill. I think I spend more time on the phone than the average telephone operator. In fact, I could almost guarantee that if I stopped making calls, A. T. & T. would drop five points.

Wherever I am, there's always someone I can call or who calls me to tell the latest stories.

Whenever he's in town, my boy Danny Thomas calls and we exchange our latest funnies. Let's tune in on a recent Cohen-Thomas conversation.

DANNY: Did you hear about the conceited actor?

MYRON: No, why was he conceited?

DANNY: When his wife sued him for divorce, she named his mirror as corespondent.

MYRON: What spoils quickly?
DANNY: A kid with overattentive grandparents.

☺

DANNY: What's the best way to make a peach cordial?
MYRON: Buy her a drink.

☺

MYRON: What's the best way to drive a baby buggy?
DANNY: Tickle its feet.

☺

DANNY: What's the best way to prevent yourself from rushing through a meal?
MYRON: Eat in a restaurant where the service is slow.

☺

Then we switch to the "longies."
DANNY: Hear any good gangster stories lately?
MYRON: Sure, let me tell you one.

A former office boy with a local stock exchange firm was brought to trial by his ex-employer on the charge of stealing $1,000 in postage stamps. He retained a clever young lawyer who made a brilliant defense plea, and he was exonerated. After the trial, he rushed over to the lawyer, shook his hand, and said, "You were great. How can I ever repay you?"

"Just pay my fee, that's all," replied the lawyer. "It's $1,000. But there's no rush if you're a little pressed."

"Well," the office boy suggested, "I can't pay you in cash right now, but will you accept stamps?"

☺

DANNY: Now I've got one for you.

A hold-up guy became slightly confused when he shoved a note at a bank teller which read: "I've got you covered, hand over all the dough in the cage," and the teller handed him a note back—"Kindly go to the next window. I'm on my lunch hour."

☺

MYRON: Now I'll toss you an animal story.

A movie producer tossed an old can of film into a lot. A goat who was passing by found it and ate it. While he was eating, another goat passed by and asked, "How does it taste?" The feasting goat replied, "I liked the book much better."

☺

DANNY: How about this one?

A tomcat and a tabby were courting on the back fence when the tomcat leaned over to her and said, "I'd die for you, you beautiful thing."

The tabby gazed at him longingly and said, "How many times?"

☺

MYRON: Let's go to psychiatrists. Not real ones, just stories.

A psychiatrist told the brother of one of his patients, "It would be wise for you to stay away from your brother for a while. He's in the midst of terrible delusions of grandeur and thinks he's Brutus."

"But what does that have to do with me?" questioned the brother.

"Well," explained the headshrinker, "he thinks you're Julius Caesar!"

☺

DANNY: Here's a good "psychiatwist": An attractive woman visited a psychiatrist and told him, "I'm in love with a wonderful man, and he loves me too. Both our parents are agreeable to the marriage, and we feel certain that we will be happy."

"Well," asked the dome doctor, "what is your problem?"

"Oh, doctor," she moaned, "I just don't know what to tell my husband."

☻

Anyone who's acquainted with Ed Sullivan knows that, despite his "smile-less" reputation, he has a keen sense of humor and often breaks up when he hears a funny story.

Ed, who recently wrote a book about Christmas, laughed when I called and told him the one about the unemployed actor who applied for a Santa Claus job at a large midtown department store. The guy who interviewed him asked, "Have you any experience?"

"Yes," replied the actor. "I worked two winters in the biggest department store in Brooklyn, and once I worked in the Bronx."

"That would be fine for an off-Broadway store," the interviewer said, "but we can only use people with Broadway experience!"

☻

Leonard Lyons, of the New York *Post*, prefers psychiatrist stories so I called and told him this one.

A disheveled man stumbled into a psychiatrist's office, tore open a cigaret, and stuffed his nose with tobacco.

"I can see that you need me," the headshrinker told him. "How can I help?"

"Got a light?" the man asked.

☻

He countered by telling me the one about the psychiatrist who was discussing one of his cases with a colleague.

"This fellow," the dome doctor said, "was under the delusion that a huge fortune was awaiting him. He claimed he would receive two letters which would give him title to two of the biggest oil wells in Texas."

"Well, what happened?" asked the other psychiatrist.

"It was a difficult case, and I worked hard on it. And just when I had the man cured, the two letters arrived."

Earl Wilson, whose "Earl's Pearls" are famous throughout the country likes "quickies" so I phoned to give him this one:

When Alaska became a state, the geographic center of the U.S. shifted from Kansas to South Dakota. Texas, however, remained self-centered.

Then he told me one:

Since Alaska became a state, the Eskimo population is rapidly becoming Americanized. In fact, some of them have even cut holes in the top of their igloos so they can stand up when they hear "The Star Spangled Banner."

George Jessel, America's Toastmaster General who's also the original "Man Who Came to Dinner," probably knows more stories than any man alive. When I get on the phone with Georgie it usually develops into a real "talk-a-thon."

He'll start off with one like this:

Two kids were talking about girls.

"Aw," said one, "Girls are a dime a dozen."

"Gee," sighed his pal, "and all this time I've been buying jelly beans."

☻

And then I'll come back with a similar one.

A little girl went to the zoo with her father. When she looked into the lion's cage she asked, "What would happen, Daddy, if the lion got loose?"

"Don't worry." smiled her father. "I would protect you."

The girl thought for a few moments and then asked, "But, Daddy, just in case the lion eats you up, what bus do I take home?"

☻

Then he told the one about the magician who was trying to sell his act to agent Johnny Pransky.

"I've got the greatest act in the world," he said. "I pull out 300 lighted cigars from nowhere, puff on each one of them, and then swallow the entire 300."

The amazed agent gasped, "You swallow 300 lighted cigars? How do you manage that?"

"It's simple," replied the magician. "I've got connections in Cuba and get 'em wholesale."

☻

I came back with the tale of the parking lot owner who called all his attendants into his office and told them. "We haven't had a single complaint about a dented fender all week. How can we make any money leaving that much space?"

☺

Marty Burden, Earl Wilson's strong right arm who also writes the New York *Post's* "Dining Out" column, chuckled when I called and reported on a recent trip I had made to California. "I went into a grove and picked some oranges. Then I went to Santa Anita and picked some lemons."

☺

Then he related the yarn about the husband who asked his wife why they never had any money.

"It's the neighbors dear," she replied. "They always do something we can't afford."

☺

The late Danton Walker, who covered Broadway for the New York *Daily News,* once called me and told about the slightly inebriated Shakespearean actor who, upon arriving home, forgot which apartment on the second floor he lived in. Standing in front of the one he thought was his, he questioned, "2B or not 2B?"

☺

Hy Gardner, the New York *Herald Tribune* columnist, who's making it big with those clever and informative interviews on his TV show, applauded when I called to tell him about the Texas cop who spotted a new Cadillac on the sidewalk in front of a large Dallas oil company.

He walked over to the fellow inside and ordered, "Let me

see your license. You know you can't park here."

"Who's parking?" replied the guy in the car. "I'm picketing."

☺

Then I told him the one about the New Yorker who lunched in a Houston restaurant and then discovered he only had one $1,000 dollar bill. A little embarrassed at its size, he figured it might be difficult for the cashier to cash it. But having no other recourse, he handed it to her. Not blinking an eyelash, she put it in the till.

"I knew you wouldn't have any trouble with that here," he smiled.

The cashier who was counting out his change looked up at him and asked, "With what?"

☺

I called Frank Farrell, the New York *World-Telegram* & *Sun* columnist, and told him about the actor who was explaining his act to an agent.

"My act is different," he claimed. "I can fly." Then, he took off, circled the room a couple of times, and made a perfect landing.

"So you can imitate birds," sneered the agent. "And what else can you do?"

☺

Speaking about agents, I like the story about the male half of a new dance team who walked into Charlie Rapp's office and told him, "Our act is sensational. At the finish, I take my partner by the hair and whirl her around for exactly thirty spins. Then I wind up the whole thing by heaving her through an open window."

Charlie paled. "You mean you heave her through an open

window. Do you do that at every performance?"

The dancer shrugged. "Nobody's perfect," he admitted. "Sometimes I miss!"

☺

And while we're on the subject of missing, I'm reminded of the banker who thought his daughter missed the boat when she married his son-in-law. One day, he met another banker on the street, and the fellow asked, "Is it true that your daughter got married?"

"That's right," replied the father sadly. "I spent $15,000 on her education, and she married a fellow who earns only $3,000 a year."

"So what are you complaining about?" observed his friend. "You're still getting 20 per cent on your money!"

☺

I called Walter Winchell, of the New York *Daily Mirror*, and he told me about the two beatniks who met on the street.

"Hello," said one. "How're you getting along?"

"Not bad," said the other. "I'm managing to keep alive."

The first beat eyed his friend for a moment and then asked, "What's your motive?"

☺

Then I told him the tale of the beatnik wife who told a surprise guest, "Next time phone before you come so I can have a chance to mess up the house."

☺

As well as being a top columnist for the New York *Mirror*, Harry Hershfield is one of the deans of storytelling. When we get on the phone together, the stories really fly.

Once I called and told him about the producer who was dissatisfied with his head writer's latest effort.

"I want you to rewrite it and put more conflict into it," he said.

"Conflict?" asked the surprised writer.

"Yes," said the producer. "Let me explain the meaning of 'conflict' to you. One man wants to be a boxer, and the other wants to be a violinist, and they're Siamese twins. That's conflict!"

☺

Then he fired this one at me.

A movie script writer who had been plagued all his life by producers who screamed of "too many comedies," "too many mystery films," "too many love stories," and "too many others," finally wrote a story about a talking dog.

"This dog," he told a producer, "is the most talented animal who ever lived. He can talk in twenty-three languages, pitch with both hands, run a mile in one minute, and sing like Frank Sinatra."

"Wonderful," screamed the producer. "We'll make a fortune. This dog sounds sensational. What kind of a hound is he?"

"Boxer," said the writer.

"No good," said the producer derisively. "We've had too many fight pictures."

☺

Bob Sylvester, who writes those witty columns for the New York *Daily News,* called and told me about the kid who brought a dozen cats into his house.

"Why did you bring them in here?" howled his mother.

"Because I heard Daddy say he smelled a rat!"

Dorothy Kilgallen, the *Journal-American* columnist, laughed when I called and told her about the law professor who was lecturing to a group of students.

"When you're fighting a case," he said, "if you have the facts on your side, hammer them into the jury. And if you have the law on your side, hammer it into the judge."

A student asked, "But what if you have neither the facts nor the law?"

"Then," answered the professor, "hammer the table!"

Lee Mortimer, a top columnist for the New York *Mirror*, buzzed me and related the anecdote about the hypochondriac who visited a doctor to have his blood tested. The doctor glanced at the test results and smiled.

"You have nothing to worry about. Your blood is fine."

"Good," said the hypochondriac. "Now give it back to me so I can go home."

☺

Louis Sobol, who writes for the New York *Journal-American*, enjoyed the tale about the fellow who visited a fortuneteller and then told his fiancée, "He told me that I'm going to marry a blonde in a month."

She replied, "That's all right. I can become a blonde in a month."

☺

Nick Kenny, the poet, who writes a TV column for the New York *Mirror* in his spare time, called and told of the photographer who quit his job at a Hollywood studio because he claimed there were so many "yes men" around that he could never get a good negative.

☺

This made me think of the tale about the Hollywood star who started divorce proceedings three weeks before her wedding and of her sister who saved a piece of her wedding cake for her divorce lawyer.

☺

Speaking about actresses, I'm reminded of the one who had her own ideas about production props.

"I insist upon real liquor in a drinking scene," she told her producer.

"All right," he agreed, "if you let me use real poison in the murder scene."

☺

Equally "kookie" was the glamorous movie queen who was taking the required blood test before her first marriage. When the doctor asked if she knew what type she was, she replied, "I'm the sultry type!"

☻

Boots McKenna tells a story about an extremely socially conscious film actress who aspired to be a member of an ultraswank Beverly Hills country club. By exerting influence, she got a friend to submit her name to the club's screening committee. Two days later the committee voted, and she was turned down. When the news was broken to her, she asked, "Were there many blackballs against me?"

"Well, I'll tell you, Betty," her friend said. "Do you know what a bowl of caviar looks like?"

☻

And while we're telling stories about Hollywood, one of my favorites deals with the high-salaried script writer who confessed to a friend, "I keep getting richer and richer but somehow I have the feeling that my work isn't up to my old standard."

"Nonsense," soothed his friend. "You write as well as ever. Your taste is improving, that's all!"

☻

Bob Williams, the New York *Post* TV columnist, appreciated it when I called and told him about the coed who sent her mother a letter.

Dear Mom:

Please send me $50 for a new dress as soon as possible.

I've had eight dates with Alfred and I've worn every dress I brought with me.

Her mother replied by return mail.
Dear Daughter:
Be economical. Get another boy friend and start all over again.

☺

My stockbroker, Adolphus Roggenburg of Newburger, Loeb & Co., called and told me that Bell & Howell had just announced a split.
"Oh, what a shame," I said. "They've been together so long!"

☺

My brother Phil, who is a partner and sales manager for Forge Mills and is one of the funniest guys in the Garment Center (it runs in the family) is always on the phone with me. (I hope his partners don't read this.) Since he's always in contact with salesmen, he'll start off with something along these lines:
Two salesmen were discussing the number of women who had taken over key positions in their organization.
"We don't have to worry," said one.
"Why not?" questioned the other.
"Because," said the first, "a woman salesman wouldn't know what to talk about. Who ever heard of a travelling saleswoman joke?"

☺

I came back with this one:
A Martian landed in a Madison Avenue ad agency and tapped a secretary on the shoulder.
"Take me to your leader," he said.
"I'm sorry, you'll have to wait," the secretary replied. "He's at the doctor's getting his ulcer checked."

☺

Then he told of the grocer who was praising a new minister.

"Have you heard the minister preach?" the grocer was asked. He said he hadn't.

"Then how do you know he's good?" someone asked.

"Because," the grocer answered, "his members have begun to pay their bills."

☺

I followed with the story of the Japanese flight commander who was briefing his kamikaze pilots.

"Fliers of Japan," he declared, "you are going on a sacred mission. I want you to shoot down all the American planes in the sky. I want you to shoot down all the American pilots, all the gunners, all the radiomen.

"Then I want you to take your planes and fly them directly into all the American ships. Sink the aircraft carriers, sink the cruisers, sink the battleships. Blow yourself into a thousand pieces for the glory of Japan and the Emperor."

Then he took a breath and said, "Any questions?"

One Japanese pilot shook his head in disbelief. "Commander," he asked, "you out of your gosh darn crazy mind?"

☺

Marie Torre, the New York *Herald Tribune* TV critic, likes gags with a video flavor.

A mother was telling her friend about her daughter's impending marriage.

"Mary and her future husband," she said, "are a very ambitious couple and refused to accept any help from us. They're starting out with just what they have to have—bed, stove, and television set."

☺

And speaking about TV, how about the TV producer who told his right hand man, "I wasn't always so prosperous. I was born poor and had to make my first pile playing a horse."

"At the races?" asked the aide.

"No," replied the producer, "in vaudeville."

☺

Bugs Baer, the New York *Journal-American* quipster, called to tell of the woman who was walking across the street when a reckless driver sped by and narrowly missed her. Realizing that it had been a close call, he backed up to apologize. However, before he could say a word, the woman noticed a pair of baby shoes dangling from his rear-view mirror and said, "Young man! I believe you should put your shoes back on."

☺

I happened to pick up the extension one day when my wife was speaking to a friend. It seems Mrs. X could not keep a maid for any length of time.

"How long was your last maid with you?" my wife asked.

"She never was with us," her friend replied. "She was against us from the start."

☺

On another occasion I caught this one between my spouse and another friend.

FRIEND: We've figured out a way to keep Harry from being late to school.

MRS. C.: What is it?

FRIEND: We bought him a car.

MRS. C.: But how did that help?

FRIEND: Now he's got to get there early to find a parking space!

☺

I phoned Atra Baer (Bugs's daughter) who writes TV columns for the New York *Journal-American* and told her this one:

Two Indians on an Oklahoma reservation were watching a husband and wife in the midst of a terrible argument.

"What do you suppose the trouble is?" asked one.

"The way I figure it," replied the other, "when they smoked the peace pipe, neither one inhaled!"

☺

Which reminds me. Did you hear about the adult western movie in which the Indians sat around the campfire, smoked their peace pipes, and complained about the high price of tobacco? Or the western so adult that the medicine man was a graduate of Johns Hopkins?

☺

And how about the one concerning the two TV stars who met at the door of a psychiatrist's office?

"Are you coming or going?" asked one.

The other replied, "If I knew, I wouldn't be here."

☺

Ben Rosenberg, the New York *Post* amusement editor, was amused when I called and told him of the teacher who was reading to her class when she came across the word *unaware*.

"Does anyone know the meaning of the word?" she asked.

"Unaware," a kid in the back yelled out, "is what you put

on first and take off last!"

☻

And before I put my phone back on the hook, I want **you** to remember this: a telephone is a device which makes it **easy to** distinguish voices and hard to extinguish them.

THE COCKTAIL HOUR

While touring the country, I've met some of the most unusual drunks. One disciple of the bottle told me he continually kept drinking because he wanted to avoid hangovers. Another said he drank to forget, but the only thing he ever forgot was when to stop. A third said he came from an alcoholic family and was fourteen before he learned toast was also a piece of bread.

I was passing a bar on Broadway one night when I saw an alcoholic actor I knew seated on a stool stripped to the waist. A sun lamp was focused on him. I walked in and asked, "George, are you all right?"

"I'm fine thanks, Myron," said my tipsy friend. "It's just that I told my wife I was spending the week in Florida."

It had been a big night in the saloon down in Tombstone Gulch. When Cactus Sam opened his bleary eyes the next morning in his shack, he was startled to see a huge, hideous ape perched on the foot of his bunk, grinning at him. Slowly reaching for his gun, Sam took careful, if wavering aim.

"If you're a real ape," he uttered grimly, "you're in a damn bad fix. But if you ain't, I am!"

☻

"A lot of men," says Dick Shawn, "would live on liquid diets if it weren't for pretzels."

☻

An alcoholic meandered into the bar and placed one foot on the rail with difficulty. "Gimme a shot of Scotch and a shot of water," he ordered.

Surprised, the bartender, nevertheless, did as he was bid. He set up a jigger of Scotch and a jigger of water. And he watched in fascination as the lush pulled a worm from his vest pocket. With great deliberation, he dropped the worm into the jigger of water where it swam around with much nonchalance. Then, carefully, he took the worm out of the water and dropped it into the Scotch. Instantly, the worm began to writhe and wriggle. In another moment, it curled up and was dead.

"Shee," roared the drunk in triumph. "That proves it. Keep on drinking and you'll never have worms."

☻

BILL: So you've quit drinking?
PHIL: Yes, I did it for the wife and kidneys.

☻

And then there was the guy who drank so much you could hear the pretzels splash as he kept eating them.

☺

The Kentucky Colonel was asked why he always closed his eyes when he drank a mint julep. "Waal," he explained, "the sight of good lickah always makes my mouth water, and I don't aim to have my drink diluted."

☺

A man who celebrated a little too much one night woke up in the hospital the next day and saw his friend sitting beside his bed.
"What happened?" he asked.
"Well," began his friend, "last night you had quite a load on and went to a window, stepped over the sill, and announced you were going to fly around town."
"And you didn't try to stop me?" screamed the injured man.
"No, at the time I really thought you could do it."

☺

The long suffering wife was about to berate her husband for staggering home at 5 A.M. "Before you begin," he warned her, "I want you to know I was sitting up with a sick friend."
"A likely story," said his spouse. "What was his name?"
The husband gave this problem deep thought, then announced triumphantly, "He was so sick he couldn't tell me."

☺

A couple of happy celebrants were weaving their way home one night.
"Shay," said one, "won't your wife hit the ceiling when you

walk in tonight?"

"She probably will," said the other. "She's a lousy shot!"

☺

Herb Rau of the Miami *News* applauded when I told him this one:

An alcoholic who wasn't feeling well went to see his doctor. After a thorough examination, the physician reported to his patient that he had too much water in his body. "But I've never drunk a drop of water in all my life, Doctor." He paused for a second, then sadly concluded, "Must have been the ice."

☺

"I'm drinking to forget."

"In that case, please pay in advance."

☺

His wife was waiting when he arrived home.

"Oh, Allen!" she screamed, "you've done it this time. Besides being a mess and a drunken bum, you've also lost me the best maid I ever had. And you know how hard it is to get a good maid."

"What'd I have to do with the maid leaving?" asked the tipsy one.

"You insulted her over the phone, that's what you did. She said she had never heard such vile, insulting language in her life, and she packed up and left."

"Gee, honey, I'm sorry," comforted the drunk. "I thought it was *you* I was talking to."

☺

A fellow came into a bar and ordered a martini. Before drinking it, he removed the olive and carefully put it into a small glass jar. Then he ordered another martini and did the same thing. After an hour, when he was full of martinis and the jar was full of olives, he staggered out.

"Well," said a customer, "I never saw anything as peculiar as that."

"What's so peculiar about it?" the bartender said. "His wife sent him out for a jar of olives."

☺

"Nobody likes to be beaten to the punch," says Ed Wynn. "Especially if it's been spiked."

☺

Sign on a bar: DO A GOOD DEED AND HAVE A DOUBLE. IT'LL KEEP US AND ALCOHOLICS ANONYMOUS IN BUSINESS.

☺

And then there was the lush who stared into a mirror, noticed his bloodshot eyes, and said, "I'll never go into a bar again. Those television sets are ruining my eyes!"

☺

A drunken intellectual was arrested for speeding and brought before a judge. "Have you anything to say before you're sentenced?" asked the man on the bench.

"No," said the drunk. "I only converse with people of the arts—Hemingway, Picasso, Faulkner . . ."

"That's enough," interrupted the judge. "Ten days. And officer, take down the list of names he mentioned and round them up. I think they may be as bad as he is."

☺

A bartender who had no money offered a lawyer several

bottles of liquor if he would handle his case. The lawyer counted the bottles, shook his head, and told the bartender, "Only eight bottles of Scotch. I can't make a case out of that."

☻

PROFESSOR: How do you explain that barrel of beer I found in your room?
FRESHMAN: Doctor's orders, sir. He said that drinking beer would restore my health.
PROFESSOR: And did it?
FRESHMAN: Yes, sir, when I bought that barrel I could hardly move it, and now I can push it all around the room.

☻

Sid Fields of the New York *Mirror* likes this one:

A comic who always seemed to be drunk had a manager who tried to break him of the habit. After endless hours of telling the funnyman how John Barleycorn would ruin his career, the manager believed he had finally reached him. However, a few nights later the actor failed to show up for a night club date. The manager waited around until thirty seconds before curtain time and then sailed out to do the bars for his comic. He found him draped across a bar in a happy alcoholic haze.

"Good God," the manager cried, "you're on!"

The comic downed another drink. "I am?" he asked. "Great. How'm I doing?"

☻

And Hinson Styles, also of the New York *Mirror,* likes this one:

The judge looked sternly down at the defendant. "Young man." he said, "it's alcohol, and alcohol alone, that's responsible for your present sorry state!"

"I'm sure glad to hear you say that, Your Honor," the man replied with a sigh of relief. "Everyone else says it's all my fault."

☻

And then there was the drunk who started to write a drinking song but never got past the first two bars.

☻

A tall muscular man walked into a bar, looked the crowd over, and said, "I'm the toughest guy in town; yes, the fightenest man in this state; in fact, I'm the toughest guy in the world."
With that a little fellow who was standing at the other end of the bar walked over and socked him right on the chin. The muscular man fell back, banged his head against a stool, and dropped to the floor unconscious. When he came to, he dopily glanced at the fellow who had hit him and asked, "Who are you?"
"Me," came the reply. "I'm the guy you thought you were when you came in here."

☻

"Why is it," says Lou Holtz, "that drunks never spill drinks on other drunks?"

☻

A lion escaped from his cage and a posse was hastily formed to track him down. Before the search began the men stopped in a saloon where they all ordered drinks. All, that is, except one.
"Oh, come on," he was urged. "Have a drink with us."
"Not me," said the guy in a shaky voice. "Whiskey gives me too much courage."

☻

"A lot of wives whose husbands come home half shot," says comic Gene Baylos, "feel like finishing the job."

☻

Returning home late from a meeting, the minister noticed one of his congregation staggering down the street.

"Let me help you to your door," he said, guiding the inebriated member of his flock gently home.

Arriving at his house, the drunk pleaded with the minister to accompany him inside. "Please Rev'ren," he pleaded, "just for a minute. I want the missus to see who I've been out with tonight."

☻

The owner of a bar told his bouncer, "Throw that drunk out

—but don't antagonize him!"

"Before we got married, my wife said to me, 'Lips that touch liquor shall never touch mine,' and I agreed with her."

"And you stuck to it?"

"Certainly, I have. I haven't kissed her for forty years!"

☻

Two drunks wandered into a zoo and stopped in front of a lion's cage. They stood watching the animal a few minutes and suddenly it let out a roar. "C'mon, let's go," said one.

"Go ahead if you want to," said the other. "I'm gonna stay for the movie."

☻

Jack Kahner told me the one about a drunk who staggered home and made his way into the house. As he groped about, he staggered into the shower and turned on the water. It made so much noise that it awakened his wife.

She was so infuriated to see her spouse making such a mess of the bathroom that she proceeded to give him a stern lecture concerning his past, present, and future.

"You're absolutely right, honey," the inebriate agreed amiably. "I'm everything you say. But please let me in. It's raining out here."

☻

"No man should drive a car while intoxicated," says Red Skelton.

"It's hard enough to get the pedestrian you're after while you're sober."

☻

A commuter approached the lost-and-found department of the Long Island Railroad. "I left a bottle of gin on the train last night," he said. "I thought it might possibly have been turned in."

"No, it wasn't," the clerk told him, "but the man who found it was."

☻

"Are you drinking again? Doesn't your health mean anything to you?"

"Yes, it means something to drink to."

☻

Two inebriated gentlemen, says Allan Bregman, stood at the bar near closing time.

"I've got an idea," said one. "Lesh have one more drink and then go find shum girls."

"Naw," replied the other. "I've got more than I can handle at home."

"Great," replied the idea man. "Then lesh have one more drink and go up to your place."

☻

"Poor man," a kindly old lady told a lush. "Is whisky your only comfort?"

"No ma'am," he replied. "I can drink beer when I have to."

☻

"Frank," stormed the corporal, "if you'd only stay sober and obey regulations you could become a corporal like me. Isn't that worth staying sober for?"

"Heck, no!" exclaimed Frank. "When I'm drunk, I'm a general."

☻

A workman was fixing one of those big tower clocks when a drunk looked up from the sidewalk and said, "Man, is that guy nearsighted!"

☺

The man went into a bar and ordered a glass of beer. He drank half of it and threw the rest at the bartender. Then he apologized profusely. "It's a nervous compulsion I have. I'm terribly embarrassed by it," he explained.

"You'd better consult a psychiatrist," the bartender said.

Several months later the man came back to the bar and did the same thing again. The bartender was naturally indignant.

"I thought you were going to see a psychiatrist," he said.

"I've been seeing one," said the man.

"It certainly hasn't done you much good."

"Oh, yes it has," the man replied. "I'm not embarrassed about it any more."

☺

Did you hear about the termite that walked into a tavern and asked, "Where is the bar tender?"

☺

"How did you spend the weekend?"
"Fishing through the ice."
"Fishing through the ice? For what?"
"Olives."

☺

A fellow was speeding down a highway when his car swerved sharply, crashed into a fence, and then rolled over several times. A farmer who was watching ran over just in time to see the driver crawl out of the wreckage. "Are you drunk?" he asked.

"You darn fool!" shouted the autoist. "Of course I'm drunk! What do you think I am—a stunt driver?"

☻

Sign over a bar: OUR MARTINIS ARE SO DRY THEY'RE DUSTY!

☻

FIRST MAN: What would you do if you had all the money you spent on beer?

SECOND MAN: I'd buy some more beer.

☻

A man bumped into an acquaintance in a bar and remarked, "I thought you'd given up drinking. What's the matter, no self-control?"

"Sure, I've got plenty of self-control. I'm just too strong to be a slave to it."

☻

Dean Martin claims his drinking goes back a long time. When he was in high school, he was voted most likely to dissolve.

☻

An airline passenger who had indulged rather freely before boarding the plane annoyed the pretty stewardess by demanding a martini. Finally, she brought him a plate with a lone olive resting in its center.

"What's that?" he wanted to know.

"That, sir," smiled the stewardess with her best smile, "is what you might call a *very* dry martini."

☻

Did you hear about the friendly alcoholic? He was always shaking hands—even when no one else was around.

And then there was the Toronto drunk who was found muttering, "It can't be done! It can't be done!" as he looked up at a big sign which read: DRINK CANADA DRY.

A husband, who came home one night in an extremely inebriated state, handed his wife twenty dollars.
"Twenty dollars," she screamed. "Where's the rest of your pay check?"
"I bought something for the house," he said.
"Oh," she replied, almost apologetically. "What?"
"A round of drinks."

A bouncer threw a noisy customer out of a bar four times in a row, and each time the unwanted imbiber would stagger back for more. At last a customer, who had watched with interest, tapped the bouncer on the shoulder.
"Know why that lush keeps coming back in?" he said.
The bouncer shook his head.
"You're putting too much backspin on him."

The much-married Hollywood actor was in a bar one night when he spotted a beautiful woman sitting by herself in the corner. He sat down next to her, turned on the charm, and said, "Pardon me, may I buy you a drink?"
"You certainly may," she replied. "I happen to be your wife."

"Today's homes have all the modern conveniences," says Hollywood *Reporter* columnist Mike Connolly, "but there are still many people who prefer to live in bars and taverns."

☻

A fellow was awakened at 3 A.M. by a drunk who pounded insistently on the door. The sleepy man opened the bedroom window and shouted to the inebriate below.

"Go away, darn it. You're trying to get into the wrong house!"

"Oh, yeah?" answered the drunk, "an' how do you know that you're not looking out of the wrong window?"

☻

Two old college classmates met after many years in a bar. They hoisted a few together, and then one asked if the other noticed the time. "Holy smoke! Doesn't your wife raise the dickens when you stay out late like this?" he asked.

"No," his friend replied. "I'm not married."

"Not married!" exclaimed the first man. "Then why do you stay out late like this?"

☻

A man raced into a psychiatrist's office and pleaded, "Doc, you've got to help my brother. He thinks he's an olive."

"Why do you say that?" asked the head shrinker.

"Because," replied the distraught brother, "he keeps sticking his head in other people's martinis."

☻

Two drunks were babbling about cradle days as they leaned heavily against the bar.

"You know," said one, "when I was born, I only weighed a

pound and a half and thash a fact."

"You don't shay," said the other. "Did you live?"

"Did I live!" exclaimed the first. "Shay man, you ought to she me now!"

☺

A fellow was drinking a Tom Collins mixed with second-rate gin one day when a friend passed by.

"Don't you know," warned the friend anxiously, "that stuff's slow poison?"

"Oh, that's all right," said the drinking one. "I'm in no hurry."

☺

A drunk was brought before the judge for the umpteenth time.

"Sam Brown," said the magistrate with severity, "you are charged with habitual drunkenness; what have you to offer in excuse for your offense?"

"Habitual thirst, your Honor."

☺

The story is told about the two men seated at a bar who became drunk after downing more than a dozen drinks each. The bartender, noticing their state, decided to give them ginger ale instead of liquor the next time they ordered. When one of the pair took a sip of the ginger ale, he bent over to his companion and whispered, "Drink up quickly! The bartender made a mistake. He gave us champagne instead of rye."

☺

He staggered up the walk with a silly grin and a faltering

step. She saw him a block away. "You're drunk again!" she shouted. "Well, if I ain't, I spent ten dollars foolishly."

☻

Danny Thomas often tells of the elderly gentleman who strolled into a neighborhood bar. He ordered two Scotch on the rocks. He drank one, then the other.

He did this for about three weeks. Then one afternoon the bartender said, "Sir, if I may suggest—why don't you order one drink at a time instead of two simultaneously? This way, while you let one drink stand until you finish the other, the ice dilutes it."

The dignified gentleman nodded. "Well," he explained, "there's a story behind my ordering two Scotch on the rocks. For years I used to have lunch with my partner, and each of us would take a Scotch on the rocks. After a while we made a pact that in the event that either of us died, the other would order two Scotches and drink a silent toast to the one who wasn't there."

The bartender agreed it was a touching ritual. A month later, however, the gentleman ordered only one Scotch on the rocks.

His curiosity aroused, the bartender asked, "Sir, how come you stopped ordering two individual drinks? Has your friend returned from the hereafter?"

"Not at all," the gentleman replied. "I'm ordering only one drink because I'm on the wagon."

☻

A friend described an alcoholic companion. "He's the nicest guy on two feet, if he could only stay there."

☻

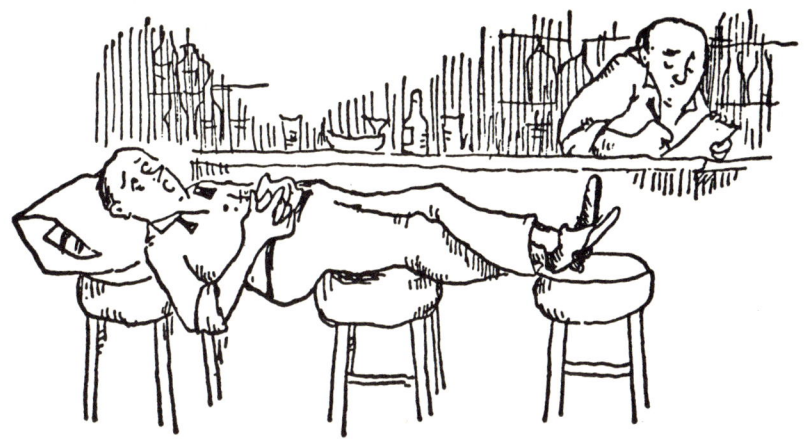

"The difference between a rich drunk and a poor one," observed Olsen and Johnson, "is that a rich one tells his problems to a psychiatrist, and a poor one tells his to a bartender."

Two identical twins decided to have some fun one night. They dressed exactly alike and seated themselves side by side in a bar, ordering the same drink. Soon, a drunk staggered in and stared at them. He kept rubbing his eyes until one of the twins burst out laughing.

"It's all right," he smiled. "You're really not seeing things. We're twins."

The drunk looked again, blinked, and asked, "All four of you?"

"Bill was held up on the way home last night."
"Yeah, that's the only way he could have got home."

My invaluable friend, Jimmy McWhan, of the Pennsylvania Railroad, added this to our last telephone conversation:

A little boy came home and smelled liquor on his mother's breath. "Why, Mother," he exclaimed, "you're wearing Daddy's perfume."

☻

At cocktail hour, a group of businessmen were downing their martinis before going home. One of them, talking loudly after his fourth drink, suddenly turned away from the bar and fell flat on his face.

"One thing about Jack," remarked the bartender, "he always knows when he's had enough."

☻

And then there was the incurable lush who was drunk more often than water.

☻

A man brought a large dog into a saloon and sat down on a stool. Immediately, the dog jumped over the bar and began to bark.

"What's he barking about?" asked the saloonkeeper nervously.

"He always mixes my martinis," said the dog's owner, "and he wants to know if I'll have it dry this time." He turned to the dog. "Dry," he said, pointing to his throat and gasping.

The dog ran along the bar, got the gin bottle and the dry vermouth, mixed them in a mixing glass with ice cubes, poured them into a martini glass, and started alternately to roll on the floor and twist into odd contortions.

"See that?" said the man. "He wants to know if I want an olive or a twist of lemon peel." "Twist of lemon," he indicated, wringing an imaginary peel.

The dog finished making the martini, grabbed the dollar bill from the bar, ran to the cash register, came back with the exact change, and dropped it on the bar.

"Say," said the saloonkeeper, "I could make a fortune with that dog. How much will you sell him for?"

"Oh, you wouldn't want him," said the owner. "He forgets to take out for taxes."

☻

Sign on a bar: YOUR WIFE CAN ONLY GET SO MAD. WHY NOT STAY A LITTLE LONGER?

☻

FIRST MAN: I have no sympathy for a man who gets drunk every night.

SECOND MAN: A man who gets drunk every night doesn't need sympathy.

☻

A skunk, a rabbit, a seagull, and a peacock were seated in a night club. They each waited for the other to order the drinks. No one spoke.

Eventually the rabbit said hesitantly, "Don't look at me, boys, I've no doe!"

The skunk shrugged his shoulders. "You can count me out, I haven't got a scent."

The seagull looked around moodily. "I pass, I've been on the rocks lately."

So the peacock spoke up and said, "Okay, boys, the cocktails are on me."

☻

Did you hear about the guy who graduated from bartender's

school with high honors? He was the highest member of the graduating class.

☺

A lush walked into a bar and told the bartender he wanted a martini, extra rare.

"You mean extra dry," corrected the bartender.

"I mean extra rare," insisted the lush. "I'm having it for my dinner."

☺

"Did you have a tough time breaking into show business?" an actor renowned for his drinking was asked.

"Tough time!" he screamed. "Why things were so bad that sometimes I had to live for days on nothing but food and water."

☺

A nurse asked the wife of one of her patients, "I can't get your husband to take his medicine. Have you any suggestions?"

"Yes," said the wife. "He'll drink anything with foam on it."

☺

"A bartender," says Eddie Cantor, "is merely a psychiatrist who works in an apron."

☺

The noted alcoholic was telling a friend about a party he had attended the night before.

"Was it a good party?" asked the friend.

"It must have been," replied the lush. "I can't remember leaving it!"

☺

Two men were standing in front of a bar.

"You're a henpecked little jerk," said the first.

The other replied, "You'd never say that if my wife were here."

☺

Sign over a bar: THERE'S NO AMUSEMENT TAX HERE. WHAT'S SO FUNNY ABOUT A HANGOVER?

☺

A wife described her husband's eating habits, "His idea of a balanced diet is a highball in each hand."

☺

The owner of a bar was describing a frequent visitor. "Although he spends a good deal of his time in my bar, he's still one of my unsteadiest customers."

☺

A lush staggered up to a cop in Times Square. "Pardon me, officer," he said, "but where am I?"

"You're at Broadway and Forty-second Street," said the cop.

"To hell with details," yelled the drunk. "What town am I in?"

☺

A pupil, aged nine, was asked to spell *straight*. He spelled it correctly and then his teacher asked, "Now what does it mean?"

The boy replied, "Without whisky or soda."

☺

The barber had a reputation for heavy drinking, and on a particular Monday morning there was a decided odor of whiskey on his breath. Suddenly the razor slipped and cut a nick in the customer's face.

"Now, Sam, you see what comes from too much drinking," the customer admonished gently.

"Yes, sir," replied the barber as he wiped the blood from the blade. "Drinking sure does make the face tender."

☺

A mink walked into a bar and ordered a double martini and explained to the bartender, "I want to taste it before I become a coat and get it spilled on me."

☺

"How would you define alcohol?"
"It's an excellent liquid for preserving almost anything but secrets."

☺

A fellow was stopped on the street by a weeping drunk.
"You've got to help me, buddy," pleaded the inebriated one. "I left home early this morning, and I haven't been seen since."

☺

And before we leave this chapter just remember this: some of the stuff they serve in bars today not only hits the spot, but removes it too.

NO PLACE LIKE HOME

The fellow who said there's no place like home must have been a bachelor. If he were a married man, he could never make such a statement. Marriage is a give and take institution. The husband gives, and the wife takes.

I like the story of the wife who told her spouse, "Jim, you don't love me like you used to. In fact, sometimes I think you don't love me at all."

"Don't love you at all," growled Jim. "There you go again. Why, I love you more than life itself. Now shut up and let me read the paper."

A lawyer's wife was complaining about the way their home was furnished. "We need new chairs, a dining-room set, and a new lamp," she told him.

"Don't worry, dear," he calmed. "Just be a little patient. One of my clients is suing her husband for divorce. He has lots of money, and as soon as I finish breaking up their home, we'll fix ours."

☺

A millionaire was being interviewed about his self-made fortune. "I never hesitate," he said, "to give full credit to my wife for her assistance."

"And just how did she help?" asked a reporter.

"Frankly," said the millionaire, "I was curious to see if there was any income she couldn't live beyond."

☺

A rejected suitor told his girl friend, "If I had all the qualities you want in a man, I'd propose to somebody else."

☺

"I dreamed last night that you gave me a hundred-dollar bill to buy some new dresses today. Surely, you wouldn't do anything to spoil such a beautiful dream, would you?"

"Of course not, darling. To show you that I'm as generous as you dreamed, you can keep the hundred-dollar bill I gave you."

☺

The shortest romance on record:
"Wilt thou?" And she wilted.

☺

An enterprising suburban housewife was all set to start her spring cleaning when her spouse came home in a state of consternation.

"Alice," he exclaimed, "there are eight guys outside with

vacuum cleaners, and they all claim they have an appointment for a demonstration!"

"That's right," his wife replied blandly. "Now you just direct them all to different rooms and then tell them to start demonstrating."

☻

"Hello there, Irving. You're looking better. How's that pain in the neck?"

"Oh, she's playing mahjong."

☻

Joe E. Lewis says the modern wife is expected to look like a girl, behave like a lady, think like a man, and work like a dog.

☻

A little girl, sitting in a chapel watching a wedding, suddenly exclaimed, "Mother, has the lady changed her mind?"

"What do you mean?" the mother asked.

"Why," replied the child, "she went up the aisle with one man and came back with another."

☻

"You can still find wives who spend two hours preparing their husbands' suppers," claims Peggy Cass. "Some of those cans are tricky things to open."

☻

Bob Marshall tells of the woman who visited a psychiatrist and complained that her husband thought he was a pigeon.

"Why don't you bring him to see me," suggested the headshrinker.

"All right, I will," replied the woman. "Just as soon as I can lure him down from the statue he's perched on."

☺

"When I can't tell whether my wife is coming or going," says Mark Wachs, "I know she hasn't been shopping."

☺

The attorney for the plaintiff in the divorce case put his client on the stand.

"Now, as I understand it," he said sympathetically, "every night when you returned from work, instead of having your wife alone and awaiting you, you found a different man hiding in the closet?"

"Yes. That's right."

"And this of course, caused you untold anguish and unhappiness, did it not?"

"Why, sure!" came the hurt reply. "I never had any room to hang my clothes."

☺

WIFE: Do you love me?
HUSBAND: Yes.
WIFE: How much do you love me?
HUSBAND: How much do you need?

☺

A guy was taking an auto trip with his wife. She looked at the road map and told him, "Darling, we're going in the wrong direction."

"What's the difference," he replied. "We're making great time!"

☺

A young fellow, just back from his honeymoon, was being enriched in wisdom by questioning a long-married friend.

"Now, about finances," he said. "Do you provide your wife with a checking account, monthly allowance, or whatever amount she requests?"

"My boy," smiled the older man. "I provide all three."

☺

"Early in life, men prefer girls with good figures," says Jack Carter. "But later, they wish they had preferred those who were good at them."

☺

Wife, reading her husband's fortune on a weight card: "'You are dynamic, a leader of men, and admired by women for your good looks and strength of character' . . . It's got your weight wrong, too!"

☺

After the court awarded the woman a large marital settlement, they met once more in the corridor.

"I suppose you always had my best interests at heart," the husband said with resignation.

"I certainly did," she replied.

"Then," he roared, "why the hell did you marry me?"

☺

FIRST MAN: My wife is very considerate.
SECOND MAN: Why, what'd she do?
FIRST MAN: She went to Florida so I wouldn't have to buy her a box of candy for Valentine's Day.

☺

"We couldn't help hearing you and your wife having a battle last night," Phil's neighbor told him the next morning. "How'd you make out?"

"Fine, fine," Phil answered heartily. "In fact, by the time it was over, she came crawling to me on her hands and knees."

The neighbor, who knew Phil's wife, looked doubtful.

"It's a fact," Phil continued. "And she said, 'come out from under that bed, you coward'!"

☻

"My dear, you're wearing your wedding ring on the wrong finger!"

"I know. I married the wrong man."

☻

Martha Raye can't understand why any woman would want her husband to run for president. "The minute you move into the White House," says Martha, "everyone on the block knows exactly what your husband does and how much he makes."

☻

"If you had to choose between marrying for love or money, Helen, which would you choose?" asked her friend.

"Love, I guess," replied Helen. "I always seem to do the wrong thing."

☻

HUSBAND: You'll drive me to my grave!
WIFE: What'd you expect to do, walk?

☻

A young woman went to a fortuneteller.

"Very soon," droned the mystic, "you will meet a tall, handsome man who will sweep you off your feet. He will shower you with gifts, take you to breathtaking night spots, and the two of you will drink a toast to your everlasting love."

"Has he any money?" she asked.

"He is president of a large concern and heir to a million dollars."

"Gee!" she stammered. "Can you tell me just one more thing?"

"What do you want to know?"

"How can I get rid of my husband?"

And while we're dealing with fortuneteller stories, how about this one?

"You will marry a dark man," said the fortuneteller, "and for the first few years of your married life you will be very unhappy."

"And after that?"

"You'll get used to it."

"Maybe clothes don't make a man," observes New York *Journal-American* columnist Bert Bacharach, "but they can break a husband."

A rather pompous fellow, hosting at a dinner said, "I wonder how many really great men there are in this world."

Without blinking an eyelash, his wife retorted, "Darling, there's one less than you think."

A Hollywood producer, who stressed realism in his films,

had a script calling for a fight between two men on the street.

Discussing the scene with his star, he said, "Bob, do you see that couple waiting for the bus? I want you to go over and start insulting the woman."

"But why?" asked the confused Bob.

"Because," said the producer, "you'll get her husband fighting mad, and he'll haul off and belt you. That'll give the scene realism."

Bob went up to the couple. "Good day, sir," he said. "Is this your wife?"

"That's right," was the answer.

"What a hag!" roared Bob, getting ready for the first punch. "Why most men would be ashamed to be seen with her!"

There was an ominous silence. Then the man turned to his wife.

"See," he demanded. "What have I been telling you all these years?"

☻

"A bachelor," says Alan King, "is a guy who doesn't have to worry about how much of his take-home pay reaches there."

☻

When asked what he did before he was married, a husband replied, "Anything I wanted to."

☻

INSURANCE ADJUSTER: Why didn't you report the robbery at once?

HOUSEWIFE: I didn't suspect I'd been robbed. When I came home and found all the dresser drawers open and things scattered all over the place, I thought my husband had been looking for a clean shirt.

☻

The woman, who was visiting her husband in the hospital, took the pretty young nurse aside and asked, "Tell me the truth. Is he making any progress?"

"Absolutely not," the nurse replied. "He's not my type."

Irv Kupcinet of the Chicago *Sun-Times* likes this story:

A wife visited a furrier and tried on a mink coat. After studying herself in the mirror, she told him, "I'll take it on one condition."

"What is it?" he asked.

"If my husband doesn't like it, will you promise to refuse to take it back?"

A wife told her spouse, "I was just as unreasonable when we were first married but you thought it was cute."

And Bentley Stegner, also of the Chicago *Sun-Times,* prefers this one:

An office worker came in one day, sporting an engagement ring. An older colleague, seeing the ring, wished the girl every happiness.

"But let me offer you some advice," said the older woman. "Don't give him his own way too much. Demand your rights. When I got married, I insisted that my husband give up smoking and drinking.

"And did he?" asked the engaged girl.

"I don't know," admitted the adviser. "I haven't seen him in twenty years."

☺

"Does your wife drive?" asked Sam, looking at his friend's car.
"No," was the reply. "It was like this when I bought it."

☺

A hillbilly found a mirror while walking through the woods. He looked into it and exclaimed, "Why it's a picture of my old Pa." He took it home and hid it in the attic. His wife suspected something, went to the attic, and found it. When she looked into it, she said, "So that's the old hag he's been running around with."

☺

Speaking about suspecting wives, I like this story.

"City Hall," said the switchboard operator, answering a call. There was no sound at the other end of the line.

"City Hall," the operator repeated. Still no reply.

Finally, after the third time, a rather nervous female voice said, "Is this really City Hall?"

"That's right, madam," said the operator. "With whom do

you wish to speak?"

There was an embarrassed silence. Then the female voice said softly, "I guess nobody. I just found this number in my husband's pocket."

☻

Mrs. Dale informed her better half that she was expecting a party of guests. He immediately rose and hid all the umbrellas.

"Why," she exclaimed, "are you afraid the guests will steal your umbrellas?"

"No, I'm afraid they'll recognize them."

☻

"Could I see the burglar who broke into our house last night?" asked a caller at the police station.

"Why do you want to see him?" asked the officer in charge.

"I'd like to ask him how he got in without waking my wife."

☻

Did you hear about the extremely lazy wife? The only exercise she gets is running up bills and jumping to conclusions.

☻

Mrs. Newlywed inveigled her husband into a shopping trip. Once she got him to the most expensive jeweler in New York, she wangled a solid gold brooch, a diamond ring, a diamond bracelet, and a pair of earrings.

"Well," the dazed, much poorer husband said when they were in the street again, "what do we do now?"

"Now," said the wife firmly and virtuously, "I'm going to save you some money. We'll take the subway home."

☻

A guy asked a recent groom, "Is your wife's cooking anything to write home about?" The groom replied, "Yes, it's got me writing home for some of Mother's recipes."

☻

When some wives start running up expenses, they leave their husbands breathless.

☻

Two matrons were talking at a class reunion.
"What kind of a husband do you have?" asked one.
"Well, let me put it this way," said the other. "If he mentions Rose in his sleep, he's definitely talking about flowers."

☻

Three commuters were discussing their wives while waiting for their trains.
"I've got a wife who meets my train every night, and we've been married ten years," bragged the first.
"Well, I've got a wife who's been doing the same thing every night, and we've been married twenty years," said the second.
"I can beat that," said the third. "I've got a wife who meets me every night and I'm not even married."

☻

"The reason some married couples don't get along," says Shelly Berman, "is that they have nothing in common to fight about."

☻

"Give one reason why so many wives are opposed to divorce."
"They don't like the idea of sharing their husband's money with a lawyer."

☻

WIFE: Doctor, my husband has some terrible mental affliction. Sometimes I talk to him for an hour and then discover he hasn't heard a single word.
DOCTOR: Madam, that's not a mental affliction. That's a gift.

☺

"Marvin, do you love me still?"
"Yes—better than any other way."

☺

A woman who was spending the winter in Miami mentioned to her friend how hard her husband worked. "Sidney," she said, "is the hardest working man in the Garment Center. He puts in sixteen hours a day and works like a horse."
"Why doesn't he take a vacation?" asked the friend.
The wife replied, "Since when does a horse take a vacation?"

☺

And then there was the guy who complained to his wife that his secretary didn't understand him.

☺

"My husband and I both like the same things," Mrs. Goldberg told a neighbor. "But it took him twelve years to learn."

☺

"For twenty years," a man told his friend, "my wife and I were ecstatically happy."
"Then what happened?" questioned the friend.
"We met."

☺

HUSBAND: I hate to admit it, dear, but I bought another

ten-thousand-dollar policy from the life insurance salesman.
WIFE: Oh I could kill you.

☺

The man gazed rapturously at the jewelry counter in a department store.
Then, he spoke to the clerk: "These diamonds are really beautiful, aren't they? I'd like to smother my wife in them."
"Oh, that would cost a lot of money, sir," the salesgirl told him. "There must be a cheaper way."

☺

One morning at breakfast a wife was cross and irritable.
"What's the trouble?" asked her husband.
At first, his wife refused to tell, but finally, she turned to him with tears in her eyes and sobbed, "If I ever dream again that you kissed another woman, I'll never speak to you as long as I live."

☺

A henpecked husband told his spouse, "If you want my opinion give it to me."

☺

And then there was the sentimental daughter of a Hollywood beauty who wanted to get married in her mother's wedding gown but she couldn't decide which one.

☺

A much-married Hollywood actor was confronted by a gay damsel.
"Don't you remember me?" she greeted him. "Five years

ago you asked me to marry you!"

"Really?" yawned the actor. "And did you?"

☻

"I didn't know your husband was artistic."
"He isn't—he's just untidy."

☻

A fellow asked his pal about his spouse, "Does your wife economize?" His pal replied, "Yes, we can do without practically everything I need."

☻

"All men make mistakes," says New York *Journal-American* columnist Frank Coniff, "but husbands just find out about them sooner."

☻

A general, a colonel, and a major were discussing matrimony. The general contended that marriage was sixty percent work and forty percent pleasure. The colonel felt it was seventy-five percent work and twenty-five percent pleasure. The major felt it was ninety percent work and ten percent pleasure. While they were arguing, a private entered the room and the general suggested, "Let him decide."

The private listened to all sides of the argument and then announced his opinion. "If you'll excuse my saying so, sirs, matrimony must be one hundred percent pleasure and no work at all."

"How did you come to that conclusion?" demanded the surprised officers.

"It's simple," replied the private. "If there were any work

in it at all, you gentlemen would have me doing it."

Two men met in a bar and soon began discussing their wives. "My wife is an angel," said one.

"You're lucky," replied the other. "Mine looks as though she'll live for years."

A young couple were exchanging ideas on marriage.
"I won't get married," said the boy, "until I find a girl like the one grandpa married."
"They don't have a woman like that today," said the girl.
"No?" said her boy friend with relish. "He just married her yesterday."

FIRST MAN: Have you noticed how reluctant the young men of today are to marry and settle down?

SECOND MAN: I've noticed many times.

FIRST MAN: They seem to fear marriage. Why, before I was married, I didn't know the meaning of fear.

☻

Hinson Styles, of the New York *Mirror,* observes that a lot of girls who seem ideal before marriage turn out to be an ordeal afterward.

☻

Harry Pavony, the accountant for the Myron Cohen Foundation, heard a new bride asked by a friend, "Does your husband expect you to obey him?" "Oh, no," she replied. "He's been married before."

☻

"Nothing gives a wife that delightfully surprised feeling," says *Variety* editor Abel Green, "like receiving the birthday gift she's been hinting about for months."

☻

"Betty, you poor girl," gushed the voice on the phone, "I just heard your husband is in the hospital. What's wrong with him?"

"It's his knee," Betty explained.

"Oh, he broke it?" asked her friend.

"No," was the crisp reply. "I found a strange woman on it."

☻

FRED: I heard you entertained your neighbors informally last evening.

SAL: Yes, the missus and I had a fight on our back porch.

☻

A henpecked husband was telling a friend about his spouse. "She's very strict," he said.

"Would you say she always gets her way around the house?" his companion asked.

"I'll say," the husband agreed. "Why, she even writes her diary a week ahead of time."

☺

"I'm getting mighty exhausted contesting my wife's will," admitted Herb to a confidant.

"I never knew she died," said the shocked friend.

"That's the trouble," sighed Herb. "She didn't."

☺

The hostess poured a cup of tea for a middle-aged man at her party and asked if he took sugar.

"No," said he.

"Yes," his wife corrected him. "You know I always put sugar in your tea.

"I know," replied her husband. "I used to remind you not to. Now, I just don't stir."

☺

"Hiding a secret from your wife," says Lou Walters, "is like trying to sneak daybreak past a rooster."

☺

A man was complaining about his new son-in-law. "He can't drink and he can't play cards."

"That's the kind of son-in-law to have," said a friend.

"Naw," said the man. "He can't play cards, and he plays. He can't drink, and he drinks."

☺

"When a man opens the door of his car for his wife," says Jules Podell of the Copa, "you can be sure that either the car or the wife is new."

The judge looked at the man who was seeking to obtain a divorce. "You claim false pretense?" he asked. "Misrepresentation? Isn't that a rather curious reason to want a divorce? You will have to explain more fully."

"Oh, I can do that, your Honor," said the man readily. "When I asked this woman to marry me, she said she was agreeable. She wasn't!"

☺

Solomon's 999th Wife: Sol, are you really and truly in love with me?

Solomon: My dear, you are one in a thousand.

☺

A bride-to-be had just shown a friend the list of wedding guests.

"Isn't it strange," said the friend "that you've included only married couples?"

"Oh, that was Phil's idea," the bride-to-be replied. "He says that, if we invite only married people, the presents will be all clear profit."

"My wife had a funny dream last night," confided a man to his friend. "She dreamed she was married to a millionaire."

"You're lucky," sighed his pal. "My wife dreams that in the daytime."

☺

"The man of the hour," says Leo Shull of show business, "is often the husband whose wife told him to wait a minute."

☺

"Didn't I hear the clock strike two as you came in last night?" the wife asked her mate at the breakfast table.

"Yes, dear," replied the husband from behind the morning paper. "It started to strike ten, but I stopped it to keep it from waking you up."

☺

Did you hear about the husband whose wife made a lasting impression on him? The doctors say the scar will never disappear.

☺

"Wives are like cars," says *Variety's* Joe Cohen. "If you take care of them, you don't have to get new ones all the time."

☺

A woman phoned the Legal Aid Society for some advice. "I want to know if I can get a divorce because of my husband's flat feet?" she asked.

"Hmmm," answered the lawyer cautiously. "I don't think so, unless you can prove his feet are in the wrong flat."

☺

"How did you get to know your wife before you married?"
"I didn't know her before I married."

☺

Two young wives were chatting. "My husband can't stand music concerts," said one. "The opening bars send him home."

"You're lucky," replied the other. "Mine is sent home by the closing bars."

☺

A wife stood in front of a mirror fixing her hat until her beloved took notice.

"That hat looks awful on you," he grumbled. "Take it off and return it for credit."

"I can't very well return it," she replied happily, "because it's the one I've been wearing for two years. But since you dislike it so, I'll buy a new one tomorrow."

☺

MRS. BROWN: It seems to me that common sense would prevent many divorces.

MR. BROWN: It seems to me that it would also prevent just as many marriages.

☺

"With all those modern household appliances," notes Danny Dayton, "a man is better off marrying a girl who's a mechanical genius than one who can cook."

☺

The young bride appeared before her dinner guests carrying a tray full of cocktails.

"I hope these martinis are all right," she said. "We ran out of olives, so I just poured a spoonful of olive oil into each glass."

☺

"It's the men from the loan company," the bride explained to her husband as the burly men clumped upstairs. "They've come for the piano."

"But, darling," her husband protested, "I gave you this month's installment."

"I know," the bride answered. "And I intend to pay them as soon as they get the piano downstairs. I've decided I prefer it down there."

☺

"Despite all its advances," says Garry Moore, "modern science has yet to find an easy way for the average housewife to get breakfast in bed."

☺

Wife to husband at breakfast:
"You and your suicide attempts.
"Look at this gas bill!"

☺

The lady of the house summoned a TV serviceman to fix the set. Spreading out his tools, the repairman inquired, "What seems to be the trouble?"

"Well, for one thing," replied the woman. "All the programs are lousy."

☺

"So," said the wife, "you love me with all your heart. Would you die for me?"

"No," said her spouse. "Mine is an undying love."

☺

"Darling," said the Hollywood bride as her new husband carried her across the threshold of her new home. "This house looks so familiar. Are you sure we haven't been married before?"

☺

The story is told of the fellow who was extremely devoted to his mother. He had lived with her for forty-three years and wouldn't wed for fear of offending her. Then, at a party, he met Mary.

After a brief courtship, the couple eloped and kept the merger secret for a year. Mary finally insisted that the truth come out or she would leave for Reno.

The couple called on his mother, and he tried to break the news gently.

"Mother," he quivered, "I hope you will understand and give us your blessing. I want you to know Mary and I have been married for a year."

The old lady looked stern.

"Mother," trembled the groom, "What is it? Don't you approve?"

"A fine thing!" cried the mother. "You and Mary have been married for a year, and I'm still doing your shirts!"

☺

A spouse who came home from a stag party with a black eye was asked by his wife, "Can you describe the guy who hit you?"

He replied, "That's just what I was doing when he hit me."

☺

"George and I had a terrible argument last night and he left home," a wife sadly told her friend.

"Oh, don't let that bother you," soothed her friend. "After all, he's done that before."

"Yes, I know," sobbed the unhappy spouse, "but this time he's taken his bowling ball."

☺

And then there was the man who met his wife at a travel bureau. She was looking for a vacation, and he was the last resort.

☻

Two housewives were discussing their mates. One mentioned that her husband was so wonderful that he treated her like a queen.

"You think that's something?" bragged the other woman. "Let me tell you how good my husband is. He treats me just like I was his mistress."

☻

Did you hear about the Hollywood couple who won't get a divorce until their son passes his bar exams? They want to be his first case.

☻

"And how is your daughter, Mrs. Scalyer—the one who got married last year? Is the marriage working out well?"

"Oh, yes, everything's fine. Of course she can't stand her husband, but then, isn't there always something?"

☻

"Well," said the husband. "I'm hardly home from the office and you're asking me for more money."

"It's your own fault," snapped the wife. "You were half an hour late."

☻

A woman who was divorcing her husband told the judge, "Your Honor, he swears at me in his sleep."

"That's a lie, your Honor," shouted the husband. "I'm not asleep!"

☻

"A gentleman," according to Bob Hope, "is a fellow who, when his wife drops something, kicks it to where she can pick it up more easily."

☻

A woman went to a psychiatrist because her husband thought he was a mink. "Your fee won't be any problem," she explained, "because he sheds a lot."

☻

And before we leave this chapter, I'd like to give one little piece of advice to roving husbands: ABSENCE MAKES HER HEART GO WANDER.

CAUGHT IN THE SPORTS WHIRL

When I have a free afternoon and the weather is nice, I like to go out to the nearest golf course and play 18 holes. It has been said that the course of true golf never runs smooth. However, one would never guess this from listening to golfers. Golf has made more liars out of Americans than fishing. In fact, nowadays, it's more popular than fishing because a golfer has a major advantage over a fisherman; he doesn't have to show anything to prove it.

One of my favorite golf tales deals with the wife who entered a sporting goods department of a large store and told the salesman, "I'd like a low handicap, please."

"A low handicap?" the man repeated puzzled.

"Why, yes," she said, "for my husband's birthday. He's always wishing he had one."

Poor Golfer: Well, how did you like my game?
Caddy: I suppose it's all right, but I still prefer golf.

☻

"You think so much about your old golf game that you don't even remember when we were married," complained the wife.

"Of course I do, honey," the husband reassured her. "That was the day I sank that forty-foot putt."

☻

"If golf is played for exercise," questions Morty Gunty, "how come the player who manages to get the least of it wins?"

☻

Frank Coniff of the New York *Journal-American* tells of two golfers who were just leaving the eighteenth green. "That sure was a great drive I made off the first tee!" boasted one for about the tenth time. "Yes, sir, a real beauty!"

"It certainly was," agreed his companion who had spent the entire afternoon hearing about that one drive. "It's too bad you can't have it stuffed."

☻

Sam Snead and Ted Williams were having a friendly argument over whether golf or baseball is the tougher game. Finally Snead drawled, "Well, there's one thing about golf. When you hit a foul ball, you gotta get out there and play it!"

☻

"My doctor tells me I can't play golf."
"So he's played with you, too."

☻

"How long have you been playing golf?" the old club member asked the stranger on the fourth tee.

"Oh, about three months," the stranger replied.

"Well, you certainly play a very good game."

"I ought to," the stranger sighed. "It took me four years to learn."

☺

Golfing businessmen have a special problem. If they shoot above par, they are neglecting their golf and if they shoot below par, they are neglecting their business.

☺

Then, there's the story about the man in the foursome who drove his ball grimly from the first tee. It rose into the air nicely, like a jet airliner taking off from the runway. Then it made a crazy heartbreaking turn and disappeared over the treetops into the woods along the fairway.

The man's partner had his back turned at the time and didn't see the awful slice.

"Well, Frank," he remarked cheerfully, "that one sure sounded good."

"Yes," said Frank. "But I'm not giving a concert."

☺

"The traps on this course are certainly annoying, aren't they?" babbled a talkative golfer to his partner just as the latter was about to make a tough approach shot.

"Yes," his companion answered. "Would you please shut yours?"

☺

"So you played golf with Jim yesterday," remarked a college girl to her sorority sister. "How does he use the woods?"

"I don't know, I'm sure," answered the friend primly. "We played golf all the time."

☻

Two friends had a date to play golf. The first one stepped to the tee, took a mighty swing and his drive was a hole in one.

The second friend stepped to the tee and said, "All rightee, now I'll take my practice swing, and then we'll start the game."

☻

The two golfers had reached the last green in the competition final and, as the excited onlookers stood in hushed silence, the first player shaped up to putt. Just as the putter blade was moving nicely toward the ball, a spectator sneezed violently. The unfortunate golfer was startled and struck the ball with a jerky and indeterminate jab. The ball hit the back of the cup, rose a good four inches into the air, and dropped into the hole.

When the applause died down, the second player advanced to his ball and just before he was about to stroke, he turned his head toward the fellow who had sneezed.

"I wonder," he said politely. "Could you possibly manage another sneeze?"

☻

"Why do you play golf?"
"To aggravate myself."

☻

Ann Marsters of Chicago's *American* tells of the golfer who was brought into the hospital suffering from sunstroke. The nurse began to read his temperature. "102-102-103."

"Hey, Doc," whispered the suffering sport. "What's par for this hospital?"

☻

Two male golfers were highly annoyed by a pair of females on the links in front of them. The women stopped to chat, picked flowers, admired the scenery, and generally made life miserable for the players following.

At one point, the two men stood on a tee for nearly twenty-five minutes while one of the women apparently looked for her ball a few yards down the fairway.

"Why don't you help your friend find her ball?" one of the indignant golfers finally shouted to the second woman who stood watching her companion search.

"Oh, she's got her ball," the woman replied sweetly. "She's looking for her club."

☻

"Nowadays," claims Joe E. Brown, "another place where men aren't safe from women drivers is a golf course."

☻

"This game is so much more fun than golf!" exclaimed an enthusiastic young lady during her first night of bowling. "You're not always losing the ball."

☻

A snooty woman came off the links, stuck her nose into the air, and announced, "I went around in 76."

To which a rival iced, "With Paul Revere, no doubt."

☻

I always thought it was an amazing coincidence that so many men lose their grandmothers the opening day of the baseball season. However, despite its high mortality rate, baseball is a wonderful sport. It has many devoted fans. In fact, some of them are such fanatics that they'll go to a ball game even when their TV sets aren't busted.

☺

One of the most popular baseball stories deals with the onetime great pitcher who retired from the game and applied for a job with a public relations firm. He was given a routine questionnaire to fill out, and one of the questions asked for his last job and his reason for leaving. To the first part he wrote: "Pitching baseballs," and to the second part: "Couldn't get the side out."

☺

Clark Kinnaird of King Features Syndicate applauded when I told him this one:

A woman raced into a psychiatrist's office and pleaded, "Doctor, you must help my husband. He finds it impossible to make decisions." "Nothing unusual about that," soothed the dome doctor. "Lots of people find it difficult to make decisions." "But doctor, you don't understand," screamed the woman, "my husband happens to be an umpire!"

☺

FIRST BASEBALL PLAYER: You didn't fare too well with the owner's daughter, did you?
SECOND BASEBALL PLAYER: Terrible—no hits, no runs, no heiress.

☺

The runner rounded second base and headed for third as the outfielder uncorked a tremendous peg from deep center. Ball and runner arrived at the hot corner in a cloud of dust.

"You're out!" roared the umpire.

"I'm not out!" roared the angry runner.

"You're not?" The ump was surprised. "Well, just take a look at tomorrow's paper."

Robert Dana of the New York *World-Telegram* & *Sun* appreciated this one:

A manager whose team was hopelessly mired in last place received a call from his head scout.

"I've just seen the greatest pitcher in the country," the talent hunter enthused. "He pitched a perfect game; twenty-seven strike-outs in a row. No one could even hit a loud foul off him until there were two out in the ninth. I've got the pitcher here with me now. What should I do?"

Without a second's hesitation, the manager replied, "Sign the guy who got the foul. We need hitters."

And then there was the outfielder who had such a weak arm, the only thing he threw out in twenty years was his old glove.

ADVICE TO BASEBALL PLAYERS: If at first you don't succeed, try second base.

The last inning was over and the center fielder, who had

muffed an easy fly, came trotting past the manager. "I've gotta get movin' if you don't mind," said the ballplayer. "I've got a plane to catch."

"Go ahead," snarled the manager. "And better luck with the plane."

☺

"It's easy to pick out the ballplayer who's gone Hollywood," says Groucho Marx. "He's the one who wears dark sunglasses—even after the game."

☺

Two rooters at a ball game were so engrossed in the contest that neither wanted to march back to the refreshment stand for hot dogs, and there wasn't a vendor in sight. They finally bribed a kid nearby to go for them, giving him sixty cents and saying, "Buy a dog for yourself at the same time."

A few minutes later, the kid came back with forty-five cents change and said, "They only had my hot dog left."

☺

"Life for a baseball bench warmer," says my good friend and personal manager, Bill Robbins, "is a many-splintered thing."

☺

When a Detroit baseball scout signed up a teen-age pitcher, the front office wired the lad to report immediately to the Tigers' farm club in Montgomery, Alabama. The following day the secretary received a collect call from the rookie. "Gee, Mr. Smith, do you mind if I don't report for another couple of days?" he pleaded.

"But why?" asked the surprised Smith.

"Because I haven't had time to make the collections on my paper route yet!"

☻

Speaking about pitchers, I heard of one who was sent to a psychiatrist by his manager who suspected a mental problem. The pitcher who had done extensive reading on muscle spasms mentioned a rare muscular disorder which he thought was the root of his trouble.

"Nonsense," protested the psychiatrist. "You wouldn't know whether you had that or not. With that ailment there's no discomfort of any kind."

"I know," gasped the pitcher. "My symptoms exactly."

☻

The baseball manager sought out his third baseman in the locker room. "Joe," he said, putting his arm around the player's shoulder, "it's all right if you forget all those batting tips I gave you. We just traded you to Kansas City."

☻

Fighters are very well-mannered people. Why? Because they always look out for the rights of others.

☻

In order to fill out the regimental boxing team, a GI was prevailed upon by his buddies to enter the divisional tournament. The soldier had never been in a fight in his life and looked forward to his initial bout with ill-concealed panic. When he came back to the barracks after the fight, he was in terrible shape; his head was both bloody and bowed.

"You poor guy," said the GI in the next bunk.

"That's not the half of it," gasped the boxer. "I gotta fight again tomorrow night. I won!"

☻

"Did you hear about the very pathetic fighter? He was on the mat so often he wore out his welcome.

☻

"My brother has a fortune in his own right."
"A coming millionaire?"
"No, a coming heavyweight champion!"

☻

"Hey Max," cried the first burglar, "let's get out of this place. We've broken into the home of the heavyweight champ."
"Don't worry," retorted the second burglar. "He won't fight for anything less than $100,000."

☻

A battered fighter was floored. The referee started the count over him, "One, two, three, four . . ." His manager shouted to him, "Don't get up 'til eight, don't get up 'til eight!" "Okay," the fighter replied. "What time is it now?"

☻

Speaking about floored fighters, how about the fellow who was knocked to the canvas midway in the third round? Although the punch which had downed him was a light one, he didn't get up until after the ten count.

"Whatsa matter, you crazy?" demanded his manager after the fight. "You wasn't hit hard. Whyncha get up in time?"

"I was so mad at being floored by that jerk," explained the defeated pug, "that I thought I'd better count to ten before I did anything."

☻

"Just think," said the conceited heavyweight boxer, "millions of people will watch me fight on TV tonight."

"Yes," retorted a boxing scribe, "and they'll all know the results at least ten seconds before you will."

☻

"Yes, sir," gloated the beaten fighter's trainer enthusiastically. "You really had him worried in the seventh round. He thought he'd killed you."

☻

A fighter was taking a terrific beating in the ring. When he stumbled back to his corner after the bell sounded, his manager looked at him briefly and said, "Let him hit ya with his left for a while. Your face is crooked."

☻

In a small fight club, the fans were disgusted with the lack of action in the ring. The two battlers did nothing but circle each other, with no punches being thrown. A forbidding silence mounted in the arena. Then . . . .

"Hit him now, ya bum," a spectator called. "You got the wind with yah!"

☻

Asked why he decided to give up fighting, an undefeated champion said, "I looked in the mirror after my last fight and saw my beaten up face and decided there must be an easier way to meet congenial people of my own age."

☻

"What did you think of the big fight last night, Mike?"
"Big fight! If my wife and I had a fight like that, the kids would boo us!"

☻

At a particularly dull fight at Madison Square Garden, an irate fan yelled, "Hey ref, put out the lights and let those bums go to sleep!"
"No, don't do that!" shouted another voice from ringside. "I'm reading."

☻

First Fighter: When I hit a man, he remembers it.
Second Fighter: When I hit a man, he's through remembering.

☻

The slap-happy fighter reeled to his corner at the end of the fifth round. His face was badly battered.

"How'm I doin'?" he mumbled.

His manager patted him on the shoulder.

"Swell kid," he enthused. "You've got the other guy on the run."

"Yeah?" cried the fighter.

"Sure thing," nodded his manager. "But just make sure he doesn't catch you again."

☺

"How did you feel when you entered the ring?"

"It was just like going to bed."

"Like going to bed?"

"Yes, I took off my robe, climbed in, and in two minutes I was asleep."

☺

A real football fan is one who knows the nationality of every man on the All-American Team.

☺

My favorite football story concerns the college president who decided to lend a hand in the recruiting of new members for the team. He toured a number of school gridirons throughout the country. When he returned to his own campus, he called his coach.

"How did you make out?" asked the coach.

"Well, I saw one team that went through a 15-game schedule unbeaten, untied, and unscored on. The amusing thing about it is that their line averaged only 135, their backfield only 125, and they had no passer or kicker," reported the president.

"Well," said the coach. "I don't suppose you wasted any

scholarships on them?"

"No," replied the president, "but I hired their coach as your successor."

☺

"Winning isn't everything," says George DeWitt, "but no college football coach ever got a raise for building character during a season."

☺

A girl told her football-hero boy friend, "You've made me the happiest girl in the world tonight, Moose. You didn't wear your football shoes!"

☺

A big college halfback bumped into an elderly man in the Assembly Hall and shouted, "Hey Bud, why don't you watch where ya goin'?"

The man replied, "Look here, Sonny, I'll have you know I'm the football coach here."

"Gee, Coach, I'm sorry. I though you were only the principal."

☺

"Tell me, sir, why do the students cheer so loudly when a football player gets hurt?"

"That's so the ladies can't hear what he's saying."

☺

Calvin Haley of the TV Coffee Shop, heard a teacher ask her pupils to list, in their opinions, the eleven greatest Americans. As they were writing, she stopped at one desk. "Have you finished your list, Bobby?" she asked.

"Not quite," answered the boy. "I can't decide on the fullback."

☺

A football coach told his high school team, "And remember that football develops individuality, initiative, and leadership. Now get out there and do exactly as I tell you."

☺

"What would happen," a football expert was asked, "if a team was trying to kick the extra point, and the ball burst in the air with half going over the bar and half under it?"

"The way I see it," remarked the expert after thinking for a few moments, "the team would be out eighteen bucks."

☺

The story is told of the football game that was played on a Thanksgiving Day in Philadelphia. In the midst of a deluge of snow and rain, the Cornell captain won the toss and bitterly

stared out over Franklin Field covered with cold, gray slush.

"Do we have to play football in that fluid?" he demanded.

"Yes," was the implacable reply. "Which end you want?"

"Well," said the player, "we'll kick with the tide."

☺

An easterner on a tour of California stopped for lunch in a small town and noticing he was opposite a college, decided to take a look at the place. As he passed a sweater-clad student on the campus, he stopped the lad and asked the name of the school.

"Sorry, sir, I don't know," the lad replied. "I'm just a football player here."

☺

It had been a terrible season for the local football team, and a friend was trying to cheer up the coach.

"At least you've taught the boys fine sportsmanship," he comforted. "They're certainly good losers."

"Good," growled the coach. "Why, they're perfect!"

☺

A doctor, who was a prominent alumnus, was asked to give the boys a pep talk at a rally before the first football game of the season.

The doctor was most enthusiastic. Throughout the speech he interspersed the following statement:

"Give 'em hell boys! When you get in that game, you want to give 'em H-E-L-L."

The next speaker was a mild-mannered minister. He arose and in a small voice said, "Boys, give them what the doctor ordered."

☺

And then there was the guy who couldn't make up his mind whether to buy a ticket to the Army-Notre Dame game or a seat on the Stock Exchange. They were both the same price.

☺

"I used to play football and I carried the ball every play."
"Were you the star player?"
"No, but it was my ball."

☺

Anyone who has spent a day at the race track will tell you this: no horse can go as fast as the money you bet on him.

☺

Speaking about horses, I'm reminded of the story about the fellow who entered an eight-year-old in a race. Since the old horse had no previous races, the odds on him were 90 to 1. But when the race began, he tore down the track like a flash and wound up twelve lengths ahead of his closest competitor. The stewards were naturally suspicious and called the owner to their stand for questioning.

"How come you never raced this horse before?" they demanded. "After all, you've had him for eight years."

"Well, to tell the truth," the owner said sheepishly, "we couldn't catch him until he was seven."

☺

MOTHER: Violet, before you get serious with that boy friend of yours, be sure he is always kind and considerate.

VIOLET: Oh, I'm sure of that, Mother. Why, only the other day he put his shirt on a horse that was scratched.

☺

A bookie was testifying before the crime investigating committee to determine the honesty of horse racing. "The boss gave me $25,000 to fix the race," he said. "There were four other horses in the race and I gave each jockey $5,000 apiece."

"That's only $20,000," interjected a brilliant senator.

"I know," replied the bookie. "I needed the other $5,000 to fix the photographer in case of a photo finish."

The horse had won the big race and was proudly telling his neighbor in the adjoining stall about it.

"And besides," added the winner happily, "I was promised, if I won the race, I'd get two extra bales of hay. And, brother, that ain't money."

ED: Were you lucky at the races yesterday?

NED: I certainly was. I found a quarter after the last race so I didn't have to walk home.

An enthusiastic racing fan made repeated trips to the ticket window to place his money on Take Courage in the last race. When he did so for the fourth time, a stranger tapped him on the shoulder.

"Excuse me," the stranger said. "It's none of my business, I guess, but if I were you, I wouldn't put all that money on Take Courage. He's not going to win."

"How can you tell?" asked the other.

"Well, if you must know," replied the stranger, "I own Take Courage, and I'm sure he's not going to win."

"In that case," was the response, "all I can say is that it's going to be a mighty slow race. I own the other four horses."

☻

At a racetrack some one asked a jockey, "How do you make a slow horse fast?"

"Don't feed him," replied the jockey.

☻

And then there was the horse who gave such a bad performance in his first race it made his parents turn over in their glue bottles.

☻

A sharpie sold a naive racing fan a broken-down filly. When the fan went to the stable to see his new purchase, he spotted a vet laboriously working over the horse.

"Is my horse sick?" asked the new owner.

"She's not the picture of health," the vet informed him, "but we hope to pull her through."

"Will I ever be able to race her?" asked the fan.

"Chances are you will," the vet assured him, "and you'll probably beat her, too."

☻

"Is horse racing a clean sport?"
"Well, it cleans quite a few every day."

☻

And before we leave this chapter, just remember this: it's easy to pick a winner at the track. Just don't take any money with you.

TALES OF SALESMEN

Mankind is divided into two classes; those who earn their living by the sweat of their brow and those who sell them handkerchiefs, cold drinks, and air conditioners. Selling is similar to hog-calling; it isn't the noise you make, it's the appeal in your voice. A good salesman, like a good cook, creates an appetite when the buyer doesn't seem hungry.

Dick Nolan of the San Francisco *Examiner* likes this one:

Lost in the back roads of the Ozark countryside, the salesman slammed on the brakes and pulled his big car to a stop abreast of an elderly farmhand, trudging along in the broiling sun.

"Hey," he called, "can you give me directions to the next town?"

"Sure," said the farmhand, wiping his sweating brow. "You turn right at the next intersection, go about ten miles until you see a big barn, turn right again and go until you see a grocery store, then go right until you come to Carson's Corners. Then turn left."

Half an hour later, the same car came along the same road and drew up near the same farmhand, resting beside the road.

"I never could follow directions in strange country," said the driver. "Would you be kind enough to get in and point the way for me?"

"Yes," said the farmhand, climbing in. "Just go straight ahead. Sometimes I send you fellers around two or three times before you offer me a ride."

The story is told of a man who tried to buy a suit at one of those "walk-a-flight-and-save-a-dollar" establishments. One of the partners tried every suit but one on the customer. Each time the fellow put a suit on, the partner would turn him around and around so he could view himself in the mirror. Finally, the other partner took over, showed the customer one suit, and made a sale.

"You see how easy it was," he admonished. "I did it on the very first try!"

"I know," shrugged his partner, "but who made him dizzy?"

Sam Mandlebaum, my accountant, overheard this at the International:

Two traveling salesmen were discussing television.

"It ruined us," said one.

"I know," said the other. "Now the farmers get the newest jokes before we do."

A salesman I know uses the same routine every time he checks into a hotel. He casually tells the operator to get the White House on the phone. Then he asks to speak to the President. His second call is to the Vice-President.

"I never get them on the phone," he once told me, "but from then on, I'm always sure to receive great service at the hotel."

☻

Speaking about hotels, I like the yarn about the salesman who spent a week at a very exclusive one. On the day of his departure, he received a two-page itemized bill. When he looked it over, he recognized every item except the very last. It was a two-dollar charge for stationery.

"But I didn't use any stationery," he exclaimed, showing the bill to the clerk.

"The stationery referred to," exclaimed the clerk, "is the paper on which this bill is written!"

☻

The greatest salesman I ever heard of was the one who sold two milking machines to a farmer with one cow and then took the cow as a down payment.

☻

"Is Jim a good salesman?"

"Good salesman! Hah! The only orders he ever takes are from his wife."

☻

Dick Friendlich of the San Francisco *Chronicle* chuckled when I told him this one:

A salesman needed $35 for plane fare home, but all he had

was $25. He took his $25 to a pawn shop and hocked it for $20. Then he sold his pawn ticket to a passerby for $15, thereby giving him the $35 he needed.

☺

And Hal Shaefer, also of the San Francisco *Chronicle,* prefers this one:

The boss and his sales manager looked gloomily at the sales chart on the wall. In one corner was a graph showing the company's descending grosses. The rest of the chart contained a map of the territory, with pins stuck in it showing the location of the various salesmen.

"Frankly," the boss sighed, "I think we have only one hope. Let's take the pins out of the map and stick them in the salesmen."

☺

A salesmen always kept his hat on while working at his office desk. When kidded about it, he shot back, "That's to remind me I have no business being here."

☺

The sales clerk went to his boss and complained, "How," he asked, "can I stop women customers from complaining about our prices and talking about the low prices in the good old days?"

"It's simple," answered the head man. "Act surprised and tell them you didn't think they were old enough to remember them."

☺

A salesman, passing through Florida, bought a dozen coconuts and ordered the dealer to send them home to his wife. A month later, when he was passing through again, the salesman returned to the fellow's store and screamed, "I bought a dozen coconuts from you, and when I called my wife, she said she had only received ten."

"Don't get excited," soothed the dealer. "That's part of our service. Two were bad so we saved your wife the trouble of throwing them away."

☻

A sales manager was getting loaded in a bar because he had just been fired. He was asked what was wrong.

"Nothing," he explained. "I'm just drunk with no power."

☻

Robert Natella was a very imaginative fellow. Accordingly, he entered a used car showroom, browsed around a bit, and picked out the worst-looking car in the place.

The auto salesman, sensing that Robert might be attracted to a more flashy model, suggested that he look at some of the other autos on the floor.

"This one's the one I want," Robert insisted. "Of all the cars you have in this place, it's the one most likely to break down, isn't it?"

"Most likely to break down? Well, er, I guess so, but I don't understand?"

"It's like this," Robert explained. "When the car breaks down and a crowd gathers around me, I'll sell them my storm windows."

☻

A traveling salesman who was driving along one of those old Ozark dirt roads stopped in front of an old shack.

"How far is it to the nearest town?" he asked an old woman sitting in a rocking chair.

"Well, lemme see," she answered, scratching her head. "Pa

figures it's about ten miles goin' and about twelve miles comin'."

"What was that?" asked the salesman, obviously puzzled by her odd reply.

"Well, ya see," she explained. "Pa walks straighter goin' than comin'."

☻

TRAVELING SALESMAN: Good morning. Did you ever see anything as unsettled as the weather the last few days?

HOTEL MANAGER: Well, there's your bill here!

☻

Bob Blackburn of the Ottawa *Citizen* applauded when I told him this story:

A young salesman decided he was tired of working for others; so he went into business for himself. Later, a friend asked him how it was to be his own boss.

"I don't know," he replied. "The police won't let me park in front of my own premises; tax collectors tell me how to keep my books; my banker tells me how much balance I must maintain; transport contractors tell me how my goods must be packed; customers tell me how my goods must be made; and the Government tells me how to keep records in triplicate.

"And on top of that, I just got married."

☻

And Ottawa *Journal* scribe David McDonald laughed at this one:

The manager of a department store was mystified by the number of "No Sale" recordings rung up on the cash register by a new salesgirl. He asked her about it.

"Well," she said, "every time I had a customer who didn't

buy anything I pushed the 'No Sale' button. Isn't that what it's for?"

☺

FIRST SALESMAN: Why don't you go on a vacation? Can't your office get along without you?
SECOND SALESMAN: That's what I don't want them to find out!

☺

The sales manager was praising the efficiency of his organization at a banquet.
"We're now making a sale every three minutes," he announced proudly.
"That's not enough," came a voice from the audience.
The speaker paid no attention to the rude interruption but went on to tell of the new sales promotion and direct-mail campaign which would insure a sale every minute and a half.
"That's still not enough," the voice repeated.
Enraged, the speaker singled out the man who had spoken and barked, "You interrupted me twice. Now I wish you'd explain your remark."
"Certainly," came the reply, "There's a sucker born every minute."

☺

A pullman porter gave a salesman special attention on a trip down South.
"What's the average tip that you get?" asked the salesman as he was leaving the train.
"An average one is usually two dollars," the porter said.
The salesman handed over two dollars and remarked that a

job on a pullman must be pretty lucrative.

"It's not so hot," the porter said. "This is the first average tip I've gotten in a couple of months."

☺

Tim Burke of the Ottawa *Journal* prefers this one:
A bartender, eyeing a tipsy salesman, remarked, "If he has one more for the road, he'll need a map to get to the door."

☺

The salesman crashed into the boss's office and screamed, "I want a bigger commission or *else!*"

"Or else, *what?*" sneered the boss.

"Or else I'll go back and work for the commission I'm getting."

☺

When a salesman's wife hauled him into divorce court on the grounds of being unfaithful, she named a comely young model as corespondent.

"Miss Smith," said the Judge to the model, "did you go to a hotel with the defendant?"

"Yes, I did," she replied sweetly, "but I couldn't help it. He deceived me."

"And how did he do that?"

"Well, he told the reception clerk that I was his wife!"

☺

A salesman, driving through Texas, overtook a young man running along the road. He stopped and invited the perspiring runner to get in.

"An emergency, I suppose?" the driver asked.

"No," puffed the young man. "I always run like this when I want a ride. It seldom fails."

☻

Sign on a California highway: THIS MAY BE THE JET AGE, BUT BROTHER YOU AIN'T DRIVING ONE YET!

☻

The salesman and his new blonde companion were enjoying a little dinner in a private room at a night club. As the meal neared its finish, he cleared his throat and said, "Honey, how about a little demitasse now?"

"I knew it, I knew it!" the blonde exploded. "I knew you weren't treating me this nice for nothing!"

☻

Jesse Berlly, who always manages the impossible Broadway ducats, heard this from a customer:

Two salesmen met one evening after work.

"I made some very valuable contacts today," the first told his friend.

To which his companion replied, "I didn't make any sales today, either."

☺

Did you hear about the fellow who stopped a woman on Broadway and told her, "You're the first white woman I've seen in six months."

"Where've you been," she inquired, "darkest Africa?"

"Nope, selling silk in Florida."

☺

A traveling salesman was showing a farmer a pair of pajamas.

"Glory be!" exclaimed the farmer. "What are those things for?"

"They're worn at night," explained the salesman. "Like to buy a pair?"

"Me?" said the farmer. "What for? Only place I go at nights is to bed."

☺

A traveling salesman, stuck in a small town with motor trouble, was a little leery about the abilities of the local mechanics.

However, having no other choice, he walked over to the nearest garage and watched one of the mechanics at work. He was amazed at the fellow's efficiency. He was really skillful. He changed the car's oil and didn't spill a drop. Before he touched the upholstery, he wiped off his hands thoroughly. He handled the steering wheel as carefully as a newborn baby. And when he pulled the car into the street, he was slow and cautious, making sure there were no cars driving by.

The salesman was truly impressed and approached another mechanic working nearby. "That fellow is a careful mechanic," he said. "He really takes pains when he works on a car."

Without looking up, the mechanic replied, "Why shouldn't he, that's his car!"

☻

A salesman, on a trip with his wife, stopped for breakfast at one of the hotels where he generally spent the night. He ordered pancakes.

When the waitress brought his order, he asked, "Where's my honey?"

"Oh," replied the waitress, "she left last week and got another job."

☻

A harassed salesman walked into the psychiatrist's office.

When he was couched, he said, "Doctor, I've really got a problem. I live in a lavish, new twenty-five-room house in the swankiest neighborhood in Westchester. It has a 40 x 70 pool, five acres of formal gardens, servants' quarters for eight, and a garage that will accommodate twelve cars. I also have a cabin cruiser that sleeps six, a summer home on Long Island, and a new plane . . . ."

"Just a minute," interrupted the headshrinker, "what has all this got to do with your problem?"

"Because, Doctor," the salesman replied, "even with commissions, I never make more than $75 a week."

☻

BOOK SALESMAN: This book will do half your work.
BUSINESSMAN: Good, I'll take two.

☺

A sales manager who had just returned from a tour of inspection of the firm's Sahara Desert branch was asked, "Is is true that there's a constant water problem out there and they're always short of it?"

"Well, put it this way," explained the sales manager. "There are times when it's so dry out there that when they mail a letter they attach the stamp with a paper clip."

☺

A company was having its annual dinner for the twenty-five-year employees, and the boss had stepped up to the refreshment stand. The sales manager, fortified by a few trips to the same stand, decided now was the time to hit the old man for a raise.

So he walked over to the boss, stuck out his chin figuratively, and stated bluntly, "Mr. Barker, I've worked so hard and so conscientiously I've ruined my health."

"I know you have, Marvin," the boss answered, and raising his glass, he said dramatically, "Here's to your health!"

☺

A salesman, who was dining in a restaurant with his latest flame, said, "If my doctor could see me with this champagne and caviar, he'd go crazy."

"Why, are you supposed to be on a diet?" the girl asked.

"It isn't that," the salesman said. "I owe him $500."

☺

A sales manager had one of his salesmen on the carpet. The

young salesman resented the call-down and becoming quite angry, said, "Don't talk to me that way. I take orders from no man!"

"Now we're getting somewhere," said the sales manager. "That's just what I'm raising hell about."

☻

A one-time salesman who had joined the police force returned from his first beat and told the desk sergeant, "I like this job. The hours are good. The pay is right, and the customer is always wrong."

☻

A traveling salesman stopped at a lonely farmhouse and asked for a night's lodging. The farmer agreed to put him up, but, as in all traveling salesman jokes, said that they were short of beds and he'd have to sleep with one of his daughters.

In the middle of the night the bedroom door crashed open, a flashlight swept over the bed, and the salesman found himself staring into the business end of a shotgun.

"Well," drawled the farmer, "worked again! This makes *five* daughters I've gotten off my hands this year!"

☻

A salesman was racing along Highway 96 at about 95 miles an hour. A motorcycle cop stopped him and growled, "Didn't you see the speed limit posted back there?"

"Why, yes," the autoist replied. "But I thought it said 96 miles per hour."

"Brother," the cop sighed. "I'm sure glad I caught you before you turned onto Highway 414."

☻

Two salesmen, Al and Bill, were discussing the fact that so many girls' names were the same as the names of cities.

"Florence, Italy."

"Helena, Montana."

"Elizabeth, New Jersey."

"Indianapolis, Indiana."

"Just a minute, Al. Indianapolis isn't a girl's name."

"Is that so? Do you know *everybody*?"

☻

SALESMAN FROM THE CITY: What's that strange odor?

FARMER: Fresh air.

☻

The secretary always knew her boss was a quick-thinking, go-getting salesman. But she never knew how sharp he really was until the phone rang in his real estate office and a soft female voice asked, "Do you sell maternity clothes?"

"No, madam," the boss replied, "but could we interest you in a larger house?"

☻

A salesman was trying to sell the young wife an egg-timer. "Your husband's eggs will be just right if you use this," he assured her.

"But I don't need it," she answered brightly. "My husband likes his eggs the way I do them. I just look through the window at the traffic lights and give them three reds and two greens."

☻

A salesman was driving through Kentucky when he noticed a man and his small daughter sitting beside a brook. The salesman stopped his car and approached the two. "You have a lovely little girl," he told the farmer. "What's her name?"

"Sybilistina," the farmer replied.

"That's a pretty long name," said the salesman.

"Look, mister," the farmer answered. "We're not city folks. We've got time."

☻

The live-wire salesman walked into the factory and demanded an interview with the manager.

"Look here, sir," he began energetically. "I'd like to talk to your men and sell them my correspondence course on how to put fire and sparkle into their work."

The manager turned pale.

"Get out of here," he roared. "Get out, you idiot. This is a dynamite factory."

☻

Two traveling salesmen met in the home office. "I hear you're going out West this trip," said one.

"Yep," said the other. "I'm really gonna take in the sights this trip."

"Be sure you see Old Faithful," said the first.

"See it?" moaned the second salesman. "I'm taking her with me."

☻

A door-to-door salesman stopped at a suburbanite's house one day. "I have something here," he said, "that will make you popular, make your life happier, and bring you a host of new friends."

"Good," said the suburbanite. "I'll take a fifth."

☻

A salesman, passing through a small town in the Ozarks, stopped for gas at a lonely filling station. On a hunch, he asked

the proprietor if he could buy some moonshine, too. After assuring himself that the salesman was no "revenooer," the proprietor came out with two jugs. "Got two kinds," he said. "Which kind do you want?"

"I don't understand," the salesman said. "What's the difference?"

"Plenty!" the mountain man cackled. "One's for courtin', other's fer fightin'."

SALESMAN: This gravy is excellent. I must have the recipe.
WAITER: Sorry, sir, this restaurant is owned by a retired newspaper columnist. We never reveal our sauces.

SALES MANAGER: I think it's a good time to sell the Joneses a car.
SALESMAN: What makes you think so?
SALES MANAGER: Their neighbor just bought a new one.

☻

A tombstone salesman and a widow were discussing the epitaph to be inscribed on her late husband's grave.

"How would a simple 'Gone Home' do?" asked the salesman.

"I think that would suit nicely," replied the widow. "It was always the last place he ever thought of going."

☻

A salesman, who was traveling through Ohio, stopped off at a diner for lunch. His bill was $1.45, and he paid it with a $2 bill. The waiter gave him a fifty-cent piece and a nickel. The salesman left the nickel and walked out with the half dollar.

"Well," sighed the waiter. "I gambled and I lost."

☻

A salesman who was deathly frightened of dentists got a terrific toothache while he was in Florida. He had always made it a habit to stay away as far as he could from dentists, but this time the pain was killing him. Accordingly, he went to a dentist, told him about the pain and also of his fear of dentists.

Being the sympathetic type, the dentist gave him a big shot of whiskey. The salesman swallowed it down in one gulp.

"Feel any braver now?" asked the dentist.

"Do I feel any braver?" snarled the salesman. "Brother, I'd like to see you try to mess with my teeth now."

☻

A salesman who stopped off to buy some blankets at an

Oklahoma Indian Reservation was introduced to an Indian family. "I'm Brave Eagle," said the oldest member. "This is my son, Fighting Bird, and this is my grandson, Jet Plane."

☻

"I don't like yes men," a sales manager warned his new assistant. "I want you to tell me what you really think, even if it costs you your job."

☻

A salesman was being interviewed by the personnel manager of a large industrial concern.

"What we are looking for," the personnel manager said, "is a man of vision, a man with drive, determination and courage, a man who never quits, who can inspire others—in short, a man who can pull the company's bowling team out of last place."

☻

Said one traveling salesman to another in a restaurant, "What's the matter, Max? You only had a sandwich for lunch. Usually you have a big meal. Are you on a diet?"

"No, on commission."

☻

Two salesmen were discussing a third. "He's probably the most conceited salesman who ever lived," said the first. "He's thoughtless, inconsiderate, and would do anything to make a sale. I guess you really don't know him as well as I do?"

"You're wrong," argued the other. "I think I know him every bit as well as you do."

"How could you possibly know him as well as I do?" snapped back the first. "I'm his best friend."

☻

A sales manager was stressing the importance of repetition to an employee. "When you're selling our product you must repeatedly praise its value because repetition is the most important factor in selling. Do you understand?"

"Yes, sir," replied the employee. "And now I'd like to ask you a question."

"What is it?"

"Can I get a raise, a raise, a raise?"

☺

"Did you ever do any public speaking?" asked the sales manager.

"Well," answered the candidate for the job, "I once proposed to a country girl on a party line."

☺

An insurance salesman was getting nowhere in his attempts to sell a policy to a farmer. "Look at it this way," he said finally. "How would your wife carry on if you should die?"

"Well," answered the farmer reasonably, "I don't reckon that's any concern o' mine so long as she behaves while I'm alive."

☺

"The cocktails on a salesman's expense account," says Phil Harris, "sometimes run into a staggering figure."

☺

A man went into a clothing store to buy a suit. The salesman asked him his name, age, religion, occupation, college, high school, hobbies, political party, and his wife's maiden name.

"Why all the questions?" the customer asked. "All I want is a suit."

"Sir, this is not just an ordinary tailor shop," the salesman said. "We don't merely sell you a suit. We find a suit that is exactly right for you.

"We make a study of your personality and your background and your surroundings. We send to the part of Australia that has the kind of sheep your character and mood require.

"We ship that particular blend of wool to London to be combed and sponged according to a special formula. Then the wool is woven in a section of Scotland where the climate is most favorable to your temperament. Then we fit and measure you carefully.

"Finally, after much careful thought and study, the suit is made. There are more fittings and more changes. And then . . ."

"Wait a minute," the customer said. "I need this suit tomorrow night for my nephew's wedding."

"Don't worry," the salesman said. "You'll have it."

☺

Jack Douglas says, "An insurance salesman sold me a retirement policy. If I keep up the payments for ten years, he can retire."

☺

JOE: I've been selling women's apparel for the last ten years.
MOE: Well, I'll bet you know all the tricks of the trade.
JOE: No, there's a blonde in Boston I never got to meet.

☺

A salesman from Ohio, stopping at a New York hotel during his first sales trip to the big city, called the switchboard to order a cab. Informed that "you don't call them—you just go down on the street and get one," he protested courteously that he had called cabs in Chicago, Detroit, and Los Angeles.

"You can in small towns," the operator interrupted, "but not in New York."

☻

"I've come back to buy that car you showed me yesterday," the man said as he stepped into the auto showroom.

"That's fine," the salesman said. "I thought you'd be back. Now, tell me what was the dominant feature that made you decide to buy this car?"

The man replied, "My wife."

☻

A salesman, stopping off at a Midwestern farm, became engrossed in conversation with a farmer. "I'm very excited," said the traveling man. "My son just won a college scholarship."

"I know just how you feel," said the farmer. "I felt the same way when my pig won a medal at the State Fair."

☻

The pretty young salesgirl who had recently been added to the vacuum cleaner company's door-to-door staff was reporting fantastic sales. The manager called her in for a word of commendation.

"What's your secret?" he asked affably.

"Simple," she replied. "I get the housewife's undivided attention because I always insist on talking to her husband. And I speak to him so softly, she strains to catch every word."

☻

Equally ingenious was the door-to-door salesman who developed an irresistible sales pitch.

When a housewife answered his ring, he would simply say,

"You should have seen what I saw at your neighbor's. May I come in?"

☻

"And remember, my friends," the lecturer told his audience. "There will be no buying and selling in Heaven."

"That," mumbled a salesman at a back table, "is not where business has gone."

☻

The salesman who returned from Florida described conditions there.

"In some parts of Miami, business is so bad that even people who don't intend to pay aren't buying."

☻

And before we leave this chapter, here's something for you to remember: few salesmen leave footprints in the sands of time, because they're too busy covering up their tracks.

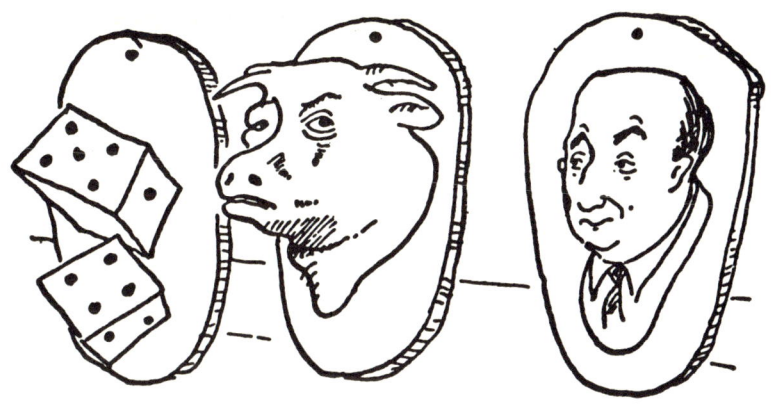

KATLEMAN'S KAPERS

If you've ever been to Las Vegas, you know that the El Rancho Vegas which is owned by Beldon Katleman is one of the most popular hotels in the gambling state.

Beldon is an extremely witty fellow and always comes up with clever quips.

I remember one time when a guest asked him what the biggest points of interest in Las Vegas were. Belden replied, "Seven and eleven."

On another occasion, a female guest who was worrying about her husband—he had spent seven straight nights losing a fortune playing blackjack—confronted Beldon and asked if her husband's behavior was more unusual than that of other guests. "I'll tell you what I tell everybody else," Beldon told her. "It's all right to play blackjack as long as you're having fun. But if you get angry, then it's gambling."

A tourist asked Beldon if there were any race tracks in the gambling state.

"None at all," said Beldon. "In Las Vegas, we prefer to put the cards before the horse."

☻

A fellow who was spending his vacation in Las Vegas wired his sister: HAVING A WONDERFUL TIME. WISH I COULD AFFORD IT.

☻

WILL: I'm going to play dice, and I'm going to win.
PHIL: How to you know?
WILL: I feel it in my bones.

☻

A New Yorker, who had heard from a very unauthoritative source that it was simple to make a fortune at the gambling tables in Las Vegas, took a major portion of his life's savings and journeyed to the gambling state.

Upon arriving, he checked into a hotel and immediately went to the blackjack table where he bet $200. But the cards were bad and he lost. Then he decided to try his luck at the roulette table. He bet $500 on a number but once again lost. Disappointed, but not disillusioned, he next went to the dice tables. Feeling certain his luck would change, he bet his remaining $5,000. However, he lost again.

Completely busted, he went over to the desk clerk and borrowed money to call his wife in New York to forward some more money.

He stepped into the phone booth and told the operator the number he wanted.

"That will be $2.85, please," advised the operator.

He put the money in the coin box and waited for his number.

But, as luck would have it, he was connected with a Chinese laundry on 14th Street.

He immediately called the operator and told her of her error and asked for a refund.

"I'm sorry, sir," came the quick reply. "Your number lost again."

☻

A gambler's seven-year old son, asked to count in kindergarten, came up with "1, 2, 3, 4, 5, 6, 7, 8, 9, 10, jack, queen, king."

☻

A guy was shooting dice at a Las Vegas Casino. He was doing pretty well when suddenly he felt a hand in his pocket. He grabbed it. Then he turned and found himself looking into a little guy's baby-blue eyes. "What are you doing?" he demanded.

"I'm just making change," the little guy alibied.

"Why don't you ask if you want to make change?"

The little guy said, "I never speak to strangers."

☻

A dishonest gambler complained, "I've got the hardest luck. Even when I'm cheating, I can't win."

☻

Gambling isn't the only thing Las Vegas is noted for. Anyone who's seen some of the shows put on at any of the night clubs on the famous "Vegas Strip" will tell you that pound for pound, Las Vegas probably has the prettiest chorus girls in the United States.

Most of these girls enjoy their work, but there are many who are looking to meet the right millionaire who will marry them and give them a life of ease.

I'm thinking specifically of one chorus girl who described her intended husband, a wealthy Midwest industrialist. "It's the little things about John that I like. He owns a small mansion, a small yacht, and a small racing stable."

☻

"I may have trouble finding the kind of husband I want," another said. "He'll have to be smart enough to make a huge sum of money but dumb enough to give it all to me."

☻

FIRST CHORUS GIRL: When I refused to marry Bill, he said that he was going to take a trip around the world to forget.
SECOND CHORUS GIRL: So?
FIRST CHORUS GIRL: So, I told him, if he had enough money for that, I would reconsider my refusal.

☻

A fellow had married a chorus girl who was one of a pair of identical twins. But within a year of his marriage, he found himself in a court of law applying to the judge on the bench for a divorce.

"But why do you want a divorce?" asked the judge.

"Well, it's this way," explained the guy. "My wife's twin sister lives with us, and I often come home and kiss her by mistake."

"But surely there is some difference between the two women," said the judge.

"You bet your life there is," exclaimed the husband. "That's why I want a divorce!"

☻

Jeanne Sager, who does my press relations, likes this story:

A beautiful chorus girl visited a psychiatrist. Before she was able to say a word, he said, "I know exactly what's bothering you. It's a man, isn't it?"

"Yes," she said. "He insists on kissing me every day of the week."

The psychiatrist told her to put her foot down and refuse.

The next day she returned and said, "Now he insists on hugging me."

The psychiatrist again told her to use her will power and refuse.

On the third day, she returned in an almost hysterical state.

"What does he want now?" asked the psychiatrist.

"It's terrible," sobbed the chorus girl. "Now he wants a divorce."

☻

NED: There was a big killing in a dice game.
FRED: What happened?
NED: A guy shot seven.

☻

Shikey Toushin, who operates the Jewel Box at the Las Vegas Sands, likes the story about the theatrical agent who died and went to heaven where he noticed an angel playing a harp. He listened for a while and then tapped the angel on the shoulder.

"I like the way you play, son," he said, "but let me give you a tip. Take up the piano. There's no call for harpists these days."

☻

A rich Texan heard that one of the leading Las Vegas hotels was for sale and that he could get it for about ten million dollars. Accordingly, he sent a trusted agent to see about the deal with orders not to offer more than twelve million.

A few days later the agent phoned in.

"We can pick it up for eleven million, boss. But we're in trouble."

"How come?"

"They want a $2,500 down payment in cash!"

☺

"A Texan, a New Yorker, and a doctor played poker. The Texan held four kings and the New Yorker held five aces."

"What did the doctor hold?"

"An autopsy on the New Yorker's body."

☺

A TV producer was telling Beldon Katleman about a new idea he had for a quiz show.

"Each week," he explained, "we'll pick a new contestant and give him the answers to the questions."

"So?" said Beldon. "What's so unusual about that?"

"Plenty," the producer said. "The answers will be wrong."

☺

Two college professors, who were spending their Christmas vacations at the El Rancho, were seated in the lobby discussing the human body and the fact that it's 92 per cent water.

While they were in the course of discussion, a shapely member of the hotel's chorus line passed by. Conversation ceased for a moment as the professors studied her.

Then one remarked, "Boy, she sure did a lot with her 8 per cent."

☺

The fellows at the Friars swear they saw this sign on an elegant Cadillac: MADE IN LAS VEGAS THE HARD WAY!

A chorus girl was having a difficult time finding a suitable man.

"You want too much of a man," a friend said.

"But all I'm looking for is a man who's kind and understand-

ing," exclaimed the chorus cutie. "Is that expecting too much of a millionaire?"

Comic Larry Best says it was so crowded when he went to Las Vegas that he had to go to a psychiatrist to find a place to lie down.

Houston columnist Paul Hochuli tells of the extremely sad-looking guy who was seated at the El Rancho Bar sipping his drink.

"Frank," asked a friend, "what in the world is the matter?"

"Oh, I'm having trouble with my wife," Frank explained.

"What happened?"

"Well, she told me she wasn't going to speak to me for thirty days."

"But," his friend objected, "that ought to make you happy."

"It did," Frank answered, "but today is the last day."

☻

A vacationing Hollywood agent was surprised when his waiter in a small Las Vegas restaurant tapped him on the arm and chuckled, "Remember me? I'll bet you're surprised to see me waiting on tables!"

"I'm not surprised at all," the agent remarked. "I remember your acting."

☻

A comic who was appearing at the El Rancho, walked into a psychiatrist's office and the psychiatrist told him to lie down and tell him everything. The comic did. So now, the psychiatrist is doing the comic's act in Miami.

☻

Four cardsharps got together and a tense, hard-fought contest ensued. Suddenly, the dealer tossed his cards down and said, "This game is crooked."

"What makes you think so?" queried the cardsharp on his left.

"I can tell," replied the dealer, "because you're not playing the same hand I dealt you."

☻

A forty-five-year-old bachelor complained to Beldon Katleman that no matter what girl he brought home as a potential bride, his mother expressed disapproval. Beldon advised him, "Find a girl just like your mother; then she's bound to like her."

A few months later the bachelor returned to the El Rancho and told Beldon, "I took your advice. I found a girl who looked like my mother, talked like her, and even cooked like her. My mother loved her."

"And did you marry her?" asked Beldon.

"No," said the guy.

"Why not?"

"Because my father hated her!"

Marshall and William were dining in a Las Vegas restaurant when to Marshall's disgust, William calmly helped himself to the larger fish on the platter.

"Fine manners you've got, William," admonished Marshall. "If I'd been in your place, I'd have taken the smaller fish."

"Well," replied William with his mouth full, "you've got it!"

A sales manager, attending a convention in Las Vegas, met a curvaceous chorine whom he found exceedingly appealing. Since he was a happily married man, he didn't know what to do.

Accordingly, he asked his boss, "I hate to appear bold like this, but I need your advice. Would you cheat on your wife?"

Shrugging his shoulders, the boss replied, "Who else—my mother-in-law?"

While we're on the subject of "faithful" husbands, how about the Las Vegas hotel owner who, while returning from a trip to New York, went to his compartment and found two lovely girls there. Checking their tickets, the girls discovered that they had boarded the wrong train. Upset, they asked if they might remain in the compartment anyway.

The hotel owner carefully explained that he was a married man, one of the most famous hotel men in the country, a highly respected citizen of Las Vegas, and he couldn't afford the slightest touch of scandal.

"I'm sorry," he finished, "but one of you will have to leave."

☺

Another passenger on the same train, who had an upper berth, was making a general nuisance of himself.

"Hey, conductor," he cried out, "will you get me a glass of water, please?"

"My goodness," replied the exasperated conductor, "that's the tenth glass of water I've gotten you in the last five minutes. I never heard of anyone drinking so much water."

"I'm not drinking it," the passenger said. "My berth is on fire!"

☺

"You beast, you animal," cried the chorus cutie. "I'm going back to mother."

"Never mind," said the guy. "I'll go back to my wife."

☺

A gambler, just back from Las Vegas, told a friend he'd undergone "Las Vegas Surgery." "I had my wallet removed painlessly," he said.

☺

Joe E. Lewis, who is one of the country's leading night club comics, often headlines at the El Rancho Vegas. Joe E. is one of the best-loved entertainers in show business, and the stories about his ability to drink liquor are legendary. Joe has many theories about drinking, such as: "An alcoholic isn't always the guy who's had one drink too many. He's usually the guy who thinks he's had one too few."

When he was a young comic breaking into the business, Joe was once working in a night club in Chicago. The owner feared that Joe might get drunk and be unable to go on.

"Lewis," he warned, "the first time I catch you drinking, out you go."

Joe worked in the club for over a week and didn't touch a glass of whiskey. One night after his act, he returned to his dressing room and was greeted by the owner who was holding a half-full bottle of Scotch in his hand.

"I warned you, Joe," he said.

"But that's not my bottle," said Joe.

"Can you prove it?"

"I certainly can," said Joe. "If it were mine it wouldn't be half full!"

Joe E. defines Alcoholics Anonymous as an organization that takes people apart to see what makes 'em hic.

One of his favorite drinking stories concerns the cop who asked a lush, "Where do you live?"

"Right here," came the reply. "I rang the bell, but nobody answered."

"How long ago was that?" asked the cop.

"Oh, a couple of hours ago."

"Well, why don't you try ringing again?"

"Aw, the heck with them," said the drunk. "Let 'em wait."

Joe E. claims you can always spot an alcoholic at a cocktail party. He's the guy who's talking to the bartender.

☻

Not all of Joe's stories deal with liquor. He often tells the tale of the local wolf who was seen at a night club with the wife of one of his best friends.

"For Pete's sake," said a friend of both, "have you no pride? Why, she's the wife of one of your brother lodge members!"

"Yeah, I know," replied the wolf calmly, "but he isn't in good standing."

☻

Another of his favorites deals with the concert violinist who had had very few engagements of late, who found it both discouraging and disturbing to see a particularly unskilled street violinist attract a shower of coins and bills every time he appeared in the neighborhood.

Not only did the passersby stop to put money in the itinerant fiddler's hat, but windows opened and envelopes of money snowed down on his miserable instrument.

"Maybe there's something to this," thought the concert violinist. And in desperation, he took his Stradivarius to another part of town and played his heart out on a street corner. He had never played so beautifully, but he collected not one red cent.

Next time the virtuoso saw the street musician, he stopped to talk to him. "How does it happen," he asked, "that with your unskilled playing you still collect so much money?"

"Simple," replied the other, "I also happen to be a bookie."

☻

"Why do you always win at cards and lose at races?"
"Because I can't keep a horse up my sleeve."

☻

Dallas columnist Tony Zoppi reports he overheard a Las Vegas chorus girl tell a friend, "What I'm looking for is a man who will treat me as if I were a voter and he was a candidate."

☻

"Bill went to Las Vegas to get away from it all."
"He did?"
"Yes, but unfortunately, it all got away from him."

☻

And before we end this chapter, just remember this: in Las Vegas or anywhere else, the only safe bet is the one you forget to make.

HOORAY FOR THE IRISH

One of the most rewarding experiences I've had as a comedian occurred last year when I was completing an engagement at Blinstrub's in Boston. On what was supposed to be the last night of my engagement, Stanley Blinstrub, the owner, had sold out the club to the St. Joseph's Guild which was holding a testimonial dinner for one of its members.

Since the Guild was composed entirely of Irishmen, Stanley thought it might be a good idea if I ended my date a day earlier and let Jimmy Joyce replace me. Jimmy is a talented young comic who's very popular in Boston where he's called the "Irish Myron Cohen."

However, being the gentleman that he is, Stanley never said a word to me. But somehow I sensed his uneasiness and felt obligated to discuss the matter with him. When I broached the subject, Stanley pointed out that Jimmy was very popular with the Irish and might feel more at home with the Guild than I would. I assured him that I had no qualms about entertaining the Guild.

I always found the Irish to be a wonderful group of people, blessed with a fine sense of humor and a rich lore.

When I stepped on the stage that night, I remembered that they called Jimmy Joyce "The Irish Myron Cohen." To break the ice, I simply said, "Good evening ladies and gentlemen. My name is Myron Cohen, but I'm also known as "The Jewish Jimmy Joyce."

The audience loved this opening and for the rest of the evening they were on my side.

One of my favorite Irish stories was told to me by my good friend Sister Mary Augustine of the Marist Missions, and deals with the pretty Irish lass who fell in love with a fellow who hadn't been to church in fifteen years.

"You're not a bad fellow, Pat," the girl's father told the suitor, "but before you marry my daughter, you'll have to become a good Catholic."

The suitor agreed and began spending a great deal of his time reading about Catholicism and discussing religion with the local priest.

For the next six months, he studied and learned everything he could about the religion. During this time, he never missed a Sunday in church.

Finally, one day, the girl approached her father and, with a tear in her eye, said, "Father, Pat isn't going to marry me."

Slightly confused, her father said, "I don't understand. He seemed like he'd developed a real interest in religion. What happened? Why the sudden change?"

"He hasn't changed, Father," said the girl.

"Then why aren't you getting married?" asked her father, more confused than ever.

"Because, Father, Pat has become so interested in Catholicism that he's decided to become a priest."

☻

An American staying in London was introduced to an Irishman who asked him, "And what country do you belong to?"

"The greatest country in the world," replied the American.

"So do I," replied the Irishman. "But where's your brogue?"

☻

A priest was writing the certificate at a christening but couldn't remember the date.

Looking to the mother of the baby he said, "This is the 16th, isn't it, Mrs. Flynn?"

"Oh, no, Father," said Mrs. Flynn. "This is only the 9th I've had."

☻

Pat and Mike were talking:

"Being that it's St. Patrick's Day, I'd like to bring home a special treat for my family," said Pat.

"I would, also," said Mike. "Let's walk down the street, and as soon as we see a butcher shop, we'll go in and buy some nice juicy steaks."

They began walking, and in a couple of minutes, they came to a butcher store.

"Let's go in," said Pat.

"Faith and begorra, Pat," said Mike. "Can't you see what the sign on that window says—KOSHER MEAT MARKET!"

"So it does," said Pat. "Say, Mike, I've seen that sign on lots of windows. Just between you and me, what does it mean?"

"Well, Pat," explained Mike, "to you that sign means nothing, and to me that sign means nothing. But for the Jewish people—that's Duncan Hines."

☺

A rich Texan, who was visiting Ireland, became engrossed in conversation with a native.

"Ireland isn't a bad country," said the Texan, "but it doesn't compare to Texas."

"Do you know that a man can get on a train in Texas early Monday morning, have his breakfast, have his lunch, have his supper, and then go to sleep. When he gets up Tuesday morning, he's still on the same train, and he can have his breakfast, have his lunch, have his supper, and go to bed again. And do you know that when he gets up Wednesday morning and gets off that train, he's still in Texas?"

"So what's so unusual about that?" said the Irishman. "We have slow trains in Ireland also."

☺

Back in the days when Brooklyn had a baseball team, Francis Cardinal Spellman was watching a World Series game at Ebbets Field. During the course of the game, a high foul was hit toward his box seat. Catcher Roy Campanella tried to reach it but missed, and the ball hit the Cardinal's knee. Campanella quickly asked whether he had been hurt.

"Don't worry about it, Roy," the Cardinal said. "A priest's knees are the toughest part of his anatomy."

☺

A priest and a rabbi were making plans for an interfaith luncheon.

"We can serve pork and beans," said the priest.

"Good idea," said the rabbi, "and we'll hold it on a Friday."

☻

A hungry Irishman went into a restaurant on Friday and asked the waiter, "Have you any lobster?"

"No."

"Have you any shrimp?"

"No."

"All right," said the Irishman, "then bring me a steak smothered with onions. The Lord knows I asked for fish."

☻

"I hear you went to the ballgame last Sunday instead of to church."

"That's a lie. And I've got the fish to prove it."

☻

Joe McCarthy, of the American Weekly, tells of the monastery where the monks were allowed to speak aloud on only one day of the year. And on that day only one monk was permitted to say anything.

One year, on the appointed day, the monk whose turn it was to talk stood up and said, "I hate the mashed potatoes we have here. They're always lumpy."

Having spoken, he sat down and lapsed into silence again. Another year passed by, until the day for talking came once more. Another monk arose and said, "I like the mashed potatoes. I think they're delicious. In fact I can hardly wait for the night when we have mashed potatoes."

Again silence for twelve months, while summer turned into autumn and winter gave way to spring. Finally, the day arrived when a third monk was allowed to speak.

"I want a transfer to another monastery," he said. "I can't stand this constant bickering!"

☺

Boston *American* columnist Alan Frazer tells of the Irishman who was stopped by a friend as he was about to enter a bar.

"Stay out of that place, Mike," warned his friend. "If you go in, the devil goes in with you."

"If he does," said Mike, "he pays for his own drinks."

☺

"The Irish are the best fighters in the world," announced Tim Connor. "They can lick anyone in the world."

"Oh, they're not such good fighters," said a Swede. "Me and my brothers Ole, Nels, and Sven Petersen and two other fellows, we licked one of them yesterday."

☺

A parishioner, who hadn't attended church all summer, met the priest one afternoon.

"Hello, Fred," greeted the priest. "I haven't seen you for a long time. In fact, I don't believe you've been to church since last May."

"Has it been that long?"

"Yes, Fred. I believe it has."

"Well, Father," said Fred, "I'll tell you the reason why. When it's hot, you can't expect people to sit in a church. Nowadays, everything is air conditioned—movies, offices, restaurants. And churches should be, too. Otherwise, attendance will drop."

"Well," said the priest, "one place has been without air conditioning for ages, and I understand attendance is holding up well there."

☺

"Abstinence," said Father Murphy, "is a wonderful thing, Tom."

"Sure, and it is, Father," said Tom, "if practiced in moderation."

☺

Did you hear about the Irish psychiatrist who used a Murphy bed instead of a couch?

☺

Irishmen are not against taking a drink now and then and Irish lore is such that many of its legendary tales—especially those concerning liquor—have been so distorted by time that they have almost reached the point of complete absurdity.

Mr. Donegan caught the bartender at Casey's bar in an unguarded moment and begged, "Pat, my mother-in-law has gone to her reward, and it's a ten spot I'm needin' for a wreath to uphold the Donegan standards. Can you advance me the ten?"

The bartender emptied his pockets and the cash register but the total came to $9.30.

"That'll do," said Donegan hastily. "I'll take the other seventy cents in drinks."

☻

Kevin: If you take another drink, you'll hate yourself in the morning.

Sean: So what! I'll sleep late.

☻

"St. Patrick's Day," according to Nick Kenny of the New York *Mirror*, "is a day on which the Irish march up Fifth Avenue and stagger down Sixth Avenue."

☻

Bennett Cerf tells of the O'Connel brothers who were dining in a strange restaurant. As usual, they had too much to drink. Near the end of the meal, brother Tim decided he wanted to wash up and asked the waiter where the washroom was. He was directed to a door to the left of the elevator.

"Go down two steps, and there you are," said the waiter. Being slightly inebriated, Tim unfortunately did not have full control of his faculties and forgot to turn to the left. He opened the elevator door, took one step, and promptly fell down the shaft.

The O'Connels came from hardy stock, and Tim was merely stunned. When his brother Mike rose to wash up, however, Tim cautioned him.

"Look out for that second step, Mike. It's a son-of-a-gun!"

☻

"Every time I see you," screamed Sullivan's wife, "you have a bottle in your pocket."

Sullivan replied, "You don't expect me to keep it in my mouth all the time, do you?"

☻

O'Leary was selling tickets for a church benefit to a friend.

The friend said, "I'm sorry I can't buy one. I won't be able to attend, but my spirit will be there with you."

"Good," said O'Leary. "I have a $2, a $3, and a $5 ticket. Where would you like your spirit to sit?"

☻

George Clarke, the Boston *Record* columnist, chuckled when I told him the tale of Pat McCoy who approached the minister who had married him just five minutes before and said, "How much do I owe you?"

The minister smiled, "As much as you think the girl's worth."

Pat handed him a dollar which the minister took without comment. Pat was reluctant to leave; in fact, the minister thought he wasn't going to get rid of the couple.

"Have I forgotten anything?" he finally asked.

"Yes," said Pat. "My change."

☻

A wealthy farmer decided to go to church one Sunday. After services he approached the preacher with much enthusiasm. "Reverend," he said, "that was a damned good sermon you gave, damned good!"

"I'm happy you liked it," said the reverend, "but I wish you wouldn't use those terms in expressing yourself."

"I can't help it, Reverend. I still think it was a damned good sermon," said the farmer. "In fact, I was so impressed that I put a hundred-dollar bill in the collection basket."

The reverend replied, "The hell you did!"

☺

And speaking about Satan's domain, Jim O'Connor, of the New York *Journal-American*, tells of the old Irishman who became so sick that a priest was sent for to administer last rites. But, somehow, the man recovered, and in a couple of weeks was hobbling about as good as ever.

"Ah, Dennis," said the priest, "it's a sight for sore eyes to be seeing you up again. I thought you were a goner for sure. You had a bad, bad time of it."

"Yes," agreed Dennis. "I certainly did."

"When you were at death's door," questioned the priest, "how did you feel? Were you afraid to meet your Maker?"

"I wasn't worrying about that so much," replied Dennis. "It was the other gentleman I wasn't anxious to meet."

☺

If I tell any more Irish stories, they'll start calling me the LepreCohen so maybe I'd better end this chapter now.

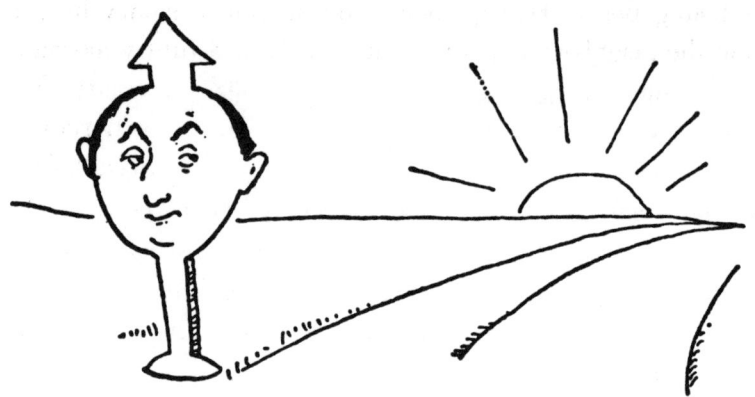

ONE FOR THE ROAD

When I went from Garment Center salesman to night club comedian, many of my friends were amazed by the relative ease with which I made the switch. They didn't realize how similar these fields really are.

The salesman's customer is his audience. He must "make friends" much in the same way the comedian establishes a rapport with his listeners. The salesman borrows even further from the comedian in that he often relies on a humorous story to break ground. Also, both are concerned with the appropriateness of his material—the comedian fits his routine to the audience while the salesman chooses just the right story for each customer.

In my salesman days, I once had a customer named Max who had three lovely children he was always bragging about. Max had more pictures of his kids in his wallet than the Rogue's Gallery has in its files. Whenever I went to see him, stories like these often helped me make a sale.

Young Bob picked up some extra allowance money by cutting the neighbor's lawns on Saturday. One Saturday morning, Bob Senior noticed that Junior was leaving a bit later than usual. He asked his son why he wasn't getting an early start.

"I found out, Dad," was the reply, "that I get more work from people who are already halfway through."

☺

Mother and daughter were in the kitchen washing dishes while father and seven-year-old Billy were in the living room. Suddenly father and son heard a crash of falling dishes. They listened expectantly.

"It was Mother," Billy finally announced.

"How do you know?" father asked.

"Because," answered Billy firmly, "she isn't saying anything."

☺

A little boy came home dejectedly from his first day of school and announced, "I'm not going tomorrow."

"Why not?" questioned his mother.

"Well, I can't read, I can't write, and teacher won't let me talk. So what's the use?"

☺

A mother, riding on a train, looked up from her magazine and frowned. "No, I don't know the name of that station where we just stopped. Why do you ask?"

"Because Sister got off there," her small son replied.

☺

"My son is certainly a smart kid. He's only four, and he can already spell his name frontwards and backwards."

"What's his name?"
"Otto."

☺

Nine-year-old Michael Mason, who brought home a terrible report card asked his father, "What do you think the trouble with me is, Dad, heredity or environment?"

☺

A fellow was trying to fix a door that didn't hang right.

"Hey, son," he called to his boy, "get me a screwdriver, will you please?"

After what seemed like a terribly long time, the youngster came back and said apologetically, "Gee, Dad, I've got the orange juice, but I can't find the vodka."

☺

TEACHER: This essay on "Our Dog" is exactly the same as your brother's.

JOHNNY: Yes ma'am. It's the same dog.

☺

A Hollywood producer's son received a very unusual report card. Instead of the customary "Poor," "Fair," "Good," and "Excellent," it was marked "Sensational," "Magnificent," "Stupendous," and "Colossal."

☺

George Q. Lewis, Executive Director of the Gagwriters' Association of America, met a friend whose wife had recently given birth to their first child.

"Can he talk yet?" asked George.

The proud father replied, "What's the sense of his learning to talk when he gets everything by yelling?"

☺

A six-year-old came home from school one day and told his father, "Daddy, my teacher takes a great interest in you."
"How do you know?" asked his father.
"Today, she told me to sit down and behave five times, and then she said she wondered what kind of a father I had."

☺

A boy in the same class came home from school and told his mother, "My teacher is mean but fair!"
"What do you mean—mean but fair?" questioned his mother.
"She's mean to everybody."

☺

The harassed mother took her incorrigible son to see a psychiatrist after every other disciplinary method had failed.
"What seems to be the trouble?" asked the medical man. "Does he feel insecure?"
"I don't know," replied the mother, "but everyone else in the neighborhood certainly does."

☺

I had another customer whose son was a doctor. When I visited him, I always came with a fresh supply of doctor stories:
The officious new nurse was determined to show her authority on her first day on the job. When a man walked into the office, she ordered him to step into the next room and undress.
"But I only want my sore throat checked," he protested.
It made no difference. Without listening further, she again ordered him into the next room. There he found another man

undressing, and again he complained that he was merely a throat patient.

"What are you complaining about?" asked the other man. "I'm the doctor!"

☻

My physician of long standing, William Hitzig, passed this one along to me:

A fellow consulted a doctor because he wasn't feeling well.
"Do you smoke excessively?" asked the M.D.
"No."
"Drink a lot?"
"No."
"Keep late hours?"
"Nope."
The doctor shook his head and asked, "How can I cure you if you have nothing to give up?"

☻

DOCTOR: There's nothing wrong with you. All you need is a little sun and air.

PATIENT: I guess you're right, but my wife is dead set against having children.

☻

The doctor at the Army base had a young corporal as his assistant to keep track of the paper work. The young man was curious about the doctor's affairs. He was always asking questions and one morning said, "In civilian life were many of your cases accidents?"

"I don't know," the doctor replied.
"How come you don't know?" the corporal asked.
"Soldier," the doctor replied, "I was an obstetrician."

☻

A woman decided to have the shape of her nose altered.
"How much will you charge?" she asked a plastic surgeon.
"Five thousand dollars."
"Five thousand dollars! Isn't there something less expensive?"
"Well," replied the surgeon, "you could try walking into a lamp post."

☺

The Mayo Clinic has worked out some extremely effective diets. One time an irritable millionaire patient was given one of these diets to follow. He looked it over with an angry eye and then snarled at Dr. Mayo, "Why do you doctors order a fellow to cut out just the things he likes?"
"Because," Mayo answered, "he never eats or drinks the things he doesn't like so it stands to reason it must be the things he does like that are disagreeing with him."

☺

A bum entered a doctor's office. He looked worried.
"Doctor," he said, "you've got to help me. I swallowed a silver dollar about five years ago."
"Good heavens, man!" screamed the doctor. "Why have you waited five years? Why didn't you go to a doctor the day you swallowed the silver dollar?"
"To tell the truth," replied the bum, "I didn't need the money at the time."

☺

"How is the patient's mental attitude?" asked the doctor.
"Much improved," answered the night nurse. "He has stopped praying for his recovery and started praying for your bill to be reasonable."

☺

A doctor stepped into the patient's room. Five minutes later he came out and asked for a corkscrew. Then he went back to his patient. In another five minutes, he was out again, and this time asked for a screwdriver. Soon after, he came out again and demanded a chisel and hammer. The distraught husband couldn't stand it any longer. He pleaded, "For heaven's sake, doctor, what's wrong with my wife?"

"I don't know yet," the medic replied. "I can't get my bag open."

☺

I once knew a woman buyer who spent a good portion of her spare time reading about the Hollywood stars in movie magazines. She knew everything about everybody in Hollywood and appreciated stories about filmdom.

A young dancer began her career in show business by getting a job as a chorus girl. Her salary was $75 a week.

When she began working, she noticed that her neighbors suddenly began acting cool toward her. The woman next door spoke to her crossly about her parents' home and how it needed a paint job and a new roof. The man across the street made remarks about daughters who were too selfish to provide their elders with new cars and vacation trips. Puzzled, the girl spoke to her father about it.

"Oh don't worry," her father said, laughing. "I've been telling everybody you're making $5,000 a week."

☺

A movie director was trying to impress a young actress with the importance of making a good entrance.

"When you enter the room," he told her, "I want every man in the audience to drop his popcorn."

☺

A Hollywood producer had just completed a real dull motion picture—a regular "bomb." It cost five million dollars and ran more than five hours. The producer was desperate. As a last resort, he called in six top Hollywood writers. He screened the

movie for them, hoping that one could come up with the magic suggestion to save the film.

The long, monotonous screening finished and the producer jumped to his feet and addressed the writers.

"Well," he said, "you saw it. Now, are there any suggestions?"

After several moments of painful silence, one writer announced, "I have a suggestion. I think this film should be cut."

Grasping at any straw, the producer said quickly, "Okay, where?"

"Right up the middle!"

A Hollywood producer, while in the midst of producing an historic film about Abe Lincoln, decided that the film was dragging. He turned to his head writer and said, "I want you to find out if Lincoln ever knew any girl who remotely resembled Marilyn Monroe."

☻

The Hollywood producer received a story entitled, "The Optimist." He called his staff together and said, "Boys, this title must be changed to something simpler. We all know what an optimist is, but how many other people know it's an eye doctor?"

☻

The story is told of the film star who was disappointed at not being asked to make a speech on the occasion of his retirement.

"What makes it really heartbreaking," he told an associate, "is that I spent five hours in the make-up department having a lump put in my throat."

☻

A noted actor was asked if he was going to allow his two-year-old son to go on the stage.

"Not for another year," he replied. "I want him to lead a normal childhood."

☻

A singer had several auditions with a talent agent and each time sang the same song.

"Tell me," the agent asked, "why do you always sing the same song?"

The singer replied, "Because it haunts me."

"It's no wonder," said the agent. "You're continually murdering it."

☻

The movie usher was visiting a dentist. "Now, Bill," asked the dentist, "which tooth is bothering you?"

"The second from the left in the balcony!"

☺

In Hollywood, a censor phoned a studio official about some stills showing a girl in a rather revealing costume.

"They're okay if that's an evening gown," said the censor, "but if it's a nightgown, the picture's out!"

☺

A famed movie queen applying for a visa came to the blank: Single——Married——Divorced——. She hesitated a moment, then wrote, "Everything."

☺

In a little Midwestern town, there's a sign that proudly proclaims it to be the birthplace of a famous movie star. "Tell me," said a tourist to the gas station attendant, "does the great star ever visit this town with his wife?"

"Seven times, ma'am," replied the attendant. "And seven prettier women you've never seen."

☺

When a salesman meets a new customer, he obviously doesn't know anything about the customer's background and his likes and dislikes.

In my salesman days, when I was confronted with these situations, I resorted to general topics which are appealing to everyone. For instance, auto stories:

A nouveau riche manufacturer took an extended trip through Europe.

When he returned, he had a large gathering at his home

and displayed all his souvenirs to his guests.

"Tell me, Ralph," one of his friends asked, "did you bring back a Van Gogh or a Picasso?"

"Oh, no," replied Ralph, "they're all left-hand drive in Europe. Besides, I've got two Cadillacs already."

☻

Paul Bruun, of the Miami Beach *Florida Sun*, tells of the prominent manufacturer who had just completed a big business deal and was thinking of his good fortune while he was crossing a busy intersection. He appeared oblivious to everything going on around him and was looking up at the sky.

A motorist passed by and narrowly missed him.

"Hey, you!" screamed the fellow behind the wheel. "If you don't look where you're going, you'll go where you're looking!"

☻

EXAMINER: When a woman puts her hand out what does it mean?

APPLICANT: It means that she's either going to make a right or left turn, or go straight through, or stop.

☻

"Why do you have MDO 448 tattooed in reverse on your back?" a doctor asked his patient.

"That's not a tattoo. That's where my wife ran into me while I was opening the garage doors."

☻

One afternoon a rickety old car drew up to an exclusive café. The driver stepped up to a man lounging nearby and asked, "Will you keep an eye on my car while I make a phone call?" The other agreed.

When the driver returned, he asked the man how much he owed.

"Fifty dollars," was the reply.

"But that's robbery! I was only gone five minutes."

"I know," the man answered. "But it wasn't the time, it was the embarrassment. Everyone thought the car was mine."

☺

A woman, trying to back her car into a parking space, smashed into the car behind. Failing at this, she pulled out of the space, and while pulling in again, she banged into the car in front. Disgusted, she recklessly pulled out of the space and struck a passing car.

A cop who was watching approached her.

"Can I see your license, ma'am?" he asked politely.

"Oh don't be silly, officer," she replied quickly. "Who would give me a license?"

☺

Herb Kelly, of the Miami *News*, tells of Boris Smolovich who came to this country from his native Poland. After being passed by the immigration officials, he took up residence in Detroit because he heard that it was easy to get work there. Sure enough, he managed to find himself a well-paying job in an automobile factory.

After his first day of work, his curious wife was anxious to learn what sort of work Boris did at the plant.

"I have a good job," he informed her. "I work on an assembly line."

"What does that mean?" she asked.

"Well," explained Boris, "I work in a unit with three other fellows. It's like a team. When a car comes down the line, the first fellow puts on the bolts, the second fellow attaches the washer, and third fellow holds both in place."

"Yes, but what do *you* do?"

"Me," answered Boris proudly. "I screw up the works."

☺

"If all the autoists were laid end to end," says comic Danny Davis, "ninety-eight percent of them would immediately pull out of line and try to pass the car in front."

☺

George Bourke, of the Miami *Herald*, observes, "It takes 1,875 bolts and screws to put an auto together, but it takes only one nut to scatter it all over the road."

☺

Psychiatrist stories have a general appeal.

After months of analysis, a patient was told that he was cured.

"You'll no longer have delusions of grandeur and imagine that you're Napoleon," his psychiatrist told him.

"That's wonderful," enthused the patient as he picked up the phone. "The first thing I'm going to do is call Josephine and tell her the good news!"

☺

"So," nodded the headshrinker to a new patient, "you think you're a dog. That is a very dangerous hallucination. How long have you been subject to it?"

"Ever since I was a puppy."

☺

A man visited a psychiatrist and told him that he'd developed the habit of making long-distance calls to himself. "Lately it's gotten worse," he said. "They're transatlantic calls, and it's costing me a fortune."

The dome doctor thought for a moment and then said, "Why not try reversing the charges?"

☺

A mother visited a psychiatrist and said, "I'm worried about my daughter because she's too fond of rock 'n roll music to have any other serious interests."

"There's a simple solution," said the psychiatrist. "All you have to do is buy some classical recordings. By taking advantage of her natural love for music, you can subtly channelize her in another direction."

A week later the mother returned and said, "I did what you told me."

"What happened?" asked the psychiatrist.

"I now have the only house in the neighborhood where they rock 'n roll to Chopin's 'Polonaise.'"

☺

A woman went to the psychiatrist and told him, "I'm awfully worried. I constantly talk to myself."

"That's not unusual," consoled the headshrinker. "Millions of normal people talk to themselves."

"I know," moaned the lady, "but you don't understand how much of a pest I can be."

☺

An advertising executive told a psychiatrist, "Doctor, I have never lost an account, and I've never had an ulcer. Also, I've never worn a gray flannel or three-button suit."

"I don't understand. What seems to be your problem?"

The ad man said, "Tell me, doctor, am I normal?"

☺

A distraught mother pleaded with a psychiatrist, "You must help my son. He spends all day making mud pies and when he gets done he tries to eat them."

"That's not unusual," soothed the psychiatrist. "Lots of boys make mud pies and try to eat them."

"I'm not so sure about that," replied the mother, "and neither is his wife!"

☻

A man visited a psychiatrist and told him, "You must help me. I have my entire ceiling and all the walls of my bedroom covered with pictures of Brigitte Bardot."

"I don't understand what your problem is," the psychiatrist said.

"My problem," said the patient, "is that I sleep on my stomach."

☻

A nurse rushed into a busy psychiatrist's office and exclaimed, "There's a man outside who claims he has a dual personality. What should I do?"

"Just tell him," replied the psychiatrist, "to go chase himself."

☻

"Doc," said the fellow to his headshrinker, "can you please cure me of snoring? I snore so loud that I continually keep waking myself up."

"If I were you," the psychiatrist advised, "I'd sleep in another room."

☻

Army stories, too, appeal to everyone.

A hoity-toity, second lieutenant was caught without proper

change in front of a cigarette machine. Accordingly, he flagged down a passing private and asked, "Got change of a dollar?"

"I think so," said the private cheerfully. "Wait till I see."

The lieutenant drew himself up stiffly and barked, "Private, that is not the way to address an officer. We'll replay this scene. Got change of a dollar?"

The private saluted smartly and said, "No, sir."

☻

It was near the end of World War II, and a German soldier, whose regiment was almost completely annihilated, approached his commanding officer and asked if he could take his long overdue furlough.

"I can't give you a furlough, Fritz," said the officer, "but maybe we can retreat through your home town."

☻

SERGEANT: What was your occupation before entering the army?

ROOKIE: Traveling salesman, sir.

SERGEANT: Stick around; you'll get plenty of orders here.

☻

A young soldier at Fort Dix was asked by his buddies how he had learned to take army discipline so readily.

"I'm used to it," he said. "My mother was an officer in the WAC."

☻

Two veterans were boasting about their old outfits.

"Why, our company was so well drilled," said one, "that, when we presented arms, all you could hear was slap, slap, click."

"Pretty fair," said the other. "But when our company pre-

211

sented arms, you could hear slap, slap, jingle."
"Jingle?" said the other. "What did that?"
"Oh, just our medals."

☺

SERGEANT: What is the first thing to do when cleaning a rifle?
PRIVATE: Look at the number.
SERGEANT: And what has that to do with it?
PRIVATE: To make sure I'm cleaning my own gun.

☺

A G.I., caught in his first barrage in a foxhole in Korea, found himself subjected to a sudden onset of hiccups. "Do me a favor, will you?" he implored his buddy. "Do something to scare me."

☺

My English cousins, Mildred and Julian Rose, tell of a British colonel visiting a United States military post, who got into a discussion with one of the officers as to which army had the better discipline. As the American was speaking, a private came in.

"Cap," he said, "I've got me a heavy date tonight. Can I use your jeep?"

"Sure," replied the captain. Then, turning to the colonel, he said, "There's proof of our discipline. He needn't have asked me."

☺

At a press luncheon in Washington, Major John Eisenhower recalled an incident during World War II, when, as second lieutenant and aide to his father, he was sent with a message to a colonel in the front line.

"My dad says to watch your right flank," the younger Eisenhower told the colonel.

"Fine," replied the puzzled officer, "and what does your mommy say?"

☺

Two soldiers were digging a trench. It was a very hot day, and both felt pretty tired.

"Do you remember the big poster saying, 'Enlist and See the World,' " asked one.

"Yes," replied his companion, "but why?"

"Well, I didn't know we had to dig clear through in order to see it."

☺

A general and a captain were walking down the street. They met many privates, and each time the captain would salute, he would mutter, "The same to you."

The general's curiosity soon get the better of him, and he asked, "Why do you always say that?"

The captain replied, "I was once a private, and I know what they are thinking."

☺

And best of all, the salesman can never go wrong by telling a story about himself.

I like the one about the traveling saleman who was driving through upstate New York when it began to pour. Soon, the visibility became so poor that he couldn't see five feet in front of him. As he was riding, he spotted a farmhouse and pulled into the driveway. He jumped out of the car, raced to the house, and knocked on the door.

In a few moments, the farmer appeared at the window,

spotted the salesman, and quickly opened the door.

"Come on in, young feller," he replied. "It's kinda wet out there."

When the salesman was inside, the farmer told him to sit by the fire and warm himself. Then he got the salesman a towel and made him a cup of hot tea.

After he was warm and dry, the salesman went to the window and looked out. It was still pouring. Turning to the farmer, he said, "It's awful outside. It would be treacherous to drive. Do you think you could put me up for the night?"

"I guess so," said the farmer, "but there's one thing I gotta tell you first."

"What is it?" asked the salesman.

"I ain't got a daughter."

"What!" screamed the salesman, as he picked up his hat and coat and raced to the door. "Of all the nerve . . . to think that I would stay with a farmer who didn't. How far is the next farmhouse?"

In a similar vein, Miami *Herald* columnist Jack Kofoed tells of the salesman who stopped at a farmhouse and asked the farmer, "Do you have a daughter?"

"Yup, and a real pretty one, too."

"Good," said the salesman. "I'll stay here for the night."

The next morning the salesman got up, packed his bag, and started to leave. As he was walking to his car, he spotted the farmer. "You old liar, you," he yelled. "I thought you said you had a daughter."

"I do," said the farmer.

"Don't lie to me," hollered the salesman, getting madder by the moment. "I was here all last night, and I didn't see her once. Did you ever hear of a traveling salesman who stayed in a farmhouse for a whole night without seeing the farmer's daughter?"

"There's a simple explanation," said the farmer.

"What is it?"

"My daughter is away at college."

A salesman and his wife arrived in Europe on a combined business and pleasure trip. Tired and hungry from the long trip, the husband ordered a large meal.

His wife made some rapid calculations, then complained, "Jim, that adds up to about eight thousand calories."

"Who cares?" demanded Jim. "I'll put 'em on my expense account."

The least popular salesman in the company was leaving and one of his co-workers was trying to get others in the office to give him a farewell dinner.

"Look," he told the other members of the staff, "it'll be a good feed, and we'll all have a lot of fun. We're even planning to award door prizes. One of you might win."

"Nothing doing," snapped one of the group. "I'd rather give that crumb a good swift kick where it would do the most good!"

"Hey!" exclaimed the party promoter. "How did you know? That's first prize!"

☺

A salesman who had been on one of the greatest selling sprees of his career accumulated a small fortune in commissions. Accordingly, he took an apartment on Park Avenue and spent his newly found wealth buying furnishings for it. He even built a garden on the roof. To accomplish this, tons of earth had to be hauled up.

Soon after the garden had been completed, it belatedly came to the attention of the owner of the building.

"What have you done?" he wailed to the salesman. "This roof cannot sustain such a weight. It will collapse."

"Are you sure?" asked the salesman.

"Of course, I'm sure. Now what are you going to do about it?"

"I'm going to move of course!" retorted the salesman. "You don't expect me to live in an unsafe building, do you?"

☺

My secretary, Ellie Malisoff, found this one very funny:

A salesman in trying to sell a refrigerator pleaded, "Lady, you can save enough on your food bill to pay for it."

"We're paying for a car on the carfare we save, and we're paying for a washing machine on the laundry bill we save. It looks like we just can't afford to save any more at the present time."

☺

A salesman, according to Herb Rau of the Miami *News*, is a man who, when right, must always keep his temper and when wrong must never lose it.

☻

The story is told of the salesman who was waiting for a train when a stranger approached and asked him the time. The salesman, ordinarily accessible, ignored him. The stranger repeated the request, but the salesman continued to ignore him. A few minutes later, the stranger walked away.

A friend of the salesman, who was standing nearby, came over and asked, "Al, that was a perfectly reasonable request. Why didn't you tell the guy what time it was?"

"Listen," explained the salesman. "I'm standing here minding my own business. This guy wants to know what time it is. So, maybe I tell him. Then what? We get to talking, and this guy says, 'How about a drink?' So, we have a drink. Then, maybe we have some more drinks. After a while I say, 'How about coming up to my house for a bite to eat?' So, we go up to my house. We're eating sandwiches when my daughter who's twenty-one and very pretty comes in. She's a very sweet and attractive girl. So, she falls for the guy and this guy falls for her. Then, they get married. And any guy who can't afford a watch—well, I just don't want him in my family."

Speaking about time, my publisher informs me it's time to end this book.

Oddly, I find it more difficult to end a book than to begin one. When I begin, I'm full of enthusiasm because I'm getting another opportunity to share some of my favorite stories with an audience. But when I come to the end, I feel regretful because no one book, or even two, can hold all the wonderful stories I'd like to tell you.

I do hope you enjoyed these stories as much as I did telling them to you. I'm looking forward to seeing you soon in night clubs and on TV.

As my closing line, I'd like to expound this bit of philosophy: may you laugh as long as you live and live as long as you laugh.